MW01045494

Still Life with Children

Still Life with Children

True Tales of Love, Laughter and Laundry

RICHARD SCRIMGER

HarperCollins*PublishersLtd*

http://www.harpercollins.com/canada

"Extreme But Typical" appeared previously in an extended version in *The Globe and Mail* (as "Time for a Trip to the Supermarket") and in *McGill Street Magazine* (as "Travel Dairy"). The following excerpts have appeared previously, in similar form, in *The Globe and Mail*: "Morning Becomes Electric," "Spare the Rod," (as "Spare the Rod and Spare the Child"), and "Cottage Life" (in five installments). The following excerpts have appeared previously, in similar form, in *Chatelaine*: "My Dinner with Everyone," "Ed and the Elves" (as "Holiday Escape") and "Disorganization Man" (as "What's Mine is Chores").

First edition

Canadian Cataloguing in Publication Data

Scrimger, Richard, 1957–
    Still life with children : true tales of love, laughter and laundry

ISBN 0-00-638486-2

1. Family - Humor.   2. Canadian wit and humor (English).*

PS8587.C745S74 1997   C818'.5402   C97-930260-9
PR9199.3.S37S74 1997

---

97 98 99 ❖ HC 10 9 8 7 6 5 4 3 2 1

Printed and bound in the United States

Contents

SPRING CLASSIC

SUMMER RUN-OFF

Acknowledgments

So many people to thank — newspaper and magazine editors, baby sitters, my agent, my parents, all the inhabitants of a rich noisy busy neighborhood — but I'd like to single out

Joe Kertes, who laughed in the right places and pointed me in the right directions,

Jill Lambert, who saw more in the stories than I ever did,

and, most of all, Bridget, for whom they were written.

To my children,
with admiration,
gratitude and
much love

 FALL DREAMS

A Present for Me

CALL ME DAD. I'm a regular hail-fellow-well-met, kingdom-for-a-horse kind of guy with four small children who light up my life but nevertheless manage to occupy a fair amount of my — *Not now, honey, Daddy's busy, and could you please take that out of your mouth* ... if you see what I mean. Thea and Sam are the oldest. They're twins, almost seven years they've been together and they have yet to agree on anything except that bedtime comes too early and dessert too late. Imogen is four, something between a princess and a dervish, and Ed is two, something between a nine-volt battery and an Act of God. My wife goes under her own name. I stay home with the children while she dashes all over the continent, but don't be fooled by frequent-flyer points, I'm the real traveler — expand my horizons without leaving the neighborhood, punch a hole in the envelope every time someone has a dentist's appointment, live the adventure in my own kitchen.

That's where I am when the phone rings. I'm making dinner — actually I'm bouncing Ed up and down on my shoulders and trying not to move my feet while I check on the pizza. I don't want to bounce too hard and flip Ed into the oven, or step on Imogen, who has wriggled across the linoleum to twine herself about my ankles, or overcook the pizza. It should have been done fifteen minutes ago, but this is a Friday and on Fridays our oven takes longer to do things. On Tuesdays and Sundays it burns things — also on holidays. On Saturdays we warm something up on top of the stove, or order in. When the phone rings I have to move fast. I close the oven door, reach for the cookies, stuff one into Ed's mouth, bend over while he slithers off, hold out another cookie for Immie, step out of her fearsome grasp and walk calmly to the phone.

That's great! I say. *We'll see you soon. Love you too.*

Sam wanders up from the basement, where he has been panning unsuccessfully through a river of toys to find the one he wants. *You know the one,* he tells me, his lower lip thrust out. *The little pink elephant with the trunk that goes up and down, only it doesn't because it's broken. One of the feet is broken too, and the tail. You know the one, Dad. Don't you?*

I shake my head, a non-verbal lie. I threw the toy out a few weeks ago when I came upon it suddenly while vacuuming. *Mom will be home for dinner after all,* I tell him. *Isn't that great?* He stares accusingly at me. Does he suspect me? The guilty flee where no boy pursueth. *Mom was home last night,* he says.

Thea's eyes brighten at the prospect of her mom coming home. *She'll be able to see your present!* she tells me. I've been hearing about this present ever since Tuesday. This is Thea's first week in Grade One and already she's made something for me. I'm touched. Sam is elaborately untouched. It's his first week in Grade One too, and all he's made is a name for himself. *See him,* I hear kids whisper to each other in the schoolyard as we walk past. *That's Ed's brother* — Ed having made an even bigger name for himself by hiding in the nine o'clock line-up with the other children and, while I was searching frantically through the schoolyard, somehow finding himself in the front row of the Grade Four class, saying, *Good morning, Miss Thompson.*

Thea is on fire to show me the present. She and I have had a guessing game about it already this afternoon. I've discovered that it is small enough to hold in my hand and that it doesn't make a noise — *Unless you drop it, then it makes a falling noise.* Thea is very literal. Imogen asked the first question she asks about everything from breakfast cereals to beachballs these days — *Is it red?* Thea's answer was, *Only a little bit is red. And another bit is yellow.*

I can only think of one thing. *Is a bit of it green?* I ask, wondering if she's made me a traffic light. She's driven with me often enough. Maybe she feels I need a reminder, something to study. But Thea, having pondered deeply, shakes her head. *None of it is green.*

We're all together in the kitchen, minutes away from dinner, and I'm not dashing around distractedly. What an opportunity for family hygiene. *Wash your hands,* I say. Thea's face wrinkles up. I hope she isn't going to make a fuss because there's no time for explanations here, handwashing is a guerrilla action, a quick in-and-out, a raid on Entebbe, compared with bedtime, which is more like the battle of the Somme. *What's for dinner?* she asks me suddenly. I know that smell. I open the oven door. *Celery sticks and corn on the cob and milk and bananas and cookies,* I say, reaching inside, *and overcooked pizza.* I take the smoking pan out of the smoking oven and close the door quickly. What I can't smell doesn't need cleaning.

SEPTEMBER IS THE START of the new year. I know there are calendar years and tax years, years of revolution, years of the dragon and the sheep, fiscal years and pig's years that you can't make silk purses out of — but for me, ever since I reached the age of four, the year has always started after Labor Day. Everything is new again then — the sharp pencils, the clean white notebooks, the nearby faces, the shoes. Babies grow up in September. They go off in the morning without you, and when you pick them up at noon they aren't babies any more. It's been a while since I was in school, but September is still the axis of my life. The pull of nostalgia is strongest then, the feelings of possibility — *this* year I'll be in the marching band, do a dislocate on the rings, find out what on earth a logarithm really is, ask Genevieve Mathis if she'd like to, you know, walk home together. *This* year I'll learn how to make pie crust, toilet train Ed, do my Christmas shopping early, remember everyone's dental appointments, get the porch repaired, win the lottery and find the perfect cottage. Possibilities.

The evenings are starting earlier than they used to. The last of the sunset catches the glass of our front door as it opens with a squeal which is echoed by the children. *Mom's home!* Sam and Thea dash down the narrow passage to the front hall. Imogen takes the detour through the living room. Ed bellows from under the tap until I let him go, and he takes off after the others. He's a hefty little guy with twinkling ankles, he doesn't run so much as bounce on the tips of his toes, looks like Babe Ruth on the basepaths.

NO MATTER HOW OFTEN I see it I love the scene in the hall, my wife knocked over by a creaming wave of children in the high tide of welcome, her stern, worldly business face dissolving into the smiling, loving one I know better. *Isn't that great!* she says, bending down. *No, did you really?* and *Good for you!* She scatters kisses and squeezes, and climbs to her feet. Her clothes look five years older than they did a minute ago but she sure doesn't.

Guess what? Imogen shouts the latest news bulletin up at her. *Dinner is all burned. Dad called the oven a nasty name. And then we had to wash our hands.* My wife has a smile for me too. *The celery sticks aren't burned,* I say.

Dinnertime follows its predictable pattern, I find myself more involved in Ed's food than my own. Tonight it's egg salad and celery — no it isn't, it's egg salad and carrots — no, corn niblets. No. Ed isn't fond of vegetables. He eats his egg salad. I don't know why I let Ed get away with not eating his vegetables. At his age Sam and Thea had them twice a day or starved. You work so hard to get everything right for the first child and, by the fourth, you take a halfhearted shot and then give up. If Ed wanted a martini I'd probably start by saying no and end up asking him if it was dry enough and would he like an olive with it. Only of course he wouldn't want an olive because it's a vegetable — unless, like so many other things we thought were vegetables, it's really a fruit.

The most surprising foods are coming out of the closet these days, declaring themselves to have been fruit all along. I wasn't that surprised about tomatoes and avocados. I knew they were fruit, they didn't ever try to be anything else. But cucumbers — I was shocked when I found out — and zucchini too. Not that I mind, some of my favorite foods are, well, fruity, it's just that zucchini and cucumbers look so very much like ... vegetables. I'd never suspected, but there they were on the front page of the supermarket flyer — *Fruits of the Season* — and I shook my head and thought, You just never know. I made sure my carrots were safely bagged, I tell you.

I've drifted off topic. I seem to need a lot of sea room under my literary lee, possibly because I float so lightly on the water, possibly because I'm such a poor sailor. After dinner my wife takes Ed upstairs for a meaningful moment — diaperful any-way — and I tidy away the dishes and wipe the counters and the table, and then wash the floor to make sure I've got every crumb. While I'm at it, I do the baseboards and vacuum the downstairs and hang the tapestries I wove during naptime and finish scoring my concerto and dash off a proposal to the UN because really that situation in central Africa is taking too long to solve. Ah, fantasy is wonderful stuff. What I really do is stack the dishes in the sink and pick up fossilized bread pills and corn niblets from under Ed's chair. Thea stops me from tidying up any more and tells me I have to sit on the couch. She has a surprise for me, she says. A present.

She hands over a small flat rectangle, about the size and weight of a license plate. *What do you think it is, Daddy?* she asks coyly, but with a big grin. Imogen trots over and asks if she can help. We pull at the wrapping paper together. From the doorway Sam says very casually, *It's a yearbook.*

Thea swells up like a balloon and chases her twin brother out of the room shouting, *Quiet, Sam!* I pretend not to hear. *I wonder what it can be?* I say. It's well and truly wrapped. Immie gets some tape on her hands and we have to pause and get it off. *Come on, Dad,* says Thea. Sam, from behind the couch in the living room, calls, *It's a yearbook.*

SAM! Thea's starting to get upset. *There there, honey,* I say.

My wife comes in, carrying Ed. He has his angelic moments, soft and cuddly, but this isn't one of them. He squirms until she lets him down, and he makes a beeline for the tape on the floor, picks it up and can't get rid of it. *So, what do you think of your yearbook?* my wife says. *Isn't it great?*

Thea puts her hands on her hips. *MOM!*

He hasn't opened it yet, calls Sam. Mom puts a hand to her mouth. Imogen starts to giggle. Ed has the tape off his hands now. It's stuck to his foot instead. He pulls at it and sticks it back on his hands. *Open the present,* my wife tells me. *Before we all die.*

Imogen and I tear and tear. The wrapping paper comes off in spaghetti strips. *Isn't this exciting,* I say. *I can't bear the suspense. What do* you *think the present is, Ed?* He's busy sticking tape on himself. *Yearbook,* he answers without looking up. Thea sits down and starts to cry. At last, all the wrapping is off. *Well,* I say, *look at that.* I hold it up. *DAD'S YEARBOOK,* it says on the front cover. Red and yellow, as advertised. Not green. *Isn't that beautiful! Thank you, Thea. Thank you very much.*

She brightens instantaneously. Her emotional weather system is one of those speeded-up satellite photos you see on the nightly news. It's hard to nurse a storm when you're already in the middle of a sustained ridge of high pressure, and anyway the latest in sports is coming up after this commercial break. *The whole class is making yearbooks. We're going to write stories and draw pictures in them every week. I asked Miss McQueen if I could make a yearbook for you because I know you write stories too. And she said yes, so I got extra sheets of paper and made your yearbook and put on the wrapping —* she says all this very fast, her face an inch from mine — *I helped,* Sam interrupts, and I thank him quickly. *SAM!* yells Thea. *I was going to say that.*

I pick her up to give her a big hug. *Thank you,* I say again. *It's one of the very best presents I ever got. I can hardly wait to start writing in it.*

Her face falls apart faster than a superhero landing on the piano keys. Poor Batman, it happened yesterday — one arm is still jammed behind middle C. *What's wrong?* I ask her. She buries her head in my neck. *I don't want you to write in the yearbook,* she says. *I don't want the pages to get messy.*

Oh.

It's not really a book, she says. *It's a present.* This makes perfect sense to all the other kids. They nod. They've given us presents before. Presents are for admiring — for putting on the fridge or putting in a bowl or putting away in a special drawer. Fair enough.

That night, after bathtime and storytime and bedtime and drink-of-water time and back-to-bed time and whimper time and cuddle time and back-to-bed time and by-the-way time and get-back-to-bed-this-instant time and Daddy-I've-spilled time and if-I-have-to-go-up-these-stairs-once-more time — much later that night, I take Thea's present out of the special drawer in my desk and admire it again. *DAD'S YEARBOOK.*

Extreme But Typical

THE FOLLOWING SATURDAY morning is typical, extreme but typical, my wife is about two hours away by plane, we've run out of everything you can run out of and still be alive, and laundry soap. Time for a trip to the supermarket, and on the way I'll finally be able to pick up the package the post office is holding for me.

Windy and wet, sheets of water rolling down like tinfoil and all of us struggling into our — *Raincoats. I said, raincoats, and do them up, Yes, Sam, up means the zipper, and it means all the way up and then you can go outside. Yes, Thea, you too. No, as a matter of fact they're on the wrong feet, Ed, but don't worry about it. And take the button out of your mouth.* Ed's very jolly this morning, full of bounce and bubbles and whatever else he can lift to his mouth. Not a challenge, Northern Ireland is a challenge, Ed's more like a good-natured volcano.

Trouble strikes almost at once. The girls, Ed and I are strolling down the block to where the van is parked, identifying rare flora and fauna on our way, when suddenly Sam, who has run on ahead, is attacked by a gaunt and spectral figure — *Yes, Thea, that's another pine cone,* I say. A full head taller than his three foot nine, Sam's assailant has both hands around the top of his raincoat and is pulling hard, despite her arthritis. He struggles in vain. With a triumphant shout she zips him up and hobbles over to tell me what she thinks. This is not my first run in with the Baba Police, black-kerchiefed grannies who haunt our part of town, looking for under-dressed kids. *He'll catch his death of cold,* she shouts at me in a language I don't have to understand to know what she's saying. Polish, probably. Most of the neighborhood is Polish. *A day like this and his coat undone. What kind of father are you?* I thank her. *You're right,* I say, and then quickly, *No, Ed, that's* not *a pine cone. Put it down and come and get your hands wiped!*

I FORGOT TO LOCK THE VAN last night and our regular petty thief has been by. I can tell because it's so tidy — toys in the tray, cupholders cleaned of candy wrappers, maps stacked neatly on the dash. The emergency mints and spare change are gone, but on the whole I'd say it's a worthwhile service. Next time maybe I'll leave the keys and get the van washed and waxed. Thea and Sam are upset. They're learning not to trust strangers in school but — *Look,* I say. *Here's a truck we thought was lost and a glove and a Barbie shoe.* Their little faces clear when I take a new pack of mints out of my pocket. My friends tell me to buy an alarm. *You'll sleep better,* they say. Are they kidding? When I hear an alarm at four in the morning, I roll right over and go back to sleep because I know it can't be mine.

Traffic is ... well, it's traffic. What do you want, if you're in a hurry you shouldn't be driving. While the kids rediscover their toys I have time to consider the phenomenon of Barbie's footwear, surely the ultimate consumer disposable, purchased by the billion and lost within minutes, often before use. If you watch closely during the unwrapping process you can actually see the shoes flying off into the dark corners of the room. In a million years, core samples from all over North America are going to show a Barbie-shoe layer just above the limestone and shale.

The way to the supermarket takes us past churches of all denominations. What are they trying to tell us, these Catholics and Baptists, United Koreans and Hindu Parthenaj Presbyterians? He Died for Us, A Living Ministry, Washed in the Blood of the Lamb. *All Welcome,* they say. The supermarket accepts coupons from other chains too.

Past the light at Copernicus Avenue is a Drive-Thru McDonald's and a Wait-To-Be-Served post-office substation, don't I wish it was the other way around. Saturday shoppers take up all the curb space. Damn. I experience a moment of sweeping envy for everyone else's ordered existence. They'll all go home successful, hair and laundry done, pictures framed, vacations planned, prescriptions filled, palms read, funerals arranged, and I can't even manage a thirty-second stop. My windshield wipers are like yours. They clear the entire windshield except for a small strip at the driver's eye level. Craning my neck to peer over this persistent smear, I can see a parking space too good to be legal, but that's no problem because we won't be here long — no problem, that is, until Thea, a real conscientious safety-first, my-way-or-the-highway big sister, waits until we're all out of the van and then locks the doors with — O my God — the motor running and, *Ed, what's that in your mouth?* still strapped to his car seat.

Vain recriminations. I should have paid more attention, counted heads, carried a spare key. Lots of things I should have done, starting with my fourth-grade math homework, but it's too late now. *Don't worry, Ed,* I shout. He gurgles or chokes, hard to tell through the window. Fortunately we're in a high-risk towaway zone. *Thank goodness you came, officer,* I say. *My baby boy is trapped inside and gas is sixty cents a liter.* I read somewhere that our van is the easiest in its class to break into and I believe it, the policeman has it open in about ten seconds. *Thank you so much,* I tell him. *I'll never do that again.* Then I feel awkward because he stands still and looks at me — does he want a tip? His rain cape flaps in the wind and there's a bit of special sauce on his chin. Those hamburgers are messy. *Thanks one last time,* I say, *will there be anything else?* He's frowning at the No Standing sign. *I just want to pick up a package,* I say. *I won't be here long.* And you know, I wasn't. The substation is closed on Saturdays.

THE SUPERMARKET IS SET a long way back from the road, like a stately home but without the trees and deer and servants, and with many more shopping carts — not too much like a stately home, I guess, except that it's imposing and open to the public. We try to park close to the automatic doors, but you can't always get what you want, can you. You can't take it with you either, and you can't have it both ways. Face it, there's not much you can do — lead a horse to water, I guess, and run, but you can't hide. The problem with those supermarket carts is that they're not big enough. Ed in the front carrier, Sam underneath like a sack of potatoes, Thea hanging off the side and Imogen in the cart — and they're hard to maneuver.

Shopping's like anything else, the key to success is speed, so we're careening down the first aisle — fresh produce, packaged meat, careful wide right turns, *Ed, take the waxed gourd out of your mouth* — when we clip another shopper. Not her fault, I'll say that right away, but she was parked in front of the harvest sausage and I was sure I could get round her. I was wrong — hey, it happens to you too. *Dad, you just knocked over an old lady,* Thea tells me. But when I look back, she's found her cane and is getting to her feet, a grizzled veteran — if looks could kill, hold the phone, central — so I nod, common courtesy, and haul the cart around to the next aisle — dairy goods, baby products, slippery when wet. Aren't they all.

Sam and Thea are getting bored with jumping on and off the sides of the cart so I let them roam around on their own. *And remember,* I say firmly, *no running.* Leaning out of the cart Immie can just reach the egg display. *I said no running, Sam, and I mean it.* His eyes glaze over and he's gone. Immie is holding a carton with only nine eggs in it, I take another one fast and move on. *Daddy,* she giggles charmingly, *you have yellow all over your shoes.*

We come across Sam in the juice boxes, tinfoil, sauces-of-the-world aisle, and what's he doing, *Sam,* I yell, *don't run, and where's your sister?* Of course he doesn't know. Twins linked from conception by a mystical bond — what a load of rubbish. Sam and Thea have nothing in common but their birthday. *Can you find her for me?* I say, and off he goes. *Don't run, Sam, don't run, when you move your legs quickly like that it's called running. Don't do it.* The only sauce we keep at home is ketchup and it's not here.

The aisle-five corner is known as Cheddar Hell Bend because a dairy display that cuts into the turning arc. You can always tell a rookie shopper. We take it fairly crisply this morning, past soap, cleanser, paper towels, into What a coincidence — *Daddy,* says Immie, *there's that old lady again.* I take a moment to help her up. *Hope you're not hurt, madam,* I say. *Can you move it? If you can move it, it probably isn't broken.* She ignores me — cold shoulders, warm heart, they say, but probably not in this case.

All quiet on the Western front now, past soup, cereal, coffee, coleslaw — *Ed, if you don't like smelly cheese, don't pick it up* — and instant pudding mix, to the aisle of great entreaty. *Please,* Imogen starts, and Ed echoes at once, so I hear stereophonically but out of sync, *Plea-ease, plea-ease, plea-ease, can we buy those cookies?* I don't know why they bother. Reminds me of dogs chasing a parked car. *Sure,* I say, and toss in a couple of bags. I wonder where Sam and Thea are. They often ambush me by the President's Travel Diary, Buy ten pounds of moussaka and win a free trip to Greece or something. Not this time. *Of course you can have another cookie now.* And so to frozen foods.

There they are, and maybe there is something to the twin theory. Both of them have their tongues stuck to the same shelf of the freezer. Waffles, I never knew there were so many varieties. *It's all right,* I tell the cluster of concerned shoppers and store managers as we trundle up. *Leave this to me.* The refrigeration unit is working hard — orange juice, fish fingers, peas and carrots loom out of the mist and then fade from sight again. Wonder where the meat pies are. At least Sam's stopped running. Grape juice works best. Insert the straw into the juice box, squeeze and stand back — no, better stand back first. *There now,* I say a moment later. *Don't you two feel foolish?* I don't know what it is about tear-stained faces, but we end up choosing three different kinds of frozen waffles before moving on to the checkout.

You can't teach slow-line selection. Either you have it or you don't. I have it. Today there's enough time to play three holes of golf, overthrow a corrupt regime, rewire the downstairs and master a Romance language. I keep Ed away from sharp objects and make sure no one dies — thank heavens for the tabloid newspapers, with their pictures of bat-winged babies and men with two heads. The checkout lady gives us all candies and a big smile. For a fleeing enemy build a golden bridge. When we see the old lady in the parking lot, we all smile, but she makes a sign against the evil eye and hobbles away. I just shrug. That's the kind of guy I am, the sum of the internal angles of a triangle must be 180 degrees, also the internal temperature of a pork roast. Winning isn't the only thing, it's something else.

On the trip home the kids have a serious argument about whether a T-Rex could eat Ed in one bite. I'm surprised. I thought they'd already settled that one. What a great feeling it is to cruise up our street and find a parking spot right in front of the house, but it doesn't happen to us today — *Here we are,* I tell them, driving by. Feeling runs high in the back seats and the telling phrase *Not fair* is introduced. We park around the block, with everyone crying except Ed, who is choking, and when he expels the Barbie shoe with a noise like a gunshot and an odd looping trajectory, he starts crying too. The rain is teeming down. *What about some hot chocolate?* I say brightly.

Morning Becomes Electric

IT'S A FEW DAYS LATER, bright and early — well, early, it's not very bright yet — and for some reason I'm just brimming with well-being. I feel like I'm inside an infomercial. I *can* have it all, a full head of natural hair, a Swiss bank account, inner confidence and the comfort of knowing that my loved ones will be provided for in the event of my untimely use of the ab-flexor. I can have it all except the morning paper. Ed has that. He and I are breakfasting together this fine and promising weekday morning, and when I ask him for the paper he says, *Okay*. It's his word this month, could mean anything. Last month it was *vacuum*. He's a lifetime supply of energy packed into a couple of years, learned to run before he could walk — in fact we're still waiting for him to learn to walk. He holds the paper away from me.

Just let me have one section, I say. *How about the one with all the nice dead people and classified ads?* Cereal spills out of his mouth onto the floor as he shakes his head. His lips say

Okay, but there's *No no* in his heart. *Come on, Ed, please give me* — in other words, breakfast as usual.

My wife drifts in, kisses us both, drifts out. *Bye bye,* she calls. *Bye bye,* Ed calls back. He doesn't say *Mama* very often. Usually I'm *Dada* and she's *Bye bye.* My wife doesn't like being a mere interjection to her youngest child, but it could be worse, I tell her. Think of all the single-interjection families. Think of those kids with two interjections and a nanny. I carry Ed to the front window and we watch *Bye bye* get in the van. She honks and drives away. We wave and go back to the kitchen where we are joined shortly by Thea in her typical morning mood, eyes bright, hair brushed, teeth gleaming. *Hello Daddy,* she says, *hello Eddie, my what a beautiful day.* Thea's trying to be independent. She spills her own cereal, her own milk and then her own juice, all by herself, and smiles proudly at me. I try to be constructive, *How about that?* I say, wiping vigorously.

Imogen enters with a ferocious frown on her face because she's a pirate, a relief to me because pirates, though impolite, are at least interested in wearing clothes and walking erect. Last month she wanted to be a dog. When she demands milk with menaces, I smile and say, *Ay Ay, Cap'n.* I could get tough, I suppose, tell her to say please and treat me with respect, but I can't lecture anyone and mean it. My mouth fills with clichés, and then my eyes roll and I begin giggling. I lack conviction, just what Perry Mason's DA used to say. Conviction and a newspaper — I can't find it anywhere. Oh well, it would only be full of news, and you can bet there'll be some more news tomorrow. There always is.

I WONDER WHERE SAM IS. School will be starting in — *damn,* my watch has stopped — soon, anyway. We live fifty yards away from the school, a brisk minute's walk, and yet both Thea and Sam are late almost every day, would you believe it?

I tap my wrist and the watch starts ticking — so what, I still don't know what time it is. Ed slinks away to be alone with his diaper. Thea and Immie begin a game of Ice-Age Barbie in the living room. The doll has her clutch purse and tennis dress but a whole host of bloodthirsty reptiles are breathing down her hairstyle, at which point I hear a groan from upstairs.

Sam is still in bed. *What's the matter?* I say, turning on the lights, pulling off the covers. *Are you tired and run down, is the pressure of modern living too much for you? Do you worry about your hairline, waistline, deadline, treeline, International Dateline, or Madeline?* He pulls up the covers. *I know what's troubling you — it's uncertainty, isn't it? Isn't it? What would you pay to have complete foreknowledge of the future — make vacation planning a lot simpler, wouldn't it? to say nothing of all the time you'd save not waiting at bus stops.* I pull him out of bed bodily. *You're not listening, are you?* I say. *Because your ears are flabby. But they don't have to be. You could have better ears, fitter ears, in just minutes a day. How would you like —* I say, How Would You Like *to be able to hear everything that people say to you. Sounds incredible, doesn't it, but you haven't tried my new Ears of Steel video, recommended by every parent organization in the country. Twenty minutes a day to firm taut super "buff" ears* — I said, TWENTY MINUTES A DAY TO —

He starts to take off his fluffy NBA pyjamas. I smile approvingly as I make up the bed. *Now what's the matter? Can't afford breakfast? Not this week, my young friend, this week only we are going to GIVE you the Cheerios and a novelty plaid tongue depressor to go with them, a great collectible.*

He shakes his head and sighs. *School is so* boring. I look up. *There's nothing to do in Grade One,* he says, and when I offer to make a list he adds, *I mean nothing fun.* Oh. And he could be right. But now is not the time for the Importance of

Education lecture, it's, *damn,* whatever time it is and getting later too, so I point him toward the bathroom and turn on the water. Immie calls, *Eddie's doing* — something, I have no idea what because the shower is running. From her tone of voice it doesn't sound too bad — taking a toy, ripping the TV guide, that kind of thing. Not like the time she raced over to say that there was blood coming from under the door. *Tell him to stop,* I yell, toweling Sam vigorously upside down — he likes that — then pushing him into his room to get dressed.

Thea yells up to ask if she can go to school now. *Yes,* I call down, *and don't forget to wear your brand new* — too late, she's gone. I run to the upstairs front window to see if she's wearing her brand new — but by the time I get there she's outside my field of view. I can make sure she puts it on when she comes home at lunchtime, if she isn't wearing it, and if I remember. Her snack is labeled. I hope she didn't take the bag of jalapeño peppers by mistake. I can hear Ed pushing the vacuum cleaner around the living room. He isn't allowed to plug it in, so he simulates its throaty electrical roar himself. He loves loud noise, always has. I remember sitting on the floor one afternoon last summer with my arms around three cowering bodies, trying to explain that thunder was just God taking out the garbage cans or bowling gutter balls, and this particularly long rumble silenced everyone except Ed, who was just old enough to pull himself up against my knee. He stood with his feet apart and his head thrown back, roaring at the thunder. It was like he and Thor were having a conversation. And maybe they were.

Right now he's *being* the vacuum, very Zen-like. I've tried it, but it doesn't work. I start to whine and overheat, then I bump into doorways and get tangled around lamps and chair-legs — and meanwhile the vacuum is being me, choking and gasping and breaking down and not making dinner. I've decided we're really better off being ourselves, the vacuum and me. Ed's diaper looks like *Picnic at Hanging Rock,* so I scoop him up in one hand and head for the change table, up and over, around and yuck. *RRRRRR,* says Ed. They advise turning off the machine before replacing the liner bag, but I've never been able to find his on–off switch.

Immie doesn't go to kindergarten until the afternoon. She yells something about her sword. *As long as you don't hurt anyone,* I say, probably the same thing Mrs. Silver told her son Johnny before he went out to play. It's tough being a pirate's parent. You don't want to spoil their fun, but you know how mischievous they can be, the little darlings. I can picture Mrs. Pugh saying, *If you aren't careful, you'll have someone's eye out with that!*

Sam wants fruit cocktail on his Cheerios, only the can opener is broken. Dammit, I meant to get a new one yesterday, and the day before that. I look at the can — *48 fl oz.; Naturally Sweetened; peaches, pears, pineapples, melons, grapes and cherries; sodium sorbitol* — as if it holds all the answers to my life, even why, only I can't get at them, and then I remember the Ginsu steak knives I bought accidentally from the home shopping channel. I was trying to pay my monthly bills over the phone, and I must have dialed the wrong number because I found myself talking with a charming operator who knew even less than I did about my current checking balance but was tremendously informative about cutlery. I was fascinated. Did you know that these knives are made of the finest tempered tungsten alloys, the same stuff they use in the space shuttle when they run out of tiles, and the knives cut through anything — sewer pipe, barbed wire, and yes even tin cans? The operator was very clear about that.

No problem, Sam, I say, pulling open the cutlery drawer — but at that moment the radio announcer informs me that it is exactly nine o'clock and Immie sneaks in from the TV room to stab me with her cutlass. If she's not careful, she'll have someone's leg off with that.

Sam gives me a quick hug before dashing off to school. *Make sure you wear your new —* I call after him, but it's too late. He's gone with his snack under his arm. No, come to think of it, his snack is still on the counter, but the bag of hot peppers is gone. School won't be boring today.

Lessons and More

THE NEAR-EMPTY STREETCAR rocks soothingly back and forth as it picks up speed. Dust motes dance in the morning sun that streams through the open windows. Imogen reaches out and sneaks her hand in mine. She's four years old and quiet, the eye of our family hurricane, the audience in our ongoing production except when she decides to come onstage and take the lead. *Will you be with me all the time?* she asks in a whisper, popping her thumb out of her mouth. *Don't worry,* I say. We're going swimming, just the two of us. Sam and Thea are at school and Ed is doing pushups for the babysitter — *Watch this!* he was shouting as we left, levering himself up for the dozenth time.

Imogen is an enigma wrapped in a favorite blankie, I don't know how much she's looking forward to our special time together, and how much she's scared stiff.

I've been after her to take swimming lessons ever since last summer. It's not a real social thing, swimming, you're not as likely to impress your friends with a backstroke as you are if you know how to spit or whistle or make a rude noise under your armpit, but it's a good thing to learn and, besides, the YMCA doesn't offer spitting lessons. Hairwashing becomes a lot easier if you're not afraid of getting your head wet. And Immie is afraid. She knows she shouldn't be, but she is. It took real courage for her to suggest that the two of us go swimming this morning. *But no lessons!* she said. I agreed. *Don't worry,* I tell her, squeezing her soft chubby hand. *I'll stay with you.* The streetcar slows to a stop in front of the YMCA and we get out. She's whimpering behind her thumb.

Imogen's eyes go wide as we enter the men's change room — *Look at that, the lockers are orange!* She reaches out to touch one. I sit her down on a bench while I change. *Dad when I grow up can I have one of those?* she asks. *One of what?* I ask, hurriedly pulling my shirt over my head. She's not pointing at a tattoo, thank goodness, though there are certainly enough of them around. *I suppose so,* I say, *but you'll have to take lessons before you can play the violin properly.* The owner of the instrument smiles over his shoulder on his way out the door. Imogen's face falls. *Lessons — like swimming?* she says. I nod, trying to pin my locker key to my bathing suit.

Isn't there anything you can do without lessons? she asks. I hold up the key, which is embedded in my finger. *You can hurt yourself,* I say. I wait for blood but there isn't any, I'm too cold, my veins are all far away from the skin, inside me where it's warmer.

Immie shivers under the shower, shivers when we get out to the pool and shivers as we walk down to the shallow end. She leans down to touch the water with her hand and gives a little shriek. *Cold?* I ask. She shakes her head. *Wet,* she says.

SAM AND THEA LIKE TO PLAY a water game they call bucking bronto — I thrash around in the shallow end and they try to stay on my back. Immie and I don't play that. Ed and I play a game where he leaps without warning into the deep end and I pull him out and give him artificial resuscitation — Immie and I don't do that either. We sit side by side on the steps leading down to the shallow end dipping our toes in the water, and then our legs, and then ever so slowly gliding in so that we are up to our — well, I'm up to my waist, she's up to her neck. I can't tell you how painful this prolonged entry is — I've always hated getting wet and cold gradually. Fortunately we have conversation to help us along. *What do you call those things deers have?* she asks. *Antlers,* I tell her. She's asked this before. *When I am older I would like a violin* and *some antlers,* she says, then with a determined face she slides another millimeter into the water. *Ooh,* she says. *That's wet.*

Then he appears, a limp and lanky teenager in a red vest and bathing shorts, with a fringe of stubble growing about his acned jaw. How many earrings does he wear? How many toys are there in our basement, how many unraked maple keys on our front lawn, how many things wrong with our van? That many. His corn-rowed hair hangs directly in front of his eyes, so he appears to spend his life staring out from behind a blond beaded curtain. He has braces on his teeth and an anklet of that plastic thread we used to call Gimp until we worked out why, now we call it that plastic thread. He nods to us, signs in at the lifeguard station, tosses the hair out of his eyes. Roberto, his name is. His hair slips down again. He yawns languidly.

Nothing languid about Imogen, she climbs out of the pool and goes straight over to Roberto. *Hi there,* she says. I swallow my tongue. *You look really cool,* she says. When he smiles the light catches on his orthodontia.

And what do you do? she asks, her face lit up with intense admiration, looking suddenly much older. I catch a glimpse of a young woman who is going to love with all her heart.

What do I do? He pushes his hair out of his eyes. *I'm a life-guard. I look after the pool, and,* his hair falls down again, *I teach little girls how to swim.*

Immie jumps in the air. *Do you? Yahoo!* She turns and calls to me, *Daddy daddy I want to take swimming lessons!*

So that's what it takes. I can hardly wait until she meets a cool tattooed violinist.

And that isn't all. She walks calmly to the edge of the pool and jumps in. She's never done it before, comes up coughing and spluttering.

I don't know whether she expects Roberto to leap to the rescue, the water is only up to her chest and, for now, I'm right here beside her.

Lost and Found Weekend

Who's Coming?

IT DOESN'T TAKE US LONG to get a school routine established — meals, mess, friends, games, stories, bed — while the afternoons get shorter and the sleeves get longer and no one has homework or a cold yet. Halcyon days, except I'm too busy to notice, and then I find myself at the end of October asking myself where the time went — probably the same place as the odd mittens and socks, and the bullets for the Destructo Robot's laser gun, and the Lego and jigsaw-puzzle pieces.

It's the week before Sam and Thea's birthday parties. Yes, I said parties. This year for the first time they each want their own party — unfortunately they want them to be on the same day. Immie mentions that Destructo's gun is out of bullets while I am wiping her — she's good about the bathroom but still needs help with the finishing touches. *I don't know where they went,* I tell her. Back in the kitchen Sam and Thea are drawing up their guest lists and Ed is eating butterscotch-tuna pudding — his own concoction. I'll bet it doesn't catch on.

Children's birthdays involve a fair amount of work for the parents. Do we have our presents picked out, guest list made up, invitations sent out and grab bags planned? Am I panicking? Did Oedipus come from a dysfunctional family? I should have done it all long ago, but I thought I had more time than I do. No excuses here. It's not like I've spent the last few weeks curing cancer, combating global warming or paring down the national debt, mostly I've been playing sneedball and Attack Dollhouse, and reading about Frances and Horton and Theseus and Persephone, and making cookies that turn all black and have to be thrown out. I let the time slip away, like Ed at a department store. It was there, and now it isn't. If only you could get in-store security to make an announcement. *Would the owner of a lost month kindly pick it up at customer service — answers to the name October.* Oh my God, October, where have you been, we were so worried about you! — actually this fantasy never works out with Ed, because security never finds him. He hides too well.

I CHECK THE COOKIES — not ready yet. Chocolate chips aren't my favorite, in fact they aren't anybody's favorite, but none of us hates them. If I made coconut macaroons, Thea would be in heaven and Sam would be in the bathroom throwing up. And anything with raisins is dangerous for Ed, he takes them out and hides them. Sometimes we find them in his nose, sometimes we don't find them. Peanut butter and apple juice are staples in our household, ice cream of any kind is a treat, but chocolate-chip cookies are a lowest common denominator, and the recipe is on the packet of chips, so we can't lose it.

Apple juice apple juice! Ed waves his plastic cup in the air, looks quite regal — picture Henry the Eighth in a high chair. *Okay,* I tell him, reaching into the fridge. We're going to have to go shopping. All I can see is a bag of milk, four carrots and a half-pound of mold. I think about throwing it out, but cheese is really only mold anyway. I wonder if the kids could be induced to eat macaroni and mold, or grilled-mold sandwiches, or I could put it in a jar and try to pass it off as Mold Whiz. Yes, I should throw it out, but I'm too ashamed. I think of cultures that use every single square inch of a dead animal, even the skin and teeth and entrails, and don't waste anything. We don't even eat the digestives in a box of favorite biscuits, or the filberts at the bottom of the can of salted mixed nuts.

Sam and Thea have been laboring hard on their guest lists. Thea has written down one name — Sam. *Isn't that sweet,* I tell her. *But he's your brother, he's going to be there. Pick someone else.* She's embarrassed. Sam is the only name she knows how to spell. I promise to help her. Sam's only party guest so far is GI Joe. I pour Ed his apple juice, sit down at the table and lend a hand. Mom gets back from Vancouver tomorrow and I told her I'd have no problem getting the invitations done while she was away — and that's true, I haven't had any trouble getting them done. I haven't even given them a thought.

THE GREAT THING ABOUT PARTY PLANNING is that anything is possible — every single guest will arrive on time, play nicely, get a corner piece of the cake, win one of the prizes, and go home happy — even Wally the Weeper from around the block, a skinny little kid who smiles and shakes my hand and calls me sir and wears a button shirt with all the buttons done up. I like Wally, but he has this habit of standing stock still on the edge of things, and when I ask him how he's doing he says, *Fine, sir, just fine, thank you very much* — and then almost invariably a single tear will steal down his cheek like a guilty thief. He blinks, and down comes another one, and soon he's crying pretty good but still without making a sound. Disconcerting, if that's the word I want, sounds like what used to happen when Miles Davis was on tour. Julius Caesar liked men about him who were fat, I like kids who are noisy.

Eddie and Imogen demand a chance to make up their party lists too, and Immie wants some milk. I'd kind of like to get the invitations ready to take to school tomorrow, and helping Ed with a list is not going to speed things up. *Don't you want to watch some TV?* I ask. *Or play with your Destructo Robot?* But they'd rather make lists. I stare around our kitchen table, frowning, the way my mom used to frown at me. *You'd rather stay here and make lists than watch TV or play games? Is that right?* They nod their heads. The world has turned full circle, and kids are still working hard to avoid doing what their parents want. I can hardly wait until they grow up and become tax inspectors or cabinet ministers. *Besides, Ed threw Destructo's laser bullets down the toilet,* says Thea. Ed covers his face. I stare at Thea. Maybe she knows where the time went.

So we all sit down together with sheets of paper that are soon covered with blobs of crayon wax and scratchings-out and arrows and pictures of trucks and fish and driblets of apple juice and milk and coffee and tears, and despite an army of names that have been bantered about — kids I know, kids I've never heard of, kids they met at a playground two years ago, kids from afternoon TV shows — the lists are still not exactly definitive. Thea has put a period after Sam's name, then scratched it out — the sort of thing Flaubert would do. Sam's list has three names: GI Joe, and Thea, and Ryan, a friend who moved to England midway through junior kindergarten — the year before last. I go downstairs to take clothes out of the washing machine and put them in the dryer. I use laundry the way some people use cigarettes, to break the action, give them something to do with their hands, pass the time. It's not exactly addictive, and the Launderer General doesn't put warnings on the packages, but every now and again I find myself going out for soap the way other people go for cigarettes. If only I liked it more.

When I get back the party invitations have been abandoned in favor of a game where they all pretend to be food, and I am teeth, and I chase them around the house. When I catch them they change to hot peppers, and I let them go. Ed starts out as Jell-O, changes into chocolate-chip cookies — which reminds me. I dash downstairs, throw open the oven door and have to stand back as the thick black smoke comes roiling out.

I get stern and order the twins to write five invitations to members of their class, and haul the little kids upstairs to have a bath. *Why is Dad mad at us?* asks Sam quietly. *Because he burned the cookies again,* Thea answers. *And he's not mad at us, he's just mad.* She sounds calm and tolerant, pretty smart for someone who isn't even six until next week.

Ed and Immie share a bath and kick water all over each other and me. It's a spiritual cleansing as much as — maybe more than — a physical one. Immie can get her own pyjamas on, almost. I get Ed into a new diaper and pyjamas in much more time than it takes to tell about it, and the three of us tumble downstairs for our bedtime story. Thea has invited Rebecca and Trinley and Charlene and Erin, all of whom I know, and Essa, whom I don't. *That's great!* I tell her. *I'll fill in the time and our phone number for you, and you can take the invitations to school tomorrow.* Sam has invited Batman.

I try not to smile. He tries not to smile. I go downstairs and put in another load of laundry. Then we all sit on the couch to read a story. Tonight it's *The Little Engine That Could.* Appropriate or what. The phone calls start the next day.

All the Help I Can Get

MOMS FOR THE MOST PART. I must know what these women look like because we all pick up our kids at the same time, but I've never heard their voices and they haven't heard mine. It's probably my ears deceiving me, but the girls' moms sound earnest and helpful and the boys' moms sound — tired. I understand. I can get tired just watching Sam eat dinner. He's like a proposition in astronomy, the orbiting body held by the gravitational pull of, say, spaghetti, for now, but in constant motion around the plate and, as the dinner mass shrinks, the orbit increases in size so that by the end of the plateful he's spinning off into space.

What's the theme of your party? asks an attractive alto, concerned that her daughter will be able to participate fully. I tell her we're traditionalists, that we thought Happy Birthday was an appropriate theme. *Do you mind if I ask what you'll be serving?* asks a keen mind. Maybe she's heard about our cheese mold and wants a recipe. I mention that Sam's favorite foods are pizza and ice cream. *But there are always hot dogs and peanut butter on hand,* I say. *Is that okay?* There's a pause on the line. I wonder if she's expecting lobster thermidor — and, if so, how I can wangle an invitation to her kid's party.

Not too many dads call, and when they do they tend to use their own names instead of their kids' so I have no idea who they are. I nearly hang up on one guy who says, *I'm Peter Tremblay,* and then waits. *That must be nice for you,* I say at last — it's all I can think of, and Ed is playing Blindman's Bluff with the stove and I don't want this guy selling me subscriptions. A few parents ask right away for my wife. That used to happen more often, but we've been in the same neighborhood for a few years now and people are starting to recognize me — not that I wear a top hat or clown suit, but it's a family neighborhood and a man in nominal charge of four young kids does get noticed, especially if he's swinging one of the kids over his head while another one is using the tail of his shirt for a Kleenex. I don't mind, most of the sexism works in my favor. *How do you do it?* asks the woman with a tot in her arms, another at her heels and a third in a stroller. *Well, how do you?* I ask, and she bridles, prepared to give me all sorts of credit but taking none herself. Unless she's objecting to the comparison because her kids are all dressed neatly with socks that match and unscraped knees. Sometimes I get to move to the front of the line at the supermarket or the drugstore because I'm laboring under such a handicap. I suppose I should get angry at this, demand to wait while all the moms ahead of me get served, but I smile meekly and push ahead. In the long run no one comes out ahead in a supermarket line.

Are you Sam's dad? one mom asks in an accusing tone of voice. The correct response to an opening like that is, *Who wants to know?* but it may not be this woman's fault that she sounds like a gangster. She's probably nervous. I admit that I'm Sam's dad. She grunts.

Michael will come to the party, but let's get one thing straight — we don't do refined sugar, or red meat, or dairy. Is that a problem?

I say the first thing that comes to mind. *What are you talking about?* She grunts again. *We don't eat red meat in this family. Or refined sugar, or dairy. Or saturated fats. All these products are inherently poisonous — bad for the human body.* Oh.

Is that a problem? She doesn't call me buster, but that's the tone of voice she has on.

Not for me, I say. I tell her my name and ask what hers is.

See you the day after tomorrow, she says.

A more usual thing is for people to ask what they can bring to help me out — for some reason they see me as a bumbling, bedeviled incompetent who shouldn't be in charge of an ant farm, let alone a group of children. I always say yes. I'll take all the help I can get. *Gas barbecue? I say. Sounds great. Picnic table with umbrella — hey, what a good idea. How many dozen wieners? What kind of veggies? A carved pumpkin? Cocktail sauce for the shrimp? Disney Greatest Hits tape? Plastic cutlery and those wet wipe-up napkins? Bring 'em all over.* I hope I'm not taking advantage of people, but they're so kind and eager and, as Charlene's mom says of her husband, *John* likes *performing. He's always wanted to be a magician. And the equipment truck won't take up too much room.* I have to laugh hysterically at this point. *Absolutely not,* I say, *I'm looking forward to his show.*

I hang up and run downstairs, I haven't heard Ed in a while and he's become fascinated by *the light box,* as he calls it. *Those are circuit breakers, Ed — don't touch them!* But every now and then an appliance will shut off mysteriously or a light that burned out an hour ago will go on again, and it usually means that Ed is standing on a chair in front of the circuit panel, flipping switches. Not today though. He's staring into the furnace room, shaking his head. *Hot!* he says to me in a confidential whisper, pointing at the boiler. *That's the idea,* I tell him.

My wife gets home after the children's bedtime, but I let them stay up because they promise to eat all their vegetables and brush their teeth extra hard and be good and quiet and not bounce on the furniture or slam doors or bother me except in an emergency — that's our litany, and then one of the kids always asks, *Could we bother you if our arms were falling off?* I can't remember when that started, but it comes out every time now. I guess armlessness must be an elemental fear. *Yes,* I say, *if your arm was falling off you could bother me.* She's been gone a week and we're all glad to see Mom. They tackle her in the hallway, a kind of munchkin rugger scrum, pushing her into the living room and clinging while she sits down on the chesterfield, climbing into her lap and pulling her face closer to theirs and somehow wiping away the care and grown-up lines around her eyes with their soft hands and wet welcome kisses.

Did your meetings make a difference? asks Thea, stroking her hair. *Daddy said your meetings were supposed to Make A Difference.* Mom smiles and shakes her head. *They made a mess, honey,* she says. *Did you get a cramp in the swimming pool?* asks Sam. His class saw a Red Cross video on the first day of school and he's become obsessed with water safety. He won't even take a bath until two hours after dinner. *What if I get a cramp in the bath?* he says seriously. Y*ou can drown in a teaspoonful of water, you know, Dad.* I do know that. I'll bet I saw the same movie when I was his age, but I can't remember it having that effect on me. I sure don't remember my parents letting me put off my bath so that I didn't become a water-safety statistic. *I didn't go swimming,* says Mom. Sam frowns, hard to imagine going to a hotel with a swimming pool and not using it — actually, I feel like that too. Then Ed and Immie ask the same question together.

What's in the big bag? they say. My wife smiles. *Birthday presents and treats for the parties on — Saturday,* she says with a questioning glance at me. I nod. Thea's party is set for the morning, Sam's for the afternoon. We've heard from everyone except Wally's mom. *And a couple of little treats for you guys to have before you go out trick-or-treating on Friday night. I can hardly wait to see the costumes your daddy has put together this year.*

I still don't get it. *Costumes?* I say.

She frowns at me. *You know, for Hallowe'en.*

Oh Yes, Hallowe'en

I REMEMBER ABOUT HALLOWE'EN, of course, but only with the part of my mind that counts socks and notices that we're almost out of bread and our phone bill is past due, a low-level holding tank of information rather than the *Tidal wave of juice, Mysterious pustules, Washing machine convulsions, Pigeon in the living room, Fall from the top step, What's that on your hands, Ed?* full-scale five-alarm red alert that is most of my life. Or the time Sam came up to me with a very serious look — *Dad, come quick. She's just lying there. I think she's dead!* — she being, as it turned out, a balloon kitty from the church bazaar. I've never felt more relieved. I guess that's why we run out of bread so often, and get these odd noises on our phone from time to time.

It's impossible to ignore Hallowe'en because the children issue Costume Idea Updates every few minutes, and also because our house is close to the neighborhood shopping street and every storefront features a trick-or-treat motif — the leather novelties, travel agency, sports delicatessen, fruit bar, family post office, used laundromat, and video rental have all broken out in a rash of orange and black streamers and stencilled cats and pumpkins. The library and adult lingerie store have outdone themselves in putting together seasonal window displays — quite frightening, both of them, Ghosts and Witches in Peek-A-Boo Nightmares, Haunted Houses and Crotchless Horsemen. The kids and I hurry past with our *Schadenfreude* carefully averted. The Christian Science donut shop stands aloof, of course, an island of rational belief in a sea of pagan superstition. *Have a honey cruller,* the motherly woman behind the counter tells me. *They're good today.* And I know she isn't just talking about taste.

Ed and Imogen like to sit at the counter on the round stools that spin. Well, so do I, and the other customers don't mind, not even when Ed works up so much centrifugal force that his donut goes flying across the room and sticks on the mirror — Ed minds, but they don't. *I'm sorry,* I tell the motherly woman, trying not to smile. I hope she believes me. It's easy to believe that Ed is sorry. I'm sure the passers-by half a block away know that Ed is sorry. I buy him another donut and smile at Immie, who is investigating the creamy inside of her donut with the painstaking care of an Egyptologist at a new tomb site. *Are you looking forward to your first Hallowe'en?* I ask Ed. He doesn't answer. His eyes are closed, his hands are holding onto the sides of the spinning stool, the entire donut is crammed into his mouth. He is humming. Hard to imagine it gets any better than this, I guess.

Imogen looks up from her excavations. *Jerry is going to be Elvis for Hallowe'en,* she says, referring to Mrs. Klesko's pride and joy from down the street, a very clean little boy I always think, possibly because I'm with Ed at the time, always well dressed and polite, with bright red hair and a history of disease that his mom is happy to tell you about.

I saw Jerry's costume, I say. This was almost a month ago. Jerry was in bed with bronchitis or impetigo or something and Mrs. Klesko brought out the pompadour wig. *I guess he'll have to be the young Elvis,* I commented. She looked puzzled. *Well, he's only seven,* I explained, feeling foolish. Mrs. Klesko smiled and quickly excused herself.

Can I wear my detective hat with my Hallowe'en costume? Imogen asks. I tell her yes. *Will it look good, Daddy? Of course,* I tell her.

I haven't actually done anything about costumes, but we've talked a lot about them. It's Ed's first time dressing up, he's looking forward to wearing Immie's pirate costume from last year, blacking his face and carrying a sword. I haven't told him he's staying home with Mom yet. Sam and Thea have been comparing characters from Greek mythology, very sophisticated. I hope they don't insist on too much detail in the costumes, the pictures in our storybook are vague and billowy but it's clear that nobody is what you'd call well dressed. Immie has moved well beyond the pirate phase. She wants to be an M&M.

Oddly enough I can do this. In the basement is a big blue piece of felt with an alphabet display on it. Ed falls asleep on our way back from the donut shop, so I throw him quickly into his crib, and Immie and I go downstairs. I cut a poncho out of the felt with the letter "m" on the front, slip it over Immie's head, and she's immediately recognizable. *Wait,* she says, *I'm not finished yet,* and scampers upstairs.

With any luck her costume won't be too dangerous. Most of my costumes are dangerous. Last year Sam wanted to be a bank robber and Thea an elephant. No problem, I made a pair of elephant ears out of coat hangers and tin foil, good-looking ones, if I say so myself. Thea identified them as African elephant ears rather than Indian elephant ears. Maybe the Indian elephants use waxed paper. Whatever continent they came from, they were wider than any doorway and, when the trunk was attached, weighed about twenty pounds. Poor Thea's head drooped so that she nearly got run over crossing the street. *Look both ways!* I called to her, and she whispered, *I can't, Daddy.* Sam meanwhile had followed another kid's dad down the block because he couldn't see out of the teeny tiny eyeholes I'd cut in his mask. At breakfast today they were talking about being Perseus and Medusa — they'll be dangerous only to each other.

I'm in the kitchen, spreading peanut butter and keeping an ear cocked for Ed, when I hear a cough from the doorway — Imogen. She uses her stage voice, *Presenting ... the M&M Detective!* I've heard her practicing this voice to herself. She usually ends up sounding somewhere between Elmer Fudd and Queen Elizabeth. She marches in as proud as a peacock, nose in the air, hands on her hips, in her poncho and a battered fedora that she and Ed use to play detectives. It fit me until it went through the wash, now it fits her. I applaud, she takes a bow, shrieks and runs off. *Perfect!* I call after her. If Mike Hammer were an M&M, he'd look just like that.

Sam and Thea have almost finished their sandwiches, and Imogen is almost ready to start hers, when Ed wakes up. We own a baby monitor, but we've never hooked it up in Ed's room, first because I can hear him anywhere in the house, and second because he's talking now, he's got lots of words and he likes to use them. *Dad, come here,* he says. *Come here right now, ha ha ha.* Listening on a monitor would make me feel like a secretary at the beck and call of a crazed and dictatorial boss — too close to the bone. *Chocolate Dad! Come here right now, and ha ha ha ha ha lawnmower.* The laugh floats eerily down the stairwell. I try to echo it as I run up to his room, but you can't scare Ed — at least I can't. He's too happy to see me.

Something to Sneeze At

IT'S TWIST-OF-FATE TIME in the old corral. I don't get to go out on Hallowe'en with the kids. Nothing tragic or important, just a few sniffles, but we all think it'll be better if I stay at home with Ed and the potful of honey-lemon tea. *Save your strength for tomorrow,* my wife says with a smile on her way out the door with Perseus (shield by Pizza Pizza, winged sandals by Converse with duct tape accents, cloak of invisibility by Hudson's Bay) and Medusa (hair by Creepy Crawlers, wings by Wabasso, stare by Maybelline) and Imogen, who has panicked at the idea of going out in disguise and is dressed in a sweater with bunnies on it and her hands over her eyes. Ed is in my arms, crying because he can't go — *Not fair,* he says piteously, with elder siblings you pick up this phrase quickly. *Not fair not — ah-choo!* I wipe my shoulder. Ed is not a neat sneezer. Not too many two-year-olds are, but Ed isn't neat even by two-year-old standards. I wipe his face, and my neck, and the wall behind me. The trick-or-treaters vanish into the night —

— returning two and a half minutes later to drop off Immie, who can't bear the pressure of performance. Apparently she went down our walk muttering, *Trick or treat, trick or treat* to herself like a mantra, up the steps of the house next door. *Trick or treat, trick or treat,* knock on the door, stand back, deep breath, wait for it — and then, under the smiling gaze of Mrs. Sagal, someone she sees every day, Immie opened her mouth and nothing came out. Beside her Sam and Thea shouted, *Trick or treat!* holding their goody baskets and smiling — and Immie burst into howls of fear and horror and was led home. Mrs. Sagal offered candy, but Immie refused. *I didn't do it,* she says when she gets in the door. I give her a hug, but she squirms and I put her down. She feels she's in disgrace until Ed hits her with his pirate sword, then she recovers enough to push him. *Now now,* I say, vaguely. I sneeze. The doorbell rings.

We open the door and smile at incredibly cute skeletons and witches. The first ones are the cutest because they're the youngest, they have to go to bed soon. *Trick or treat,* they chorus tentatively, nudged by parents. Immie stares at them. They're her age, how do they do it? Ed is showing off his pirate sword and sneezing. None of the kids blenches, but I notice a couple of parents take a step back. Then we hand out the candy.

Ed is puzzled. He had no foreknowledge of this. No one told him that that we were going to take the candy from the big bowls and offer it to people we don't even know very well. He lowers his cork-smeared eyebrows and scratches his cork-smeared nose — what with tears and mucus and a fair amount of rubbing, Ed's costume has undergone a sea change, Blackbeard into blackface. I've been trying to get him to sing *Fifteen men on a dead man's chest,* but I think now that *Mammie* would be more appropriate. *Bye!* we all call out together.

The doorbell rings again ... and again ... and with each new arrival Ed's suspicions deepen and darken. We're simply *giving* the candy away. All of it. That's our plan — hideous in its simplicity. He tries to hide the bowls when I'm not looking, he tries to hold some of it back, he tries reaching into the other kids' bags, he tries telling them to go away, he even tries some more tears, but nothing alters the steady outflow, the steady depletion of what he might call our cherished natural resources — and it's one-way traffic, we aren't even getting advanced technology in exchange. Ed's face is set in a scowl. He stares at the trick-or-treaters as if they were from the income tax. He folds his arms across his chest. He stares at Immie, who is starting to enjoy herself giving out the candy. He looks like that guy in *The Invasion of the Body Snatchers* when he finds out his family are really pods.

Hello, Jerry, I say, looking down on a familiar pompadour and dark glasses. *Great costume. Do you sing as well?* He smiles politely, wrinkles his nose the way Elvis used to and sneezes. *Very nice,* I tell him. Immie gives him a handful of candy and he just stands there. She gives him some more candy, then some more, and he finally smiles and moves off.

Ed snaps. Jerry must be the last straw, unless he can't stand the thought of Elvis getting candy. Anyway Ed screams, *NO!* and runs out of the house. *NO NO NO,* while the rest of the street looks on interestedly. *Give it BACK!* he shouts. Jerry does what anyone would do when pursued by a diminutive but furious Al Jolson — he starts to run. But high-heeled cowboy boots aren't made for speed, and neither is Jerry, and he tumbles before he's taken four steps. Thank heavens he's not the old Elvis. You can't get grass stains off of white bellbottoms. Ed jumps on top of him. *Stop!* I shout, running up to grab his collar and then, *Hi there, Mrs. Klesko.* She glares at me while I separate Ed and Elvis, reprimanding the former and returning the wig to the latter. The Kleskos limp off without a word. Ed, in my arms, is smoldering. He looks like Othello in the big scene, until he sneezes.

Immie has been doing great on her own. Most of the candy is gone. *You can have a piece too,* I tell her and she tries to say thank you but her mouth is full. Ed opens his mouth wide enough to fit a Batmobile, but before the scream gets out, I pop in a caramel I was going to eat myself. Ed subsides.

Next ones through the door are Perseus, Medusa and Mom. The children grunt a greeting and head for the kitchen to gloat over their loot. Immie follows, she remembers this from last year. My wife yawns, hopes I haven't been too bored. I smile. *The jack-o'-lantern on our porch is out,* she says. I know. Our pumpkin always goes out, except for the year we put it on the window sill inside, then it rolled off and burned the carpet. *Time to be shutting up shop anyway,* I say. *Immie has a generous hand with the candy.*

WE WASH OFF MAKEUP and put the kids to bed and tell each other the funny bits of our evenings — Thea convinced she'd turned a garden gnome to stone, Sam wearing his Hudson's Bay blanket of invisibility over his head and unable to find his way down from the Lewises' porch. I drink lemon tea and sniff a lot. I can feel my own cold coming on just in time for the birthday parties tomorrow. And then we hear the roar from upstairs. Ed with a stuffy nose. I carry him down to sit with us for a bit. He's half asleep and wearing a sticky snot mask over his entire face, neck and shoulders. I suppose you'd pay good money for this at a spa but it looks pretty disgusting. I dab at it ineffectively with a washcloth, what it wants is a steam hose.

The bell rings. Who can it be at this time of night? I carry Ed to the door. We're both surprised to see a loutish seventeen-year-old with long greasy hair, a black leather jacket and a ten o'clock shadow, also a cup of coffee and a cigarette. Is he collecting for his college fund? He is not. *Trick or treat.* He smiles nastily, sips his coffee, flicks his cigarette into our garden. Is this a local Jaycee dressed up as a dangerous and disaffected youth? If so, it's a good costume. He's even got the dirty fingernails and teeth, and the bolts of metal piercing his cheek and forehead. I'd have to say he's real. I'm wondering what kind of trick he has in mind if we don't give him a treat. Somehow, soaping the windows doesn't sound right. I'd like to be able to help him, I know what it is to have a craving for Nutty Buddies and not enough money, but all our candy is gone. And I have to ... I have to ... And so does Ed. As if we'd rehearsed it a thousand times, we lean forward together and sneeze right in the young man's face. And Ed's is a messy one.

Sorry! I call as soon as I recover my breath, but by then he's down our front steps. I wipe my nose and Ed's. *Bless you,* I say to Ed. Who yawns.

Two-Party System

NO MATTER WHAT COLOR balloons are, they always look festive. I'm blowing up green and purple ones for Sam, and pink and yellow ones for Thea, and there's something about the inflated roundness that cannot relate to tragedy. You don't blow up balloons for a funeral, not even tasteful black ones with *SORROW* stencilled on them. In this respect they're not like flowers, which seem to serve weddings and birthdays and funerals equally well. They talk about a language of flowers. I don't believe I've ever heard of a language of balloons. Probably because they're so vulnerably here and now, and so unexpectedly gone for good. Come to think of it, that would explain why there aren't too many balloons at funerals. The most moving expression of sympathy for, let us say, a husband's hunting accident would lose a lot of its emotive power if, in the middle of the eulogy, it went POP. Flowers wither and balloons go pop and there you have all the difference, except that you can't twist little squeaky kitties out of a handful of flowers.

Wow, keen, can I have one? All the kids want a balloon to bounce in the air — another difference, I've never heard of a six-year-old who said, *Wow, keen, can I have one?* to a bouquet of flowers. Flowers are to gather for Mom. The joy is in the picking and in the giving of a gift that will make her happy and not break the giver's little heart.

It is birthday party day, Saturday morning, and Thea's friends will be coming in a few minutes. Station wagons and vans have been arriving all morning with supplies. *Where did the streamers come from?* my wife asks. She's been working upstairs. *And this HAPPY BIRTHDAY THEA cake?* I shrug, I have no idea whose parents have offered to bring what. The cake was left on our front porch like a charity baby. Someone rang the bell and then drove away before I could say thank you.

I suddenly realize I have a clean diaper in my pocket. Not where it belongs. Steve and the barbecue arrived during the last changing of the guard, at least an hour ago. *Ed, come here!* I call. He runs away. That's the thing about Ed — he always does what I tell him. *And be careful!* He's holding a balloon in front of his face. I'm afraid he'll fall down the basement stairs. He doesn't, he runs into a wall. The balloon pops and he sits down hard and starts to cry. At least I can catch him now. He's desolated at the loss of the balloon and, more important, he's dry and clean after an hour without a diaper. Part of me is saying I should take this opportunity, we've been thinking he might be old enough to start toilet training ... and another part of me is saying, Shut up, you idiot. Shut up wins for now. I wrestle Ed into a diaper while he's trying to stand up — this is position number 201 in the *How to Enhance Your Diaper Changing* book — and then blow up another balloon for him. Like first love, the loss of a balloon is devastating and quickly forgotten in the joy of a new one. Ed runs off, holding it in front of his face and rubbing his drippy nose against it. Now it'll stick to the wall all right. The doorbell rings.

Dad! Speaking of sticking to the wall, Sam's balloon has lodged in a ceiling cornice. He can't get it. Neither can I. I blow up another one for him.

The girls all arrive within five minutes of eleven o'clock. All the moms ask if they can stay and help. My mouth is open to invite them in, but my wife thanks them and sends them on their way. *They were just being polite,* she tells me. Oh.

I know little girls. The idea is to say something goofy right off and let them get their giggles at you. That way no one feels left out. And don't worry about what to say — anything in your head will do. A group of six-year-old girls will giggle at paint drying, if you point it out to them.

Now, girls, does anyone want something to drink? This isn't my goofy line, I'm just trying to get them comfortable, but they giggle anyway. The doorbell rings. *Or something to eat?* I say, and they giggle harder. *That's a pretty dress, Trinley,* I say. They collapse on the floor, tears starting in their eyes. Thea is laughing as hard as any of them. I thank them because they're a very receptive audience. These aren't really good jokes. Sam's balloon comes floating down, bouncing against the top of my head. The girls laugh so hard I start to worry for their health. Good thing they aren't drinking anything or they'd all pee their pants.

Darling — my wife's voice is loud enough to carry over the din, but carefully noncommittal — *did you arrange for ... donkey rides?* I am puzzled and somewhat irrationally guilty.

You see, I can't remember *not* arranging for donkey rides. I run to the front door.

A man I have never seen before is standing on our front lawn holding, yes, a donkey on a halter. The man is smiling. The donkey's nose is in our flower bed, nuzzling the dry twigs and hollow husks I keep meaning to rake out if only I can find the time, and the rake, and a bag to put them in. What is that poem, never the time and the place and the loved one all together — something like that.

Hello there, says the man with the donkey. *I'm by way of being a friend of Jack Zlavin.* It takes me a minute. *Charlene's dad.* We smile at each other. I introduce myself. He nods. I never seem to be able to get people to tell me their name.

Can I get you a cup of coffee? I ask him. *Or a thistle or something?*

That's when I notice the smoke coming from the side of the house. My wife asks if I've seen Imogen recently, and I haven't, but I'd really like to find out what's burning. You know what they say — where there's smoke, there are higher insurance premiums. I pelt around the side of the house, and the black clouds are stronger and thicker, but I don't see any flames. I follow the smoke down the laneway between the houses, and there in the backyard is a busy barbecue, wieners and burgers and onions, two chefs in tall hats and aprons, holding tongs and spatulas.

Clouds of aromatic smoke march across the landscape like an invading army. Dogs are barking, people are coughing. It may be fancy but I think I can hear smoke detectors going off in nearby houses. The big chef is Steve, Erin's dad. I remember he offered to come over with the barbecue and food from the butcher shop down the street. He looks quite at home in front of a smoky grill. The small chef is Imogen. Her hat is falling over her eyes and her oven mitts go right up to her shoulders. She squeals whenever a tongue of flame shoots up from the coals.

Take Back the Meat

I THINK THEA HAS A GOOD TIME at her party. She certainly eats and talks and giggles a lot. We all sing *Happy Birthday!* even Sam, and when Ed realizes that it's not his birthday, he has to be carried away. I get him upstairs and check his diaper, fine, but he's holding this dark brown mess in his hands and I panic. *It's cake,* he says and, feeling like some weird fetishist, I smell it. *Cake, all right,* I say, relieved, though not relieved enough to share with him.

I'm worried when the games don't go over very well. I'd planned on a jolly few minutes of Musical Chairs and Visually Challenged Person's Bluff, but all they want to do is stand in corners and whisper, and shriek whenever Ed sneezes or pops a balloon. And pet the donkey. Forget about pinning the tail on it or riding it, they all want to stand in the front yard patting its muzzle and offering it blades of grass. At least it's nice and warm for the day after Hallowe'en — golden leaves, autumn sunshine in a blue sky, black smoke from the barbecue.

Sam and the Donkey Man seem to have hit it off. They're engaged in earnest conversation, holding plates of cake and plastic cups of juice. Guy stuff. The donkey nods every now and then too, looks like a cocktail party out there. Immie is certainly enjoying herself, smoke-grimed and productive, carrying dirty plates into the kitchen, filling big green garbage bags with crumbs and cups and half-eaten hot dogs — Ed likes to peel the skin off before eating them, I can't watch, I get squeamish at a *bris* too. Am I exploiting Imogen? Child-labor laws would probably have something to say about four-year-olds engaged in heavy physical activity, but when I offer to do it for her she gets angry. *Daddy — let me!*

My wife has a deadline, so I try to keep the kids away, but

when I sneak a moment to check on her up in the third-floor office I find a hive of activity: Ed chatting up a storm and parking his little matchbox cars in rows on his diaper-change pad — talk about your pit stop — and Thea's friend Margaret whimpering quietly in the corner. In an old movie, my wife would be barking *Sell* into one telephone and *Buy* into another, and working a lit cigar around her face without using her hands, but this is the nineties, she's e-mailing articles to Hungary while explaining to Margaret that lots of people make a mess of their braids. *I can't do them either,* she says. *Why don't we put your hair in a ponytail? There, that's lovely.*

Margaret looks up at me. *Thea's hair is so beautiful today — did you put it in braids?* she asks. I shake my head. I've attempted French braids more than once. I always think I'm getting it and then, after pulling this strand this way and crossing that one over, pulling tight and repeating a few times, I end up with a freshly shampooed Gordian knot. Actually, once I managed to tie a perfect bowline. Great if I wanted to moor Thea to the kitchen table or something, not much good as a party hairstyle. Her hair today was done by Eva, a nice older lady from down the street who neatens children up as they go past her house. She handles her stretch of the sidewalk like an assembly-line worker, tucking in a shirt, doing up a button, brushing away dust, and then starting on the traffic going the other way. She and Thea hit it off very well. I think Thea reminds her of the granddaughter she never had, the one whose parents don't know how to look after her.

What are you making, Eddie? I ask him. I don't want him to feel left out in all this birthday hoopla. He stares at me as if I am too stupid to breathe on my own. *That,* he enunciates clearly, *is the highway.* Four rows of cars, very neat, bumper to bumper, unmoving. It's the highway all right.

The fax rings. Hungary calling.

Come on downstairs, Ed. Let Mom finish. And you too, Margaret. It's time to open the presents, I say. Ed's eyes light up. *Not for you,* I remind him. His eyes go out again.

STEVE IS A NICE GUY, big and friendly, a good-natured bear with those longhorn mustaches that Lech Walesa made so popular a few years back. *Hey, Richard, come out back,* he says. *Just a minute,* I say. I hope nothing has caught fire. I count heads in the living room. Everyone is accounted for except Sam. I run to the front window and there he is, waving good-bye as the Donkey Man trudges away. I dash out on the porch and call, *Thank you!* The donkey turns around to sneeze at me. The man keeps walking.

Did you know, Sam is very excited, *that the donkey pooped every time a streetcar went past?* We live close to the streetcar route, I can hear them squealing late at night. They don't do anything for my bowels, though. *Oh really,* I say without much enthusiasm. The evidence is unmistakable. I examine it as if I were Sherlock Holmes, and conclude that four hundred and eighty-three streetcars have gone by in the past couple of hours. Why isn't there that kind of service when I want to go downtown? *Do you want to pick up the poop in a plastic bag,* I say to Sam, *or come inside and watch Thea unwrap her presents?* Sam's jaw drops. *Is there another choice?* he asks piteously — probably what Hobson said. I smile. *How about watching Steve burn something in the backyard?*

THEA IS A METHODICAL PRESENT-UNWRAPPER, and her friends don't seem to mind. She holds each card in her hand, opens it slowly, reads as much of it as she can aloud, asks questions about it, passes it around and only then — only then — does she approach the squishy gift-wrapped parcels, and they too are discussed, unwrapped slowly, handed around and admired in turn. Everybody has something to say about each one, no matter how small it is, how fragile, how soon-to-be-lost. A black nylon handbag no bigger than a thimble — I'll swear I vacuumed up its exact duplicate less than a month ago — is analyzed down to its atom-sized beads. *It'll go with her cocktail dress, you know. The bias cut with leg-of-mutton sleeves,* says Erin, with a considering cock of her six-year-old head. *And the faux-fur wrap,* adds Margaret, her ponytail swinging happily, back in the thick of it. *And the black pumps will be perfect — hey, wait, where did they go? Thea just opened them.* After Trinley's and Erin's gifts have been dealt with, I look at my watch, expecting it to be suppertime or Christmas or something. One-thirty.

Ed pulls me down so that he can whisper in my ear. I wince in anticipation. Ed's whispers are usually loud enough to be heard through a load-bearing wall. *These are not real presents,* he informs me, *sforzando,* so that I have to shake my head to clear it, the way you do after an explosion. *They are just clothes.* I nod my head. *Prêt-à-porter* Barbie reposes on the couch, her wardrobe gathering around her like a warrior queen's honor guard.

The last gift draws gasps of amazement, admiration and envy from the crowd. Thea teases it out of the wrapping paper inch by inch, until she sees what it is, and then even she cannot resist pulling it free. *Look, it's Polly Pocket's Riding Stable!* No point in looking. I know I won't see anything without a magnifying glass. Polly and her entire world are designed to fit into your pocket. When Thea and I play together I have to use tweezers and a jeweler's loupe in order to move Polly around. If video games train future jet pilots, Polly Pocket trains microsurgeons. Highly competitive fields, both of them, you have to start young and spend a lot of time sitting still. The girls cluster round, Ed pops a balloon, there's a collective shriek, and Polly and her thumbnail palomino stallion fly through the air to land somewhere in the crumb-strewn wild hand-woven Persian yonder. *Don't worry,* I assure Thea. *I'll find Polly tomorrow.*

I just hope she doesn't jam in the vacuum.

ON THE BACKYARD DECK, Steve has been struck dumb. He doesn't notice the beer spilling out of the bottle in his hand. I worry about whether his jaw is locked in the wide-open position and he's never going to be able to close his mouth again. It's a good posture for the dentist's chair but you don't spend more than an hour or two a year in the dentist's chair, and meanwhile you have bugs and soot and airborne debris collecting inside you. I'm relieved when he closes his mouth, takes a swig from the beer bottle and stares at me.

Sam here tells me that you don't — he pauses, he can hardly say it — *you don't have a barbecue.* Sam glances at me apologetically. He didn't mean to give away the family secret. I wink at him. *That's right,* I say.

When Linda told me to get our barbecue over for the party, I just assumed ... another pause ... *it was because your own barbecue was broken. And now Sam tells me he's never eaten anything ... never eaten anything that you've barbecued. Good God, man.*

Nice to know I can still amaze people. *We just fry our steaks and chops,* I say. It's a treat to see his face.

And your wieners? he asks, but he's actually afraid of my answer. I get like that when I'm watching a horror movie — don't say it, don't say it ...

Through the back window I can see movement in our living room. *Boiled,* I say over my shoulder, just to hear Steve scream, and head inside. Thea has unwrapped her presents, Imogen has put all the wrapping into a garbage bag, and

Charlene's mom is standing in the doorway. *Good-bye,* I say, *and thank you so much for coming to Thea's party.* Charlene is a skinny no-nonsense kid. I like her. She waves good-bye to Thea, then turns to me, puts her hands on her hips. *Where's the grab bag?* she asks.

Oh right. Many parents spend the entire arms budget for a developing country on grab bags. My kids have brought home semi-precious stones, limited-edition collectibles and imported Belgian chocolates, but I've gone into the matter in some depth and the things they like tend to fall into two categories — they either Make A Noise or Make A Mess. I try to cover both ends. This year everyone gets a chocolate bar, mini-harmonica, stamp pad and, my favorite, a Whistle Spray Paint Top — you wind it up and let it loose on a big sheet of paper, and it shoots paint through holes that open and close as it whistles a tune. Talk about opportunity, I can hardly wait to try it myself. The boys will get one too. *I don't want a stupid little harmonica,* Sam told me when I bought them. *There are no stupid little harmonicas,* I told him sternly. *Only stupid little harmonica players.*

The other girls leave shortly after, except for Erin. I go out to the backyard, where her dad is holding the barbecue tongs like they're the Olympic torch. The barbecue itself is still smoking away. *I thought you might like to try it,* he says. *It's easy. I'm going to take my little girl home now. I'll leave the grill on. There's lots of hamburgers left. Why don't you try cooking them for the boys.* I don't say anything.

Empower yourself. He sounds like what's-his-name on TV with the big smile. He hands the tongs over to me. *Take back the meat,* he says. *You can do it.*

Thanks, Steve, I say. He salutes, marches off through the house. I turn off the barbecue, put my arm around Sam's shoulder. *Pizza for dinner,* I say. I don't know if I'm ready to barbecue yet, and besides Michael's family doesn't do meat.

The doorbell rings. I can hear Thea's voice calling *Jason's here! Hurry, Sam, or your party will start without you!* Sam starts into the house, turns and looks back at me. *Happy birthday, son,* I tell him. He smiles and runs inside.

Dream Catcher

SAM TAKES HIS FRIEND UPSTAIRS so they can hit each other with plastic weapons and jump on beds and shout and fall on each other. They call it Superheroes but I think they must be getting mixed up, unless Giggle Man or The Human Door-Slam are some of the new crime-fighters. Thea and Ed retreat together to play Barbies. It's an unlikely pairing, but Ed loves to have his ideas taken seriously. I'm assuming it was his idea to cram Ken headfirst into the big cauldron and dance around in a diaper. I must have looked surprised, because Thea asks if there is anything wrong. *No no,* I say hurriedly, I'm all for multiculturalism, and really Cannibal Barbie looked quite hungry for her Long Pig. Imogen puts the finishing touches on a tidy living room, I don't know whether to encourage this behavior or not. I hope she isn't feeling oppressed or anything, but at the same time it's nice to have cleaning help. They talk about having a doctor in the family, but we don't get sick that often and the house gets messy almost every half-hour.

The bell rings, and as soon as I open the door I know it's her. I don't even have to hear her voice. For one thing her car is parked on the sidewalk with the motor running. *Come in come in!* I say to Michael, who reminds me of young Prince Hamlet, fat and scant of breath and dressed in black. *The guys are upstairs killing each other. There's food and drink in the kitchen and a few balloons still unpopped in the living room. I'll take your present. What do you want to do?* He smiles at me uncertainly. Maybe he doesn't know what he wants yet, maybe he's not used to being asked. He drifts upstairs slowly, uncertainly. He'll act only when compelled. His mother sniffs the air, not appreciatively. *I smell barbecue,* she says. *Michael doesn't do barbecue — and he doesn't like the preservatives in most snacks. You said there would be pizza — that's all right for a treat, but please only one piece, and only plain tomato. The party's over at four o'clock, right? I'll see you then.* She clatters down the steps, jumps in her car and speeds away. The wind changes, warmth returning to a momentarily chilly afternoon, and then a gigantic THUD from upstairs shakes the whole house. Those noises are always louder when you're listening to them than when you're making them. *What on earth is going on?* I yell up the stairway the way my parents did, and hear, faintly, reassuringly, *Nothing.* Just what I used to say.

The doorbell rings again. And again. More superheroes, including one in costume. *You made it, Batman!* I cry, shaking his hand. *Sam will be so glad. He invited you specially.* His mom — should I call her Mrs. Wayne? — looks confused, not used to her son being greeted so effusively I suppose. Shrieks from upstairs followed by the pitter-patter of running feet, and Ed comes sliding down on his shirtfront, hotly pursued by — *Give it back!* Thea is probably talking about the arm protruding from between his clenched teeth. I catch Ed, tickle him until his jaw muscles relax, toss the arm back upstairs.

Ken? I ask. Thea returns to her room and slams the door. Well, I can't blame her. A moment later another enormous THUD brings plaster dust down in a cloud. Ed and I scamper up to see — *What on earth is going on?* my wife calls from the third floor. *Nothing,* apparently, but I open the door to make sure. The Incredible Bed-Jumper has met his mortal enemies The Pillow People and, under the influence of the infamous Dr. Gravity, everyone has fallen in a heap. *Anyone hurt?* I ask — they all wear masks of guilt, except Batman, who has his own. *Okay then, the crimewave's over. How about snacktime,* I say and they run downstairs. The thunder of their passing evokes Memories of the Serengeti. I wonder if President's Choice has done that one yet.

I've decided what to do about Immie. If she's going to perform menial work, she should get menial wages. *Here, honey,* I say, reaching into my pocket and pulling out a quarter. *And thanks. The living room looks great.* Her eyes light up. *Money — yahoo!* She's got the right attitude but no pockets, so she gives the quarter to me to keep.

ORANGE POP COMES in giant two-liter bottles that need slings and derricks to be properly maneuvered into position for pouring. Sam and Batman have the brilliant idea of laying the pop bottle on its side before unscrewing the top and letting the orange fountain spill out into the cup. A great idea, but it requires a level surface for the pop bottle to rest on, and the surface they have chosen is, alas, the kitchen table, which slopes down to every point of the compass. I enter the kitchen just as the top comes off the bottle, too late to avert the crisis, especially with all these small bodies between me and the rolling, spewing bottle, but I'm better at damage control anyway. I make a series of rapid springs for the pop, tea towel, tap, sink, table, back to the tap, knocking children around like ninepins, and then knocking the bottle over myself in my haste to get it closed properly. Not much left in it now. The good thing about orange pop is that it blends pretty well with our kitchen decor. I force a smile. *Has everyone had something to eat?* I ask. Universal headshakes, so I pass around the bowls of potato chips, almost stepping on — *Sam, get up!* he's lying underneath the table with his mouth open, catching the last of the dripping orange pop.

So far it's a routine party — camaraderie, high jinks and pizza coming. I've got the boys nicely charged up, but I notice a single quiet figure on the outskirts of the general electricity.

Is everything okay? I ask Wally the Weeper. *Are you enjoying yourself so far?* He looks at me with his spaniel eyes. *Yes, sir. It's very ... very ...* He swallows. He can't finish what he was going to say. His eyes are moist and full. *Have some potato chips,* I say, putting the bowl in his hands. *Then we'll play games, kick the can or tag or — Oh no, Michael!*

He startles like a guilty thing upon a fearful summons. *How are you feeling, Michael? Fine, I hope.* My smile is artificial and full of preservatives, just like the potato chips in his mouth. If he doesn't do meat or junk food, what's he going to make of sour cream and smoky bacon flavoring? Already his mournful black suit is covered in fragrant dust. We all like the chips. To me they have come to represent one of the four basic food groups — the light brown, along with butterscotch and peanut butter. But it would be hard to justify them as health food, considering that they are designed to evoke the flavor of something that is already artificially preserved.

Sorry, Michael, I say. *I wasn't thinking.* I lead him out of the kitchen, squat down to his level. He's chewing enthusiastically, not foaming at the mouth yet. *You'd better not have any more of that stuff. Would you like —* I stop, what do we have in the house that his mom would approve of — *an apple,* I say, kind of lamely. *No, no. I love these chips,* he says. Increase of appetite has grown by what it fed on. Damn.

How about just a bite of an apple? I say, brushing surreptitiously at his clothes. *Just a bite.* Serpent, that's what I am. Except not as persuasive. *No no! Please don't give me an apple,* he says. *Please.*

What can I do? He doesn't want to leave Paradise. *Okay,* I tell him. *You won't have to eat an apple.*

I AM A FIRM BELIEVER in gender equality. My consciousness has been raised so high you can see it from way down the block, and I have done my level best to offer all our children the same opportunities and options, but there's no getting away from it — boys and girls eat chips differently. Boys move around. Our kitchen is a tornado of male movement with a bowl of chips at its eye — and Thea, standing still beside it. *Hi, honey,* I tell her. *Nice to see you.* She smiles around a mouthful of chips and absentmindedly tweaks Batman's ears as he hurtles past. He falls down.

Do you want to go and get your present for Sam? I ask her. It was actually her idea to give her brother a birthday present. My wife and I fell over ourselves with approval, and Sam buried his head in his hands because he knew that now he'd have to give her one.

Of course there are other sex differences. Girls seem quite capable of holding two thoughts in their heads at once, though neither one is exactly what you'd like them to be thinking about. *Thea, why don't you get Sam's present and put it with the others.* She smiles at me, doesn't move. Boys, on the other hand, have no thoughts in their heads for long periods of time. Then they want to discuss God or refinish the basement.

Let's play a game, I say. *Everyone grab a chair and carry it to the living room.* I must say I had thought of this as a prelude rather than the main event, but it turns out to be pretty popular all by itself. Before I can say another word everyone except Thea is carrying a kitchen chair and running around, shouting, bumping into walls and each other and falling down. Another sex difference — boys like falling down. Thea is washing her hands at the kitchen sink. She smiles tolerantly as the boys, having made a circuit of our downstairs, run through the kitchen again, knocking into each other and puffing with pride. *My chair is the biggest,* claim several of them. Thea tweaks Batman's ears and he falls down. She giggles.

What on earth? My wife squeezes down the hall with a doubtful look but, like me, she doesn't want to stop a group of children having a more or less harmless good time.

Musical chairs, I answer straight-faced. *What do you think?* She winces at a crash which results in four human and eight chair legs waving in the air.

I think it would be better with music, she says, and then bursts out laughing. When I see what she's laughing at, I have to smile too — inch by inch across our dining room floor, glacierlike, huge, undeflectable, inevitable as the end of the world, the overstuffed armchair I inherited from my grandfather is moving toward us. From beneath it comes a series of short, powerful grunts. *Ed, are you okay?* I ask.

The doorbell rings and I run to answer it, not a straight course, more like a steeplechase — leap the orange puddle, climb Grandpa's chair which is stuck in the kitchen doorway, hurdle a collection of stools and children, then, realizing the *50% OFF* coupon is stuck under a fridge magnet, backtrack, grab the coupon, slide through sticky orange — *damn* — climb the chair again meeting Ed unexpectedly at the summit, tumble down the far side in a heap, no bones broken, and limp toward the front hall. The doorbell rings again as I cross the finish line.

One plain pizza, one with pepperoni, one with everything else. My coupon is for another pizza chain. The delivery guy has change today — a portent. I'm not superstitious but I tell him to keep it.

SAM OPENS HIS PRESENTS before I can clear the dirty dishes off the table. By the time I get to the living room, it's all over except for a heap of paper and cards and empty boxes that my wife is putting into a green garbage bag — I wonder if I should offer her a quarter — and a learning game from, just a guess, Michael. The boys are upstairs shooting each other with lasers. I can hear the firing from here, and the whine of the ricochets and the screams of the wounded. I used to make the same noises myself. Imogen and Eddie are playing trains. He has his arms around her waist and she is chugging placidly around the room. He sneezes and wipes his nose on her shirt. What are sisters for?

And standing at the foot of the stairs, gazing peacefully up into the gunfire, is Wally the Weeper. *How's it going?* I ask him. *Did you get enough to eat?* He swallows and says, *Yes, sir.* He's holding something in his hand, a circle with thread stitched around it, looks like a basketball net for elves. *It's a Dream Catcher,* he says. *Sam gave it to me. I'll hang it in my bedroom to catch all my dreams. Isn't it beautiful?* Wally sighs, stroking it. A tear rolls down his cheek.

My wife looks up. *That's the present Thea made for Sam,* she says. Immie and Eddie chug past us. I can understand how Sam might not want his sister's present but — *Did Thea mind when Sam gave away her present?* I ask. BANG! A very loud noise — from upstairs? We all wait, but it doesn't repeat. *Thea hoped I would like it,* says Wally *And I do. Oh I do.*

I don't have a problem with this. An artist is appreciated and a Dream Catcher goes where it will do the most good. Next time the train comes past, I hitch on behind Eddie. *Let's go pick up Mom,* I tell Immie, and we steer over. Wally hitches on too, so that when Thea and the boys tumble downstairs to ask if we can hear the sirens, we're stretched all the way across the living room. They hitch on one by one, with Thea and Sam at the end, making a giant birthday train winding its way around our downstairs.

It's been a good day, I think to myself, enough excitement to last until next time and no kids threw up or peed their pants — another difference between girls and boys, by the way. Imogen is still at the front of the train. She's making a quiet pigeon noise as we shuffle down the hall. The little engine that cooed. *You know,* my wife says thoughtfully, *those sirens are awfully loud. I wonder where the fire is.* Next thing we know the front door is knocked open and the hall is full of asbestos uniforms. The fire is in our backyard.

*   *   *

I'M SORRY, I tell the firefighter with the notebook, a hectic and smelly few minutes later. *I'm not very experienced with these things — I thought I was switching* off *the gas.* He explains it to me several times, but I still don't really know what happened, something about negative pressure and reverse fuel flow toward a nearly empty tank — the bottom line is that the barbecue blew up.

My wife is on the phone to the hardware store for a replacement when the doorbell rings again. A dramatic figure stands on the front porch, cloaked, top-hatted, sneezing. A magician, but he can't make a stuffy nose disappear. *Sorry I'm so late,* he says. *I've been in bed all day with this cold. I just got up, and Sue made me change and come over. Birthdays are hell, aren't they. Hope all the kids aren't driving you crazy — any of them left?* I tell him no. He takes a bottle of aspirin from inside his cape and shakes a couple into his hand. *Oh. Well, do you think I could have a glass of water?* He swallows the pills, hands me back the water glass, turns to go. *I really feel lousy,* he says. What can I tell him? *Magician, heal thyself.* I shut the door.

Disorganization Man

WITH THE BIRTHDAY–HALLOWE'EN conjunction safely past, I am no longer able to put off all the little tasks that have been piling up around me like leaves which I really must rake up one of these days. I like to think of myself as an organized kind of guy — hey, there's no harm in thinking, is there? I like to think about exotic faraway places too, and high-seas adventure and a girl named Nancy who was in my first-grade class — so that when the chores pile up I immediately MAKE A LIST. The books on how to organize your life, make a million in real estate and achieve total complete inner peace always begin by telling you to MAKE A LIST. They probably go on to say other things, but by then I've been called away to referee a fight between Godzilla and Sailor Moon and, when I finish tripping over toys, stacking laundry, dancing to the radio with Ed — he likes the CBC gardening shows best — rescuing lost platoons of GI Joe soldiers from behind the fridge and taking them back to base camp for a little R&R

with glamorous PX Party Barbie who comes with these teeny weeny little — Thea tells me they're balloons — anyway, when I get back the book on how to organize my life has vanished and I haven't got past the part that says MAKE A LIST.

Today there's a lot to do, reminds me of yesterday, but looking back all I remember doing yesterday is separating laundry into two piles, both of which were dirty. And playing Detectives with Imogen. She was Inspector Sharp and I was Inspector Strong. *What do you think, Inspector Strong, is that a clue?* she'd say, pointing at a bush. *Definitely,* I'd say. We had the two important detective accoutrements, fedoras and donuts. Mine had a gray silk band, Immie's had chocolate icing. Then Sam and Thea came home from school and we all built a fort in the playroom out of the toys we were supposed to be putting away. And then, before I knew it, it was dinnertime, and another chore opportunity had slipped on the stairs and fallen down.

But that was yesterday. Today is Saturday and I'm sure we'll get a lot done. I begin my list right after breakfast. I find a pencil and a scrap of paper with only one important phone number — whose, I wonder — and write firmly on the back until I have to use the bathroom. Not the one upstairs, my wife is cleaning that. She doesn't believe in lists. I use the bathroom in the basement, and while I'm down there I decide to start the laundry, only we happen to be out of detergent. That's okay, shopping is right at the top of the list. We'll go at once.

Come on, you buck privates, into the van, I call, me and GI Joe, except Thea insists on being a doe private. The van sputters and starts and sputters some more. I had a teacher like that back in public school — you had to pity the kids in the front row. Our van doesn't have a speech impediment, it's almost out of gas. That was item number four or five. It moves up the list. But on the way to the gas station we pass a lawn sale — and Sam needs a new dresser, and there's one for sale. *Hang on!* I shout, stopping suddenly and bumping up onto the curb. The kids say it isn't nearly as much fun driving with Mom. The nice lady in charge of the sale stands protectively in front of her collection of porcelain miniatures, but we ignore her, check out the dresser, climb on it, pull out all the drawers, rock it back and forth, try to lift — *Not yet, Ed. We haven't paid for it.* We decide to buy it, also a book about bees, *So we'll be ready when they take over,* says Sam. He was stung for the first time last year. The dresser is heavy and the lady in charge is wispy and ethereal-looking, so I try to lift it by myself, then I try with the kids helping, but I trip over Ed, who is supporting from underneath. Finally the ethereal lady takes one end and we take the other and we get it beside the van. Fortunately our vehicle comes with roof racks. Unfortunately it doesn't come with a boy scout to tie the knots. I decide to come back later for the dresser.

The kids are milling around like gnats in a horse pasture. We seem to be the only people interested in this lady's lawn sale. Other cars slow down as they drive by but no one is stopping. I thank the lady. She nods calmly, full of a kind of grim inner peace, but as we drive off her face breaks into a beautiful smile. I can see it in the rearview mirror.

Three blocks later our front tire goes flat, I must have punctured it going over the curb. The last time I changed a tire it took hours, and I sprained my wrist so badly I was in a soft cast for two weeks afterwards. And that was a bicycle tire. I'm not confident, but I am a member of the motor league. There's a phone booth across the street — *And bring some gas,* I say. Might as well be efficient.

The kids have finished climbing over the seats and sitting on each other. Now they're getting hungry. Fortunately I keep some emergency mints right beside the tire jack I'm afraid to use. We're all chewing happily when the motor league shows up. His name is Brian. He changes the tire and adds gas to the tank. Talk about your full service. I wish I'd asked him to pick up laundry detergent on the way over. Brian frowns at my membership card. *This has expired,* he tells me. He makes me promise to renew my membership today. *Make that the first chore on your list,* he says. How does he know about my list? *Okay,* I tell him, *I'll do it right now.* He's shaking his head as we drive away.

Our front hall is tidy. So is the living room. From upstairs comes the noise of the vacuum cleaner. I find my list on the kitchen table where I left it. At the top, beside *Go Shopping,* I've written *Sandwich Bread* and *Milk* and underlined them. Oh no. I wonder what we'll eat for lunch.

Water Sports

SATURDAY AGAIN, a whole week has steamrolled over us, smoothing and flattening our rough surfaces and leaving us slightly sticky to the touch. My wife is in Montreal facilitating something. I'm in bed in the dark, listening to a small voice murmuring, *Dada Bye bye chair Eddie Sam Thea vacuum Immie lawnmower duck.* Ed runs through his vocabulary as soon as he gets up. I can hear him very faintly from the warm but precarious edge of sleep, seems I'm always close to the edge of sleep, and that edge is always crumbling underneath me.

Ed tries the words he has trouble with. This morning it's *elbow,* and all the time in the background I can hear the crib groaning and squeaking as Ed bounces up and down. He lives to bounce, it's his form of self-soothing, like a blankie or a thumb, only he's less likely to require orthodontia than treatment for concussion. Ed might have been an aerobics instructor in a previous life, only they haven't had aerobics instructors for very long, have they. Maybe he was an india-rubber ball.

Ellboy, elbow — that's it. He repeats it to make sure he's got it right, *elbow elboy elboy*. Then he stops, and I know I'm about to be pushed off the precipice of sleep into the free-fall of urgent summons, *DADA ... DADA ... DADA*. No other call of nature is so strong. *Coming, Ed* — that's me fumbling for my glasses in the dark, deciding that my bladder can wait. *DADA DADA* — louder now. *All right, Ed, all right.*

I never look at the clock until I have my coffee because I don't want to know, and besides I'm too busy making sure Ed doesn't turn on all the elements, jam the sink with Cheerios and lock himself in the cupboard with the adult-proof lock.

Ed's a jolly morning companion, smiling as he feeds himself and flings his spoon into the corner, smiling as he grabs everything within reach — juice, newspaper, napkin, hot-water tap. I pull his high chair away from the sink and he laughs and grabs my glasses, flings them after the spoon — at least that's where I think he flings them, so it's where I start looking. I take a firm step in that direction and, by one of those coincidences that Thomas Hardy used to think were so ironic, it turns out the glasses are a step away, exactly a step. There's a *scrunching* sound underfoot and another in my stomach. I pick up the pieces and try to remember where we keep the Scotch tape.

The other kids come down about the same time as the sun comes up. The kitchen is filled with light, finally, and the floor covered with cereal, spilled milk and useless tears, and I tell them that we have to go to the place in the mall that fixes glasses while you wait. *And if you get dressed right now we'll buy some toys too,* I say. That's not a bribe, a bribe is where you give them the toy first — and it never works. They start playing right away, and then they offer you a turn and you forget what you wanted them to do. I've taped my glasses a little bit off center, and, you know, the dirt on the floor is starting to look like part of the pattern on the linoleum. Maybe I shouldn't get them fixed.

Fall Dreams

*   *   *

OUR MALL LOOKS LIKE YOUR MALL, so I won't describe it
except to say that the glasses place is near a courtyard with a
series of low posts which are perfect for resting against if
you're a grown-up, or playing Leap Frog or Slalom Racing or
Bounce Dancing or Slide 'n' Stop — our favorite — if you're
not. And, oh yes, there's a tinkling fountain in the middle,
irregular shaped, thin and twisting like a stream, with rocks
on the bottom. A charming spot.

We always have a great time in the mall. There's so much to
look at and fondle — people and shoes and goldfish and popcorn and ashtrays with real sand in them. Our voices bounce
around off all the concrete in quite a satisfying way, and so do
we. Then we get to the glasses place, where the lady holds out
her hand. *Give me your eyewear now, Mr. Scrimger,* she says,
causing a moment's confusion because the word doesn't regis-
ter. Ralph Lauren may sell eyewear, but I don't have any, what
I have are glasses. I can hardly wait until he gets into disposable diapers with a picture of a little pony on the front, and all
the drugstore clerks will be talking about *Tushwear.* Heavens,
give the designers time and we'll be able to walk into a hardware store and order an Armani U Bend or a Nike Ball Float
— advertised as *Water Jordan,* maybe. Where was I, oh yes,
the lady asks for my eyewear — *And we'll replace your broken
frames and get them back to you in ... half an hour,* she says.

Maybe I haven't given this quite enough thought. *That's a
long time,* I say, plucking Ed from the top of a Calvin Klein
display case. *Eddie chair yes!* he shouts piteously. I put him
down. *Eddie chair no,* I say. I'm quite fluent in Edspeak. *No
no chair no, climb no,* driving the point home. Ed's shoulders
slump. And with a gulp I take off my glasses, plunging myself
headfirst into a familiar shadowy half-world. I'm kind of surprised to be here with my clothes on, usually I'm in the swimming pool or getting ready for bed. The world is an amiable

blur to my naked eye, a colorful fog I drive through without headlights. Can I really do this? I wonder, can I keep track of four small children in a mall, relying only on my sense of touch? The short answer is no, but you have to remember that in his day Napoleon was a short answer and look what happened to him. Can I do it? I tell you, for a second I'm ready to cancel the deal, tell the eyewear lady I'll wait until my wife gets back from Montreal or the kids are old enough to drive. Then the little man who lives on my shoulder, the little crooked man with the raspy voice who tells me to do things — the little man I shouldn't listen to, but he's right there beside my ear and he sounds so encouraging, so devil-may-care; the little man who tells me to grow a beard, buy a thirty-six-speed bike or answer the phone in a Scottish accent — says, *Go ahead.* I give over my glasses and grab hold of Ed. Once you have found him, never let him go.

Five minutes later we're on our way to the muffin place. I figure if I can keep them all seated around a table with their mouths full I'll be all right. Only, the muffin shop is *that* way from the glasses place and I unknowingly lead us *this* way, past a perfumed haze and a leathery haze and a popular-music haze toward the unmistakable tinkling sound of the fountain courtyard. And before I know it they're all having fun, sliding and leapfrogging and bouncing among the posts, and I don't have the heart to stop them. *Careful,* I shout over and over again, and *Don't run, Sam.* Maybe this'll work after all, I think to myself — as they say, no man is as blind as he who cannot see.

IT'S THE SLIDE 'N' STOP that does us in. Ed masters the slide perfectly but doesn't stop against the post. Doesn't stop at all, as far as I can tell. I hear a pretty solid plunk and a splash, and Imogen screams.

Where's Ed? I cry, groping forward to grab the the nearest child — Thea, it turns out. You know she looks very pretty with her hair like that. *Ed's in the fountain,* she answers matter-of-factly. *Where? Where? Thea, show me where he is!*

Ed is the worst kind of non-swimmer because he thinks — no, he *knows* — despite a huge body of evidence to the contrary, that he can swim just fine. Time and again and again and again he has jumped into a swimming pool and been dragged back choking and spitting water. I used to think he was fearless, but I'm starting to wonder if all that bouncing in his crib is really good for him. Stubborn belief in the face of overwhelming data makes for great TV but it's no way to handicap a horse race.

A crowd is gathering. I can't see them, but I know they're there. I hear a murmuring in the background, a vague and minatory sussuration, like curtains being pulled open and shut by a whole streetful of disapproving old ladies. I get right down to the water's edge, but I can't see Ed, or feel him. I scrabble around but I can't find him. *Over here, Dad,* shouts Sam from the other side of the fountain. Well, I'm not going to worry about my dignity. I wade in. It's up past my knees and surprisingly cold. *Ed! Ed!* I feel around — rocks, water pipes, a candy wrapper, a quarter, another quarter, a Styrofoam cup, something so soft and hideously squishy that I'm glad I can't see it, another quarter, and then I hear a splash right at my feet and bend down and there he is. I pull him out by the boot heel, dripping wet and shivering. *Sam!* I say to his upside-down face, *what are you doing in here? Where's Ed?*

I'd laugh if I wasn't so worried. Sam's one of those blond skin-and-bones kids, looks like an eel when he's wet. He points wordlessly. When we get closer I make out a blur on a nearby rock, repeating very quietly to himself, *Dada Sam Bye bye Immie Thea lawnmower vacuum* in between sneezes.

*   *   *

I'D LIKE TO BE ABLE TO REPORT that the crowd of mall shoppers is sympathetic, but they aren't. Many of them say I oughtn't to have done that. Several of them say I can't do that. None of them has a towel.

My favorite is an annoyed older woman who has, perhaps with justice, some doubts as to my competence as a parent. *Young man, you should pay more attention to your children,* she says. *Several of them are quite damp.*

And I'd like to be able to report that I convince the policewoman in the parking lot that I am allowed to park in the handicapped spot. *But, officer,* I say, *it was physically impossible for me to see the sign.* She doesn't even look up from writing the ticket. *You don't understand. I was blind at the time.*

I would have thought blindness counted as a severe handicap, but she nods, she's heard this one before. *Hey, I didn't know they had a swimming pool in there,* she says handing me the ticket. *Bit late in the year, isn't it?* Then, staring intently, *Nice frames — Ralph Lauren?*

I drive off without answering. Before we're out of the parking lot Thea remembers that I'd promised them a toy. I apologize and say we'll have to come back when we've changed into dry clothes.

I can report that, when my wife calls that night from her hotel and I tell her the story, she bursts into an uncontrollable fit of laughter that lasts for two minutes, and finally has to hang up the phone without saying good-bye, and that she tries to call me again an hour later to apologize and can't even get a word out without going off again.

My Dinner with Everyone

DINNER HAPPENS EVERY NIGHT. You'd think I'd remember it. Mind you, Christmas takes me by surprise too, and it's not like they're keeping that a secret. This afternoon we're in the middle of a hectic game of Red-Light-Space-Explorer-Green-Light-Crazy-Eights — what, you don't play that one? I can't explain all the rules, but there's plenty of running around and lasers and wild cards, and Ed isn't obeying any traffic rules — when I suddenly realize it's too late to roast the chicken that's in the fridge. We'll have to try again tomorrow. If memory serves, I was too late for the chicken yesterday too. You know, in a few days I'm going to have to buy a new one. Thank heavens we live in an age of instant gratification — speed chess, divorce by phone, headaches that disappear by the time you finish this sentence, and dinosaur pasta, easy to heat and serve. *Dinner,* I call a few minutes later, and the cry is taken up all over the house — *Dinner dinner* — feet thumping, voices raised, lights flickering. Thea wins the race by a short head but Sam files a formal complaint to the stewards. I tell them I'll consider it. Ed is attempting a difficult traverse across the scarp of his high chair — *You should never climb alone,* I tell him, helping him to the summit.

The can says tomato sauce, but I've never seen a tomato that color. Actually I've never seen anything exactly that color, though a hummingbird outside a Florida hotel window in 1987 came close. But who cares about purity. The kids love it, except Ed, who is afraid of the tyrannosaurus shape. *It's made of pasta,* I tell him. *You can crush it in your fingers, in fact you already have.* But there's no convincing him. *I scared,* he says. *I scared.* How can I make him eat his own nightmare? I'd be eating the income-tax people. I get him a peanut-butter sandwich. *But you still have to eat your vegetables,* I tell him sternly. He's relieved, I'm amenable and the other kids are orange, so everything is more or less normal when the doorbell rings.

Sam flickers and is gone. Getting him to stay still through an entire meal would take hypnosis or one of the Borgias. *It's for you, Dad!* he calls, and then, *Hey Thea, there's a guy here with a clipboard!* I can't leave Ed, so in the end we all troop into the front hall to meet a smiling parka-clad young man from Save the Children Aluminum Siding — I think I have that right. He has stencils and graphs, and pictures of smiling tots and Easy-To-Maintain siding in Many Popular Designer Colors. I don't quite understand how the scheme works — sounds like the Rainforest Pencils I bought last week for ten dollars each. We all start to ask questions at once. *How old are the children?* we ask, and *What are their names?* and *Do they like to play tag? We like to play tag.* Turns out we're all for saving children but we don't care much about the aluminum siding. I suspect the young man may feel differently, especially after shaking hands with Ed.

Back in the kitchen the radio is telling us about storing our bulbs over the winter. Ed's the only interested listener. I dial vigorously and end up with Bach. The kids giggle over the name. *Can you say Bach, Eddie?* I ask. *No, at the base of the throat — Bachhh. Whoops, those peas came right back up didn't they. Maybe you'd better stop saying Bachhh.* Immie is swaying quietly to the music. *Isn't that pretty, it's a minuet,* I tell her, and she nods, chewing with abstract gentleness as if she doesn't want to hurt what's in her mouth. Dinner for Imogen is like evolution — slow change over time. With the others it's more of a nightly *coup d'état.*

Sam gets that No Honestly I Really Do Mean It look on his face and tells me he's afraid of his vegetables. Thea chimes in, *Me too, Dad. I just know I'm going to be dreaming about celery all night long.* She has a gurgling laugh, very infectious. I can't help joining in even though Ed's dinner chooses that moment to stage a counter-revolution. *Three more bites,* I tell everyone, wiping vigorously with a damp rag, *and we'll see about fruit and dessert.*

Instant quiet. Dessert, like bedtime, imposes order with ruthlessness. Parents have such power. I feel almost Napoleonic as I spoon applesauce into a plastic bowl for Ed, and then I open the cupboard which used to have cookies. Yes, that's what I said — used to. Now it has a ketchup packet, an empty tin and some crumbs. The doorbell rings but I ignore it, trying not to think ahead to Waterloo. I hope they won't cry, and it's my own fault too — I ate the cookies. *Finished my vegetables, Dad,* says Sam. I toss him an apple absently. The doorbell rings. I pull open drawers at random, looking for something sweet, spilling birthday candles, extra packets of ketchup, napkins, notes for a short story, elastic bands, a corkscrew that would have come in handy a couple of nights ago, an empty Tim Horton's bag — talk about an anticlimax — and more ketchup packets. *What's for dessert, Dad?* says Thea. The highlight of the day as far as she's concerned, my poor little girl; been eating dessert for almost seven years now and I'm going to have to look her in the eye and say — what?

Donuts! she shouts. She's seen the bag. I tell her no. Sam frowns, he's been worried ever since I told him who Tim Horton was. *I just don't understand how he can be dead and his donuts are still here,* he says. I must remember to break it gently to him about Laura Secord. *But, Dad,* Thea asks seriously, *if there aren't any donuts, what's for dessert?*

I'm wondering if I can sell them on a new squirt-in-your-mouth candy that comes in tomato flavor — hey, there's weirder stuff out there — when the doorbell rings again. Imogen is still massaging her pasta with her teeth. Ed's finished spreading his applesauce on the arms of his high chair, no doubt to provide himself with a surer grip next time he tries the ascent. I pull him out and we all follow Sam down the hall to the door. And there on our front porch, her breath smoking in the chilly night air, stands a vision from heaven, by which I mean a schoolgirl, shortish, stoutish, sincere, with glasses, a slight overbite and a familiar uniform.

Would you like to buy some Girl Guide cookies? she asks.

Special Projects

MY KIDS SPEND A LOT OF TIME pretending, and that's good, it prepares them for later life — you never know when you might meet an old friend who has gone into the insurance business. I used to pretend too; in one week I was John Glenn, Lawrence of Arabia, Professor Moriarty, Bobby Orr, Kit Carson Trail Blazer and Scout, Gawain, Johnny Quest, Muhammad Ali, Athos and the Scarecrow — and that wasn't a particularly exciting week. I like the kids pretending. I like it that they pretend together. But I confess I'm a little puzzled at what they pretend to be. Mostly it's animals. *What does your favorite fish look like, Dad?* Sam asks after school on one of those late fall days that can't make up its mind whether to rain or snow, so it's not doing anything. I'm upstairs changing Ed, a task that is becoming more and more difficult for both of us as we slouch together toward toilet training.

I don't know whether to think of training as a milestone or a minefield, an opportunity or obstacle, a thrilling ascent of the summit or a long and nauseating tumble down a scree-laden slope, rolling over and over and over and covering yourself in dirt and filth and grime until you can't breathe and then the doorbell rings and it's your next-door neighbor saying, have you noticed the trouble we're having with the drains? I guess it's not a thrilling ascent of the summit, after all. Whatever else it is, though, toilet training is obsessive — it's like a weird cult thing. It takes up all your time and you can't help assuming everyone else is in on it. We ate out only once while we were toilet training the twins, perhaps because I kept going up to complete strangers and asking them if they were *sure* they didn't have to use the bathroom. Most of them were quite sure. A few humored me and went, but you could see they weren't really happy about going — which of course only confirmed the parallel.

At the moment I'm engaged in a species of all-in wrestling. Ed's on his back, feet in the air, pinned except for one shoulderblade, and I'm manipulating the diaper with my free hand — anyway I can't give Sam's fish question all the attention it deserves. *Poached,* I tell him, without thinking, *in a simple herb-butter sauce — why, what's yours?* Ed squirms free, one point to him, and I get one shoulder down again, a point to me. *I like sharks,* he says, and I take a moment to stare at him. The only fish he likes has batter all around it. I can still remember him discovering caviar at my wife's office New Year's Eve party, one of those dress-up affairs that kids hate except for the cocktail swords. You know, it's hard work making polite conversation with other spouses while holding an exploding boy under my arm.

He's got Jerry from down the street with him this afternoon. *Hi there,* I say. I hope Jerry is over his scarlet fever — I think that's what Mrs. Klesko told me it was this time.

I relax momentarily and allow Ed to wriggle free again. He stands up with his fists clenched in front of him. He's got a fighter's build — if you can imagine a midget John L. Sullivan piddling on the bed you've got Ed. *Jerry and I are pretending to be fish today,* Sam tells me. *That's nice,* I say, wondering who they're going to get to play chips. I manage to hypnotize Ed with the swinging telephone cord and get the diaper on him — he doesn't try to fight it, now that he's marked his territory. Ed's not a fish, he's a dog.

THE CHILDREN CHASE ONE ANOTHER all over the house, making swimming motions — even Immie, who still won't put her head under water, and Ed, who probably doesn't have any idea what is going on. From the front window I can see Thea and Rebecca on the lawn, arguing about something. Rebecca is a recent best friend, unmemorable herself but with a truly impressive mother. She came to our house to pick her daughter up from the birthday party and I practically did myself an injury straightening to my full height and deepening my voice. I've met Rebecca's mom a few times now and she always looks like she spent the last eight hours making weighty decisions — Balance of Trade, Future of Third World Health Care kind of decisions, and here I've been worrying which Parcheesi man to jump and how to get Barbie's head out of the dollhouse chimney (actually the head isn't the problem, it's the hair). Everything about Rebecca's mom is meaningful, even her handshake, even her briefcase. I'd never met anyone with a meaningful briefcase until I met her. I don't know her first name but I'll bet it isn't Jou-Jou.

Rebecca is pointing something out, gesturing with gloves that match her scarf and natty fall coat. Thea isn't wearing gloves. She has her hands on her hips and is shaking her head. I know that pose. *Nothing you say will convince me,* she's saying. I knock on the window and wave. Rebecca waves back tentatively. Thea ignores me, keeps shaking her head.

Sam's different; he smiles and says nothing and keeps on going his own way. Just the other day I tried to convince him that Max the Monkey didn't need to sit at the dinner table with us because he was already stuffed. Sam smiled and casually covered the monkey's ears. When I turned away, he whispered, *Don't worry, Max. I know you're real. My dad doesn't know any better.* I guess I didn't, but I'm learning. I apologized to both of them and now use Max as a source of inspiration. *See how straight Max is sitting,* I say to Sam. *And he never leaves the table until he's finished.* Max is actually a lot less trouble at the table than any of the other kids. Not much of a conversationalist, mind you.

I trawl upstairs with a box of cookies and lead the fish down for a snack. Thea joins us in a bad temper, slamming the door, dropping her coat and slouching into the kitchen. She takes a cookie and stuffs it in her mouth. Never let the sun go down on your hunger. *Rebecca is* not *going to come here again,* she says with her mouth full. Always sad when best friends fall apart. *What's the problem about?* I ask. She swells with righteous indignation and explains that Rebecca has stolen her idea for the Science Fair.

She wants to do her project on leopards and I already told her that I wanted to do my project on leopards and there can't be two projects on leopards and hers will be better than mine and everyone will laugh at me, and yesterday Sam got an extra cookie at dinner and I didn't and I can't find my library book and my life is ruined! She buries her head in her arms and sobs heartily, breaking off every few seconds to chew her mouthful of cookie.

It's a heart-wrenching scene. *What Science Fair?* I ask. This is the first I've heard of it. Sam explains while Thea sneaks another cookie. My heart falls lower than a sinking bullet.

TOO FAST, I'M THINKING, it's all happening too fast. I knew this moment would come — just as Achilles knew. There's no getting around your fate. When you choose children you're choosing glory over length of days, it's part of the contract. But not yet, surely. They're only in Grade One. When I was in Grade One homework was tying your shoes. Make a loop, wrap the other end around the loop, pull through to make another loop, pull tight. That took us months. Then on to printing. Science Fairs were another world, the sort of thing your babysitter worried about, like dating or acne or SAT scores.

Thanks to Velcro my kids don't have to tie their shoes. Too bad, I could have helped them. What I can't help them with is a Science Fair project involving — as Sam's does — salt, flour and water. This is the real problem, the rattling skeleton in my closet of fatherly inadequacy. Salt, flour and water are simple household items which, when combined in the right hands, not mine, can be used to make beautiful and effective science projects. Sam can't decide whether he wants to do his project on Central America or the Himalayas. I can't decide whether to whimper or scream. I can barely listen to him talk about it without my blood running cold. I take a cookie. It's something I can control. And it tastes pretty good.

What's your project about? I ask Jerry with a sigh. His father is an engineer.

Jerry starts talking. After a few minutes I leave because I have a load of laundry in the washing machine. When I get back Jerry is still talking. As I understand it, his father is helping him to build something that will be part convection oven and part missile silo — come to think of it, you could put those two ideas together and get our toaster. It has a tendency to fire burned bread at Mach 1 or 2. If we aimed it due east and set it for *very dark,* I'll bet we could hit Libya with a following wind. Use a really heavy rye bread and you might do some damage.

Sam is nodding intelligently. Thea has gone upstairs to her room. I can't help picturing a map made on a board with salt and flour and water and fluorescent paint — a map of, say, Central America, complete with mountain ranges and chief exports, only there'd be a big earthquake wiping out half the indigenous population and changing the shape of the Yucatán peninsula because I got the ingredients all mixed up.

The doorbell rings with a strangely meaningful note. I should have been prepared. I open the door and there is Rebecca's mom, all six and a half feet of her. I abruptly stiffen my spine and wish I'd combed my hair. *Good evening,* I intone huskily.

She looks as if she spent the entire day firing the board of directors. *I think Thea left this at our house last Saturday,* she says, handing me a library book and taking a step back.

Gee thanks, I say. Her car is parked right in front of our house — I can never find a spot there — with the motor running. *I wish I could return something to you but Rebecca never leaves her stuff here.* It's a joke, but you'd never know it from her response. I deepen my voice even further. *You shouldn't have gone to all the trouble,* I say, sounding like the six o'clock news with Darth Vader.

We were on our way to the library anyway, she allows. *Rebecca needs some help with the foreign language sources for her Science Fair project.* Is that a joke too? It sounds like one to me, but you'd never know it from her delivery. I try a neutral smile. She nods and turns in a stately sweep of executive trench coat and designer boots.

Jerry's putting on his hat and boots in the back room. After he leaves and just before Thea screams, I say to Sam, *Do you understand what Jerry's project is about?* Sam shakes his head. Good boy, all that pretending is paying off already.

Thea screams like a madwoman, a maenad on her way to devour the sweet-singing youth who charmed her lately. I'm talking about — *ED!* she screams, racing along the upstairs hallway.

Ed has a peculiar way of getting downstairs. He flings himself down on his stomach, like a fireman shooting down a ladder without touching the individual rungs, only Ed touches each individual stair. Thumpthumpthumpthump, he goes, fast as lightning, and he reaches the bottom of the stairs and keeps going, Thea shaking her fist and screaming at him as she descends more normally.

Look at this! she shrieks, holding out a familiar figure. *What's wrong with your doll?* I ask. She looks the same to me — golden plastic skin, long blonde hair, head tilted kind of coquettishly, bare feet. I don't want to make fun of Thea's distress but I don't see the problem until she explains that the head and body don't go together. The head belongs to another doll. Ed has created a hoax — Piltdown Barbie. I'm impressed that Thea could see through it so quickly, and without carbon dating. *Where's the rest of her?* she shrieks at me, pulling off the mismatched head. Now if she tucked it underneath her arm it could be Anne Boleyn Barbie — probably not a popular model.

I think maybe you and I had better take a look in the dollhouse chimney, I tell Thea, putting my arm around her shoulders. *And honey, prepare yourself. It's not a pretty sight.* Immie comes up behind us at this point, gives my leg a good pinch. Thea screams. I guess she got pinched too. *Stop that!* I say, but Immie just moves away, chuckling to herself. *I am a stingray,* she says.

I'm Fine, Daddy

THE HARDWARE STORE has that distinctive odor of tarred twine and oil paint and hot metal and fresh-cut wood, makes you want to go out and kill something with your bare hands, I wonder if they get it in a can, like air freshener. *I want some wood,* I say. There's no reason to feel inadequate just because I'm not much of a handyman. These people are here to help.

Wood. The hardware guy says it incredulously, as if I've gone into a library and asked to see a book. Ed wanders away in his strangely tight-fitting sweatpants. Without a diaper he looks different, especially from behind. *What kind of wood?* He stares at me through narrowed eyes, Bert his name is, or if it isn't he's wearing Bert's shirt. I know what I want, but it's difficult to put it into terms he'll understand — I suppose kids feel that way all the time. *A flat piece about, oh, this big,* I say, holding out my arms. *Give or take.*

You got any measurements? Bert asks with a frown. Ed is over by the fertilizer — very apt. We had an accident at lunch, and another accident on our way to drop Immie off at afternoon kindergarten, so we should be safe for a while. Ed has been without a diaper for a few days now, nothing between him and the seat of his pants except Fruit of the Loom and these accidents. Most of them are harmless spills, mind you, that's what the nuclear industry calls its occasional accidents, and we have had a couple of Chernobyl-type disasters too — in fact, so far the only clear winner in the war on diaper dependence is Procter & Gamble or whoever it is who makes our laundry detergent.

No no. It doesn't matter what size it is, I say. *Not really. As long as it's about this big.* I show him my arms again. He turns away, he doesn't want to look. I've offended against one of his ten commandments. I suppose there are other hardware commandments, but *Thou Shalt Measure* would come pretty early in the decalogue. *Okay, how about three feet square,* I say. Bert whips a tape measure out of his leather apron. Billy the Kid wouldn't have stood a chance against him, Bert would have had him all measured long before Billy got his own measuring tape out. *Three feet is that long,* he says, pointing. *Is that right?* I pretend to stare at his thumb. Really I'm looking for Ed, who has moved out of sight.

Sure, I say. *Sure. Or ... or maybe a bit bigger.* Bert's breath goes out in a long hiss. He wipes his thinning hair back from his forehead. *How much bigger — this much?* He stretches his tape longer. Is his hand trembling? I can't tell. *Excuse me,* I say, *but I came in with a little boy and I'm worried about him. Can you see him? A little boy in a yellow coat and blue sweat pants.* The store is pretty cluttered, and the aisles are narrow — it's a hardware store, you know what it's like inside. Bert peers around, shrugs his shoulders. *Don't worry, the kid's fine. He's just wandering around, amusing himself.* I nod. That's what I'm worried about, and so would Bert be if he had any sense.

Didn't you wander around hardware stores when you were a kid? he says with a scowl. *No, probably not. But it's all right. Leave the kid alone, give him a chance to have fun. Now, you're looking at particle board, I guess.* He stares at me. I stare at him. *How about three-eighths inch?* he says. *Or three-quarter inch.* I lean toward him. *You pick,* I say. Then I hear Ed's voice and I forget about the wood.

Oh no, I'm fine, he says loud enough to be heard all over the store.

Oh no is right. I'll bet I know where he is. *I'm fine* is what he says to me when he's sitting on the toilet and I ask him if he's done. He likes sitting on the toilet. This whole training thing is as much his idea as mine, so I hear *I'm fine, Daddy* fairly often. It doesn't mean he's done anything. It means he's fine. We're together and he doesn't mind sitting and waiting for — sometimes it seems as if we're waiting for Godot.

The last line of that definitive play is a stage direction, *They do not move.* Neither does Eddie, not even when I try to encourage him by singing motivational songs from Broadway. This afternoon I tried *Every time it rains, it rains pennies from heaven* and *Another Op'nin, Another Show.* We waited and waited, but there was no opening and no show for Ed. With Immie in her coat, and kindergarten about to start, I abandoned Broadway for Madison Avenue. *Just do it,* I told Ed, and he didn't.

I run down the narrow aisles toward the plumbing display and sure enough there is Ed, perched atop a very nice-looking porcelain throne with copper fittings and all the pipe you would need to install it yourself. Ed's pants are around his ankles. His brow is wrinkled in a very familiar manner. Several customers are smiling. I relax. Bert doesn't, he turns nasty. *If there's any crap in that toilet, you've bought it,* he tells me. *Listen, I'm toilet training the kid — if there's any crap in the toilet I'll insist on buying it,* I say. And of course there isn't. Bert mutters to himself while I get Eddie back into his pants. A very nice but nervous hardware lady gets my attention, smiles, lowers her voice. *He can use the staff toilet. It's through there.* She's whispering like a nervous alpinist, but I know there's no danger of an avalanche with Ed. I'd be surprised by a brief flurry.

I HAVE THREE CHILDREN out of diapers now. Over the years I've stood and sat and hunched in any number of staff bathrooms. This one is cleaner than average, but I'm a little put off by the dozens of plungers stacked along the far wall. I sing some more encouraging songs. *Drip Drip Drop Little April Shower* always did it for Immie, but it doesn't work here, and neither does *Chitty Chitty Bang Bang.* I try a sample of Europop. *À cause de l'amour mon coeur fait Boum!* I sing, but Ed doesn't *Boum!* He doesn't even sigh.

At the back of the store Bert selects a thin sheet of board. *I hope this is thick enough,* he says. *What's it got to hold, anyway?* I smile. *Either Central America or a volcano.* He doesn't say anything, just turns on the saw.

I can carry Ed and the piece of board out of the store, but it's a long way home and the board is awkward. The best plan seems to be to put the wood in the stroller and carry Ed. It's pretty hard work. By the time I get home I'm dripping with sweat — no I'm not. I'm dripping with Ed.

I carry him upstairs so I can change both of us. I don't want to traumatize him. *Don't feel bad,* I say, *but let's try to use a toilet next time. You'll be going to school in a couple of years and you don't want the other kids to make* Exxon Valdez *jokes. Now are you* sure *you don't have any more to do?* He shakes his head, doesn't look the least bit traumatized. I must be doing something right.

We go down to the basement to add our dirty clothes to the laundry mountain. Our washing machine has started hiccuping in the middle of its cycle, and I don't have a cure except to drink out of the other side of the glass. *What are you eating?* I ask Ed, not that I really want to know. *Smartie,* he says, opening his mouth to prove it. I risk a quick peek. Looks like a Smartie all right, but — *Did you find it inside the couch?* I ask. It's the usual place. He shakes his head. *In my nose,* he explains. Oh well, then.

My wife calls to say she'll be working late and to ask if anything exciting happened. She likes to stay in touch with the real world, as she calls our house. I don't know what that says about her job — or mine. I tell her that Thea and Rebecca are best friends again, that Sam's project for the Science Fair will be on volcanoes, and that Ed has promised never to climb inside the fold-up couch again, no matter what Imogen says. The two of them are discovering they can do more together than either of them can alone. Cooperation, *Sesame Street* calls it, but *Sesame Street* is not convincing. Folding up the sofa bed with your little brother helping from inside it — that's convincing. *Any progress with the toilet training?* my wife asks from the safety of her fortieth-floor office. *Any forward movement at all?*

I laugh. *No movement,* I say. *No movement of any kind.*

I hear a howl from the basement and Thea's calm measured voice. *Don't worry, I'll get Dad. He'll know what to do.* Then the smoke alarm goes off. *I think I'd better hang up now,* I say.

How to Do It

THEA AND I ALWAYS have a good time together. She likes it that she can beat me at rummy, that we both like apple crisp, and that we both hate combing her hair. She sits at the kitchen table after dinner, folds her hands and says matter-of-factly, *Leopards have spots. I want my project to be about spots. What do you think I should do?* I'm wiping and putting away and keeping an ear out for Ed and the washing machine.

I never say, *What do* you *think?* to Thea. She knows what she thinks. For what it's worth, I don't bother saying it to Sam either, because he has no idea what he thinks. When kids ask you a question it's because they want to know what *you* think — or because they don't want to go to bed. Around sundown Imogen becomes a hard-nosed and rigorous seeker after truth. I cannot possibly tell her all she wants to know. Mike Wallace isn't in her league. *That's not right,* she says when I tell her why the bath water goes down the drain. *You're lying. Tell me the real reason* — frowning as hard as she can, dripping all over the mat as she struggles against time. She's trying for Sixty Minutes but she'll take any number she can get — even five is better than none.

You want kids to come and look at your project, don't you? I say to Thea. *They'll come if they've heard about it — that's called* advertising. She nods. *And if there's candy,* she says. I hear the washing machine begin to hiccup, and dash downstairs. I've found that if I open the lid of the machine and stir the clothes around by hand for a minute or two, the hiccups go away. Like so many cures, this was discovered by accident.

Thea and I discuss her idea of bribing the other students with candy. We agree it's a good one. All we have to do now is find what I call a delivery system. *You mean how to do it,* she says.

I ALMOST NEVER WORRY about how to do it, I'm too busy tidying up after it, whatever it is. Solutions come to me out of thin air, out of the mouths of babes, out of the hand of God or the UPS truck. And sometimes they don't, and I'm left alone and vacant on the stage — full house and empty mind, as the song says. The very next day the postman delivers a mysterious package from a mysterious place — well, from Michigan. Cindy is a friend of ours who Means Well and Talks in Capital Letters. Her only son is named Mel (I've got to admit I *love* that her son is named Mel. Mel is such a great name. All the Mels I've ever heard of were great guys, Mel Tormé, Mel Coolee. It's got a grand, mythic, Old Testament ring to it — Joshua son of Hezekiah son of Mel. With a name like Mel you can be anything from a baseball star like Mel Ott to a poet like Mel, Lord Tennyson). The kid Mel is a bit older than Ed, and for the past six months Cindy has been cajoling, entreating, begging, threatening, whining, wheedling and imploring Mel to use the toilet. She hasn't thought to bribe him with candy yet, but she's tried gold stars on the calendar and stickers with Happy Faces on them. And now, as she says in her letter, she's found How to Do It — which reminds me, Ed hasn't had an accident since breakfast. It's time to see if he's made another one.

His backside is sticking out from underneath the sofa in the living room. He discovered a rich Lego mine there the other day. I thought we cleaned it out, but he may have found another adit. I crawl in beside him, his face is screwed up with effort and his arm is stretched toward a cardboard bottle cap. *Puck,* he mutters under his breath. I reach them for him, bring out a handful of those bottle caps the kids all play with and collect and forget about. It's as good a racket as restaurant coffee or retail heroin, the things can't cost more than three cents a dozen to make, and kids and parents will pay a dollar for them. *Puck,* says Eddie — these ones have pictures of gargoyles on them. *Pog,* I tell him. *Puck,* he says, flinging them in the air to shower down upon us — which reminds me. Does he have to go? No.

Cindy's gifts are wrapped carefully. They're in packets of six, and Cindy's sent us four packs, and I don't believe what they are. Even after I read her note I don't believe it. What they are is — *Life-savers, my God I was absolutely at my Wits' End with little Mel and then I saw these advertised, and I Rushed out to buy them and they worked like Magic. You simply Must try them* — Cindy is not talking about pills that cure forgetfulness or make you tall, she is not talking about gum that lasts forever or cigarettes that taste like a nice dry white wine, she is not talking about telephones that answer back or blinds that go the wrong way, or pills that cure forgetfulness. I wish she was. What she is talking about are targets that dissolve in urine. Yes, that's what I said. They're made of specially treated paper and they float in your toilet bowl. Wait, it gets better. The targets are suggestive of a video arcade, there are Spanish galleons, space invaders, panzer tanks and fighter planes and grim-looking monsters. In my mind's eye I see Cindy floating a picture of, say, Cruella De Vil in her toilet (*Be careful not to flush prematurely,* it says on the instructions — because of course the target hasn't dissolved yet, has it, and you don't want to flush undissolved targets down your toilet. There are signs to that effect on airplanes) and little Mel concentrating hard as he pees and destroys. I can't imagine what fun a girl would have, be kind of a night attack in dark glasses, but the whole idea has got to be a guy thing. The name says it all: *Ready, Aim, Water.*

Daddy, why are you laughing? Imogen has a pre-snack look on her face, but the breakfast dishes haven't been put away yet, and she and Ed are still in pyjamas. *Bathroom humor,* I tell her. *Come on, let's get dressed. Then we can go to the park and play.*

IT'S A BEAUTIFUL MORNING, crisp and smoky, with the sun climbing up the sky using the bare branches of the trees for a stepladder. Tots and moms and grandparents are all in crisp winterwear fresh from the shop or the dry cleaners. Ed and Immie like the park. There's a dinosaur for Ed to fall off, and a slide for Imogen to climb to the top of and then decide she doesn't want to go down. *Come on, honey,* I shout from the bottom. I have to shout because I'm about a hundred feet away, the slide goes all the way down a hill. *Come on.* She waits in line at the top and when it's finally her turn she dithers, takes deep breaths, sits down, wriggles into a seated position with her legs dangling, and then — while I'm waving and calling for her to come on and the rest of the line is fidgeting and holding its collective breath — and then and then she — sets like cement.

Come on, Immie, you can do it, that's my girl, just one little push and then away we go, that's all it takes, just one more little — I talk encouragingly to her as I climb the hill myself, but she doesn't move a single tensed muscle and in the end I have to pick her up, locked in the seated position. They say rigor mortis takes a day or so to wear off, but she's got to be at kindergarten this afternoon. I don't have time to exchange more than a quick and sympathetic smile with the other parents because I notice that Ed has left the dinosaur. From this height I can see a pattern of little dints in the sand all around it where he has fallen. Now he is headed toward — *No no no, Ed,* I yell at the top of my voice, turning awkwardly and, yes, slipping onto the slide with Imogen frozen in my arms. She shrieks. I sit down — *No, Ed!* — very suddenly, and away we go, quickly and bumpily, Imogen shrieking like a banshee and me yelling *Stop, Ed! OUCH. No — OUCH — No!* At the bottom of the slide Immie has this huge smile on her face — *Daddy, can we do it again?* — But I don't have time because Ed is deaf to my entreaties. His little legs are carrying him closer and closer to — the swings.

Galileo discovered useful stuff about pendulums, but I've always subscribed more to the Edgar Allan Poe view — they're dangerous and untrustworthy. Like cats and cliffs and fast-running water and silk dresses and cream-colored rugs and just-washed floors, moving swings exert an irresistible fascination for all very young children. They're hypnotic, *Come closer, closer,* they call with their weight of clanking chains and creaking canvas. *Come closer and let me hurt you.* At any given moment on a busy playground there are six pendulums swinging back and forth, and twice that number of rapt toddlers lurching across the sand toward concussion, as Eddie is doing right now. I can see his head move back and forth as he follows the arc of the juggernaut nearest him. *Stop, Ed! Stop!* And of course he does, the moment he's in the swing's path. *No, go! GO!* I say, and he turns to frown at me as the swing comes down — only a brawny arm picks him up in the nick of time and sets him down out of the swing's path. I come panting along a few seconds after the nick of time. *Thank you, thank you,* I say to Ed's stout, elderly savior.

My ninth, the man rasps. He has a voice like a forest fire in a dry season. He jerks his head at Eddie. *My ninth save this morning.* I tell him again how grateful I am, bending down so that Imogen can slide off me. All the swings are occupied, so she and Ed stand and watch them going back and forth, back and forth. *My record is fifteen,* says the man. The corners of his mouth turn down. *I save around eight or nine hundred kids a year. There was an article about me in the neighborhood paper — "Larry the Lifeguard of the Playground," they called me — maybe you read it?*

I don't answer because there's a little girl who, unlike the hero of the poem, is going to lose her head while all about her are keeping theirs unless I grab her. *Hey!* rasps Larry, as I lift her from the path of destruction, *what do you think you're doing?* I put down the girl and her mom comes up to thank me. In the background I hear Larry grumbling to himself.

I thank him again, and then, *Time to go,* I tell Immie and Ed, who launch immediate protests. They would rather play than go shopping, and I don't blame them, but we have to buy potatoes and jelly beans for Thea's Science Fair project and, *ulp,* salt and flour for Sam's.

Imogen pushes the twin stroller until she gets tired and wants to get in herself which is — well, if a New York Minute is the length of time between the light in front of you turning green and the car behind you honking its horn, then Imogen pushes for a couple of New York Minutes. Then it's my turn to push until I hear a shout.

Hey you! I look back. Across the playground, Larry holds a struggling toddler — I guess that's a tautology. *Number ten,* he shouts triumphantly. I keep pushing.

Luck! cries Eddie, pointing at a fallen tree branch that

blocks our way. *No silly, that's a log,* says Immie. *Luck,* Eddie insists. I kick it out of the way and hurt my toe. I start to hop around and swear. *Bad luck!* says Eddie. I don't know whether he's talking to me or it.

I HAVE TO CONFESS to a sort of morbid fascination with the dissolving targets. I'm almost glad Ed doesn't want to sink the *Bismarck,* so that I can. Very satisfying. I wonder about the possibilities for an adult line of sinkable targets. I mean the *Bismarck* is okay, but what about a portrait of your landlord? or your boss? or your mother-in-law? Wouldn't you like to piss all over the Dallas Cowboys? I would. A guy like Richard Nixon's probably been splashed on enough, but there are lots of other politicians who haven't, some of them still in office. And what about those deserving people at the income tax — or your ex-spouse's lawyer? How'd you like to soak him the way he soaked you? Piss on all of 'em and feel good about it. You could probably deduct the targets as a legitimate medical expense. They're bound to be cheaper than Prozac. Of course you might spend most of your day drinking water, but that's good for you too.

If you stop and listen, usually you can hear which piece of furniture Ed is bouncing on. Sam's bed has a distinctive squeak, and there he is. He smiles calmly at me and keeps bouncing. His eyes are open, but his whole face is at peace. Bouncing is his way of getting his ducks — not dogs, ducks — in a row. Most people have down time, Ed has up-and-down time. If Immie can be alone with her blankie, I don't see why Ed can't be alone with a set of bedsprings and a reasonable clearance. Doctors talk about oral gratification, I figure this is some kind of vertical gratification.

＊　　＊　　＊

THEA'S SCIENCE FAIR PROJECT is going to be an immense success. After dinner we get together in the kitchen to carve raw potatoes into leopard-spot stamps. *Do they look real?* Thea asks anxiously. I assure her that, considering they are made from potatoes, they look incredibly real. Thea's plan is for the other students to use the stamps to help draw their own leopards, with a jelly bean given out for each spot and a grand prize of jelly beans going to whoever can guess the number of spots on the leopard Thea is drawing herself. I tell her I think it's a great idea for a project. My wife overhears us from the mud room, where she's putting on little shoes. *You're bribing your friends, aren't you?* she says. Thea smiles down at her drawing. It's not the bribe that counts, it's the delivery system.

Ed and I are going for a walk in the dark, my wife calls. *Does anyone else want to come with us?* We all do.

It's getting dark earlier, but it's not cold enough to freeze. The stores are still open, lots of street traffic clustered around the outdoor fruit markets and delicatessens and streetcar stops. The six of us often take a stroll. It's a way of winding down as a family without worrying about spilled food or who gets to pick the TV show. I try to explain about the soluble targets to my wife, who cannot see the potential for an adult market. *For the political activists, you could have a line of anti-patriot targets,* I say — *draft cards, flags, Norman Rockwell paintings.* She nods and helps Ed out of the stroller. *Or take the situation in Bosnia. If only the UN peacekeepers handed out targets with what's-his-name on them, the populace could whizz on each other instead of killing each other.* She nods and helps Ed into the stroller. *It'd work in Northern Ireland too. It's a magnificent sublimation of all negative feelings — I speak from experience. I have no, repeat no, anger toward the* SS Bismarck. She nods and helps Ed out of the stroller again. He wanders a few feet away to look more closely at a huge stuffed animal in the toy-store window — Kermit the Muppet. Somehow, no matter which direction we start off in, we always end up in front of the toystore. We aren't alone either. As usual there's quite a crowd milling around in and out of the place. *You don't understand where this thing could go,* I whisper, *I see myself in Stockholm accepting the Nobel Piss Prize ...* At last she breaks down into a snort of laughter which is choked off very shortly when Ed, at the top of his lungs, calls out *FRUCK!* — only of course that's not what it sounds like.

Boy, talk about your attention grabber. If all of us who drew in our breath let it out at once we could blow out Methuselah's last birthday cake. Ed couldn't care less. He has a point to make here. *FRUCK FRUCK FRUCK,* he shouts. He's getting excited. By now I'm at his side. He's pointing at the window, got a huge grin on his face. *Fruck, Daddy,* he says.

Frog, I say firmly. I don't think I can let him get away with this one. *Frog frog frog.* I pick him up, smiling around at the crowd. Some are convinced but not a few shun me. *Poor kid,* I hear more than once. My wife and the other kids are on the far side of the street. I wave, and they head away from us. My wife's shoulders are shaking with laughter, I can see them from here. Ed and I hurry after them.

The Mountain Stands Tall

I DON'T KNOW ABOUT YOU, but I get cranky when I'm covered head to toe with yucky sticky grimy, can't stand it, can't control it, can't get it out of my hair or off my clothes, and it stinks and sticks to me and I never want to see any more of it again as long as I live. I'm not talking about Ed's toilet training — that's going fine, in fact this afternoon we had a breakthrough when I sang *Looking Out for Number 1*. Can't think why I haven't used that before. No, I'm talking about Sam's project for the Science Fair tomorrow. Yes, tomorrow. I've been on it since school got out and now it's dinnertime. The girls are whining and I don't blame them, and Sam, who has been hopping from foot to foot and getting his hands almost as dirty as mine, is saying, *Aren't we done yet?* and I don't blame him and I'm saying, *NO, WE'RE NOT. NOW EVERYONE STAND BACK OR I'LL EXPLODE,* and Ed says, *Daddy, peepee,* and I say, *JEEZ, ED, Do you have to go NOW?* and I don't blame me either.

I feel as if we've emptied the Dead Sea of salt and drained Niagara and kneaded most of the Nation's Breadbasket. We've made Towers of Babel that turned into Valleys of Destruction. We've made Dry Gulches and Floating Islands and Swamp Things and about forty pounds of ready-mix concrete molds in the shape of various bits of Ed — he *will* try to help even when thanked politely and told not to.

I don't hear my wife get home. She marches across the kitchen, leaving little high-heel footprints in the white dust that coats everything from the light fixture down to the peeling linoleum. Taking in the situation at a glance, she suggests take-out — which isn't as easy as it should be because the 1 on the phone key pad hasn't worked for a few days now. It's a faulty hook-up, you punch 1 and get # by mistake. The usual result is a disconnect but I've ended up talking to people in the bowels of big companies who always ask me *how* I got this number. I keep meaning to call the phone repair service, but there's a 1 in their phone number. Our long-distance bill is down and that's good, but I have to bother the neighbors or go to the corner phone booth to order pizza or chicken wings, and what's the point of inconvenient convenience food?

Daddy! An urgent summons from upstairs. I can't recognize the voice at this distance. *I need some toilet paper!*

Well, I know it can't be Ed. And it isn't Sam, I can see him, and anyway he's got to be glued to the floor like me. My wife looks up from the phone book but I tell her I'll get it. *One more layer,* I tell Sam. *Not too thick. And be careful of the lava squirter.* He nods grimly and picks up a handful that looks like snow and feels like mud. And sets like Plaster of Paris. I have to slip my feet out of my shoes to get out of the kitchen. *Coming!* I call upstairs.

*   *   *

GUESS WHAT, there isn't any toilet paper. I'll swear I bought some just the other day, but toilet paper, like ketchup and mittens, is just one of those things I should buy every time I leave the house even for a few minutes. I hunt around and finally find some Kleenex on top of my wife's dresser, and Immie is very upset. *This is not our regular kind,* she says, sounding like the TV housewife who lives for Johnny's socks. I love those commercials. It's a peek into a lifestyle impossibly removed from mine, people with obscene, vast, incredible amounts of — time. Imagine having enough time to worry, and I'd like to believe she really does worry, about how white your child's socks are. I confess to an almost visceral yearning for time — not eternities of it, no great vistas of leisure spreading before me like an earldom — but time I can hold in my hands, a half-hour here, a couple of hours there. It's a peasant mentality, I know, scrabbling for little bits of soil I can call my own. I guess I have more in common with Johnny than with his mom. *This paper is all soft and girly,* says Imogen when I hand it to her. Ever since we read a story about life in an Iroquois village, Imogen has been comparing our home comforts with theirs. I don't know why, she already spends the winter in a smoky, leaky house. I suppose she'd really like me to find her some birchbark or maple leaves. *I'll get our regular kind of toilet paper tomorrow,* I say.

She folds her tissue in half. *Daddy,* she says, as I am about to go downstairs. I stop. She folds the tissue again, very deliberately. Everything she does is deliberate, from the finding of the right posture to sleep in, to the location of the exact corner of her blankie that she would like to hold while she sucks her thumb, to choosing her wardrobe — even if it's always the same corner of the blanket, and the same clothes. *Daddy, would you sit and chat?* she asks, and my breath goes out of me.

Sure. I hoick myself up to sit on the vanity — and it occurs to me, sitting there, my legs dangling, that this is a chunk of time. Instead of leaping around downstairs with clean-up, dinner, laundry, Science Fair project, *Eddie, take that out of your nose,* dirty dishes, laundry, garbage, and whatever I happen to have forgotten, I will chat with my younger daughter about — *What would you like to talk about?* I ask. About animals.

IMMIE IS A LITTLE WORRIED about her favorite animal. She unfolds her Kleenex and then folds it again. It's something she always does with toilet paper, trying to create a perfect white square. I think of it as a kind of functional origami. Thea's favorite animal is the leopard. It is strong and fierce and has big sharp teeth. And Sam's favorite animal, the orangutan, can climb trees and swing on vines, and the adult male has a red beard. Imogen is worried that her favorite animal is not a good choice. It is not very strong, she says, or very fast or able to fly. *The other animals always run ahead and they get to do things and I have to wait,* she says. It's the same at dinnertime, Ed and I are both wearing his vegetables and Sam and Thea have half-emptied their plates and been told to sit back down three or four times before Imogen finishes settling her napkin on her lap and saying her grace. *Do you want to be faster?* I ask. She nods quietly. *Then why not change your favorite animal? Pick something glamorous. Peregrine falcons are fast, kodiak bears are strong, buffalo are — well, they're usually beaten in the Super Bowl but ....* I stop, she's shaking her head. *I like my animal,* she says, *even if it is slow.*

I get down from the vanity and squat beside her. *Good for you,* I say. *You stick with your favorite animal and it'll stick with you. Because your animal is the most feared animal in all the forest. Did you know that, Immie?* She is so pleased she drops her Kleenex and all the tedious folding comes undone. *I have to go now,* I say, *but I've enjoyed our chat. Good luck, my little skunk.* I give her the Kleenex. She commences folding carefully. I shut the door gently, not to disturb her concentration.

I enter the kitchen as my wife is saying, *You know, Sam, this stuff really is sticky.* I pause to put my shoes back on, then realize I can't move in them and take them off again. *Dinner should be here in ten minutes,* my wife informs me. *I found a place without a 1 in the phone number.* Sam is kneeling on a chair by the counter. He has no shoes either. *What are we eating?* I ask. My wife doesn't know. *They're local and they deliver. It'll cost twenty dollars. The money is on the table in the front hall. Sam, what's happening to the volcano?* I look away. I know what's happening. It's happened before. *Oh dear,* says my wife.

SAM'S VOICE QUAVERS AS HE ASKS if we think it's possible to glue the pieces of the volcano back together. *Or we could use tape,* he whimpers, echoing my own sentiments. I've taught him there's a right tool for every job, and the right tool is tape. If tape won't work you have to fall back on that other great tool, the checkbook.

The volcano hasn't so much cracked as splintered into many, many heaped-up pieces, some of them the size of matchsticks, some smaller. The same thing happened to the first few pie crusts I attempted. And the next few. I wonder if Sam would consider doing his Science Fair project on Shards. *No, son,* I say. *I don't think there's that much tape in the world.* Sam sinks to the ground and starts muttering to himself. He's praying, I think. He has his contemplative side, pays attention in church, asks questions like *Does God ever have a bad day?* I can picture him as a teenager getting together with a few friends to form a garage choir. Low and away, out of the corner of my eye I see movement. It's Ed, I wondered where he'd got to. He's stuck to the floor by the seat of his pants, a humiliating but effective trick, I'm surprised I haven't tried it before. He too is saying something under his breath as he kicks at his clothes. A different kind of prayer — what he is saying is, *Got to peepee.*

Oh my God, I lunge forward, pull him into the air, leaving his pants behind him, and take a step ... where? *Good for you!* I remember to tell Ed, he's really getting the hang of this training. *Now hold on!* He's bone dry, but for how long? I'm holding a live grenade in my hands, and I don't know how many seconds I've got left. I suppose I could fall on Ed. It's what you're supposed to do to a grenade, but it's so messy and I don't want a medal on my coffin. I compromise and stand him on the counter, aiming him at the kitchen sink. *Okay,* I tell Ed. He peers down, is he expecting to see a target picture of a U-boat or something? I'm trying to think of an inspirational song. All that comes to mind is *Moon over Miami,* maybe because that's what I see. I'm pointing Eddie away from me. No one moves when the doorbell rings. It's one of those tableau scenes. And then the doorbell rings again. Thea calls from the living room, *I think there's someone at the door!* She's watching TV. My wife is up to her elbows in flour, I'm not. She takes Ed. I move down the long corridor to the front door.

You really ordered from Karl's Restaurant? He sounds surprised. *I guess I've seen everything now. How are you? Jeez, is it ever getting chilly, eh?*

I've noticed him around the neighborhood, a big barrel-bodied guy with a head of hair like a radioactive Brillo pad and stained false teeth. Hard to say if he's thirty-five or fifty, or sober.

Yeah, chilly, I say, taking the food from him. *How much do I owe you?* His bicycle is leaning against our porch. He's usually on a bicycle, running a mysterious errand. The bag in my hand feels wet. He wipes his hands on his jeans, looks blank. *My wife told me twenty would cover it. Is that right?* I say. *Twenty? Yeah, twenty's fine. Thanks, thanks.* His eyes are very wide, very dark, very distant. *Say, your porch needs a little work. Are you thinking of getting it fixed?* he asks surprisingly. I can't remember the pizza delivery guy ever mentioning home improvement. Mind you, I don't remember the pizza delivery guy on a bike. *Maybe next year,* I say instinctively. It's what I tell Thea when she inquires about a dog. He nods and pats his pockets. I half expect him to pull out a business card or paint samples, but he just wants a pen and, when he gets it, he leans over and scribbles on the brown paper bag. *That's who I am,* he says. *When you want anything painted or repaired. I'll do a great job, if I say so myself, and I'm cheap. Ask for me.* I tell him I will. *Bye, then. I've got to be getting home now,* he says. I guess there aren't any more take-out orders from Karl's Restaurant. *Sure is chilly,* he says, mounting his bike and wheeling uncertainly over our front lawn. I carry the dripping bag inside. On it is written the single word *ROY*. That's who he is.

The kitchen sink and table are clean. The Science Fair project is in the mud room. Ed's in new pants and Sam's in tears. *Dinnertime!* I call, opening the bag and recoiling, *I think,* from the smell. *Did Ed pee on the table?* I ask. Sam shakes his head, sobs louder than ever. *On my project.* Oh. But if it isn't Ed I'm smelling, then it must be the food. Karl, that optimistic soul, has enclosed a menu, which is almost unreadable because the ink has run into the tomato sauce. At least I hope that's what it is. One word leaps out. *Peruvian?* I say. *Is that the latest thing?* My wife shrugs. *It was the only place I could reach by phone.* I spread out the food and we all sit down together. Thea and Imogen are clean. The rest of us look as if we've been plastering all day.

After a few bites I start to feel better, because I know that no matter how chaotic and horrible my life becomes at least I won't ever have to eat food from Karl's Peruvian Restaurant again. My wife swallows a couple of times with difficulty, and pushes away her plate. I give Ed a spoonful of his regular dinner — tuna salad and chopped carrots — then I try a bite of the tuna myself. I'm hungry. *Hey,* says Ed.

No one eats a lot except Imogen, who has discovered — *What are these called again?* she asks, holding one up. *Lima beans,* we all tell her. They're the only part of the meal I can identify with any certainty. *Hey,* says Ed to Thea on the other side of him, *that* mine *food.*

I end up making sandwiches for all of us.

AFTER DINNER I RETRIEVE THE PROJECT board from the mud room. Sam and I have agreed to give it one more try with a bit more liquid in the mix. *And it'll have to be a smaller volcano,* I tell him. His face falls. No one likes to have his mountains turned into molehills. But something odd has happened over the course of dinner — something strange and wonderful, probably related to urine. *The mountain stands tall!* I cry. Sounds like one of those sentences you read in a Swiss language textbook — *Which way to the hotsprings? Your ski poles are longer than those of Gutrune. What a jolly little goat.* Sam's volcano with the flattened top, in which we have cunningly inserted a novelty squirt-your-friends boutonniere filled with fluorescent orange paint, is ready to go. We all burst into applause, even Ed, who seems to have provided the missing ingredient. *Thank you,* whispers Sam with his eyes closed. I don't think he's thanking us. *Do you want this?* My wife holds up the bag with *ROY* on it. I shake my head. She doesn't ask about Karl's menu, I notice, just throws it straight out.

*   *   *

THE ANIMAL GAME PROCEEDS smoothly without the orangutan, who is busy painting his miracle volcano. I notice that the skunk is walking proud and the leopard is giving her a fair bit of respectful space. Of course that could be the lima beans. Both the animals run squealing when Ed comes crashing into the room. *Who are you?* I ask him. *What is your favorite animal?* He scowls and stomps on my foot. *I am Godzilla,* he says.

 # WINTER LIGHTNING

Infectious Laughter

SAM GETS SICK FIRST. He's the sensitive one, meaning the one who sees the most of Typhoid Jerry, that boy has germs the way other kids have freckles. Anyway, Sam lies perfectly still in bed with his little black Dutch cap on, hands clasped on his stomach, eyes wide open — scares me when I check on him before going to bed myself because he looks about ready for the formaldehyde.

Hi, Sam, are you awake? How are you feeling? I say quietly, checking his forehead. I don't want to alarm him — or me, for that matter.

I might as well say now that I don't take temperatures. I tried when the twins were small and succeeded only in traumatizing all of us. They'd be crying and hot, and I'd be swearing and stabbing at rapidly closing orifices. I never got the mercury to move above room temperature except once when, for some reason, it read Well Done. Maybe I was using the meat thermometer. There are books that say to monitor your child's temperature every half-hour for the duration of the illness, but there are books that say that gardening is the secret to inner peace. There are books that say $y = mx+b$ or that you should choke the goose as you're killing it to make sure the blood stays in the chest cavity — I mean you can say anything in a book. As far as I'm concerned the kids are either Fine or Hot. If they're still Hot the next day, it's time to see the doctor. This evening Sam is Hot. I spoon out some kids' Tylenol and a lot of instant coffee. It's going to be a long night. And it is.

DR. IMRE IS BALD AND BUSY. He starts to write the prescription before we get our coats off. *Get that filled. If the kid isn't better in a week, shoot him.* Sam giggles, he remembers Dr. Imre from last time. *Is it the pink stuff?* he asks. Dr. Imre says it is.

We used to get the white medicine but something happened, maybe we used it all up. *Shake well and give him a teaspoonful not less than an hour before a meal or two hours after,* says the pharmacist. I used to pay attention to that stuff — wake the kids up at three-thirty in the morning, run to school at ten forty-seven — but I don't bother anymore. Familiarity, I guess, *Have a slug,* I tell Sam in the car, uncapping the bottle with difficulty at a red light. The sooner we start, the sooner we're done.

Ed's sick by the next morning. Not that he slows down or anything, but he starts to drip, leaves a trail like an accent border all over the house — I just don't know if we want a greenish accent border two and a half feet above the ground. The girls are sick too. Imogen is quiet and Thea isn't.

When Thea's sick, you know it all, throb by throb. It's a kind of sharing, I suppose, like telling you ALL about her day at school, beginning with what the teacher was wearing. Sam is more likely to say *Fine* and disappear in the direction of crayons, TV or hockey stick. When she describes a ringing in her ears and a dry throat — *Like tree bark inside, Daddy, and every time I swallow it scratches* — I know what I'm in for. I phone Dr. Imre to reserve a block of seats, but his answering machine says that he's sick too, so, on a bright but chilly Tuesday morning, with frost crackling underfoot, we all head for the clinic at the hospital. Ed tries to climb out of the stroller a couple of times but his heart isn't in it. Maybe he's sicker than I thought.

WHEN THE RECEPTIONIST SEES US she cries, *Oh no!* in an audible undertone. She must be thinking of the last time we came and had to wait and wait before the doctor could see us. I had so much fun playing trucks on the quarantine carpet that I forgot about Ed for a moment — I'll swear it was only a moment.

Hi there, I say with my biggest smile. *Remember us?* I don't hold grudges, even though the hospital clearly over-reacted, broadcasting an Emergency Code Green over the internal loudspeaker. Green is supposed to be a plague warning, and all Ed had was chicken pox.

Stay close, I tell him now. *Remember what happened when you wandered off.* He shivers. How could he forget, poor little guy, cranky and spotty and chased all over the place by what looked like alien beings from the Infectious Diseases department, I'd have run the wrong way myself. The gift shop was full, but it wasn't Ed who caused the customers to scream and run away. Those sterile suits with the masks and ventilators are quite scary — and if Martians were going to invade the Earth, they might well choose a hospital. No wonder the lady at the cash counter fainted.

When the president of the hospital asked for my Health Insurance Card, I thought he was going to cut it in half, the way they do at the Wal-Mart when you can't pay, but he just shook his head and handed it back with a tight smile. *Well, I think we've all learned something,* I began, but he'd already turned away.

This time we get seen fast, no waiting, and it turns out that the sickest one is — Imogen. She gets two bottles, pink and purple, and starts to feel better at once. *I have more medicines than anyone!* I like the doctor, she's the old-fashioned type with a frown and a bag of lollipops who doesn't bother with the latest type of thermometer. Have you seen them? They use ultrasonic waves and the Earth's gravitational field — I think that's what the nurse said — and look like terrorist weapons. Our doctor grimaces down at the kids and feels their foreheads.

Hot! she pronounces. Good to have my diagnosis confirmed.

A Seasonal Saga

Trumpets and Togas

DECEMBER COMES EARLY this year. Seems I've just taken down the last of the balloons and eaten the last of the kids' Hallowe'en candy, and suddenly everyone is sending me Seasonal Greetings. Do I resent other people's efficiency? I do not. I am amazed at it. The afternoon post brings us a card from Hilda, our very first babysitter. She said a tearful good-bye to us just a few months ago, it seems, and since then she has been graduated, married, employed, promoted and delivered of a beautiful baby girl. Maybe it was more than a few months.

There's a seasonal family photo with the card. Hilda is already more organized than I will ever be. I haven't even shoveled the walk after the weekend snowstorm. I can't help it, I keep getting sidetracked. Just yesterday morning Immie

[113

and Ed and I went out with every intention of shoveling, but we ended up building snowpeople instead. They're still there this afternoon, frozen sentinels lining the path I must make. While Ed tries to knock them over and I bend my back to the accumulated and compacted task, I find myself thinking again of Hilda's photo, so poignant, not because of the baby who looks, let's face it, like Winston Churchill, but because of Hilda herself. She's grown up. In a way she's changed more than Sam and Thea. They're still kids, but she's not anymore. I hope she's having fun. Looking at her picture I can more easily see the grandmother she'll become than the giggly blonde I used to ask about homework and boyfriends. I couldn't possibly pay her now. I'd be more likely to vote for her for something. *Watch out, Ed!* I say. He has picked up an icicle and is alternately licking it and stabbing the snowpeople. It all looks like some kind of weird blood drinker's burial.

Twilight comes early now, a blessing for me. Summer sunsets mean it's almost nine o'clock. No wonder everyone is asking when we're going to have dinner. Today I can take a moment to rest from shoveling and gaze up at the darkening sky and hear the school bell ring down the street. It's not nighttime after all — it's just dark. The kids run up with their eyes bulging, every December day that passes is another notch on the Frenzometer.

Imogen swishes down the street in her parka and leggings and floppy hat and mittens and boots, every zipper zipped, every button done up. How do kindergarten teachers do that? I don't send her to school that well dressed. In fact, one day last month she was having trouble with her coat and we were late so I said, *Forget it*, and Ed and I ran her over, and as she was following the other kids into the school I noticed that the reason she was having trouble was that her coat was on upside down. If I taught kindergarten, I'm sure I'd spend the bulk of my time dressing and undressing the students — throw in a couple of trips to the bathroom and that'd be the afternoon. I wouldn't get anything taught and I'd be exhausted too — burned out after a couple of years. Forget what the curriculum guidelines say about cooperation with peers, color and number recognition and fine motor skills, my report cards would read, *Imogen stands in line well, and can correctly pick out her snowsuit. Emile stands in line well and can correctly pick out his snowsuit. Maria need some work on standing in line, and for three days in a row she has picked out someone else's snowsuit.* No point sending Maria to summer school though, no one wears snowsuits in summer.

I go back to the front walk, feeling like a hero of song, Roland or someone. With my great shovel Joyeuse in hand, I fight the billowy white giants and push them to the side of our walkway, where they completely cover my children. Sam can't stay still for long — there's a guy who'd get a bad grade in my kindergarten. He bursts to his feet and runs in circles, but Ed and Immie settle into the middle of the snowbank. I think they're trying to eat their way out. Thea is helping me by standing in front and telling me where to shovel. She is singing a seasonal song, *Oh Hanukkah, oh Hanukkah, we'll light the minora. Let's have a party. We'll all dance the Torah.*

Sam runs up at this point to shout, *Not Torah, stupid. Torah is the Holy Book. You can't dance a Holy Book.* I interrupt the theological discussion on a point of order, *No calling names,* I remind them. Sam, who's having a difficult time right now, says he's sorry in such a way that we all know he's not. Thea's expression sets firm. She has a good memory and knows what she knows. *Amanda says Torah,* she says.

Immie staggers out of the snowbank, weaves over to me and says, *I'm full, when's dinner?* A sentence that defines childhood for me. *ED?* I call, but there's no answer from the snowbank. He's still hungry, I guess.

When's dinner? Immie asks again. It doesn't bug me that

kids repeat their questions. It means I have another chance to get the answer right. *Soon,* I tell Immie and her face falls. I'll bet that's a word that sums up childhood for her. *Guess what, though — Sally's coming to look after you!* Her face lights up again. No one is more despondent than Immie and no one bounces back into hope so fast, it's almost dizzying at times. Meanwhile I can't see any part of — *Ed?* I call again. No answer. *Ed!* My great shovel turns over the snow carefully but he's not in the drift anymore. *When's Sally coming?* Immie asks. *Very shortly,* I tell her, and speaking of shortly, *Ed come on, where are you?* The evening is drawing in but I can't believe he can get very far. Mind you, that's what they said about Columbus.

Help comes around the corner in a pair of fur boots and a muffler and a knapsack. Sam sees her first, *Sally!* he says. She waves cheerily. Immie and Sam set off at top speed to meet her. Sally is our current favorite babysitter. She lets them do whatever they want, and then tidies up afterwards, so we're all happy. And I've never seen her without a smile on her face, except when something sad happens to cartoon animals on TV. A jolly, bouncy arts major. I didn't know anyone like her when I was in university. My crowd were all too busy smoking and sneering. Takes a lot of time, sneering, and makes you cough if you don't do it right.

Sally! Sally! A familiar head pops up above the porch railing. Ed, he must have crawled out the back of his snowdrift when I wasn't looking. Sally waves. He waddles to the top step, calling *Watch, Sally!* She comes puffing up with Sam and Immie just as Ed steps off into space. He's learning to walk down steps instead of doing his fireman-down-the-ladder act, but he's forgotten what a scientist friend of mine calls the drag coefficient of the snowsuit — anyway he tumbles forward in a perfect flip, landing right in Sally's arms, thank goodness. The two of them sit down together and she bursts out laughing.

Thea is tugging at my sleeve. *Can I tell Sally about the Winter Concert?* she whispers. I nod. *But Thea, be nice about it. You know what I mean, don't you?* She nods responsibly. I collect my shovel and finish off the walk while Sally herds the kids inside.

CAN YOU COME TO THE OFFICE GET-TOGETHER? my wife asked, and I said, *Sure,* because I like parties, even office parties. *Is there a theme? What should I wear?* My wife paused. *It's mid-December. It's what they used to call a Christmas party.* Reminds me of the rock star formerly known as Prince. I guess I have to wear my suit. Too bad, I was hoping to dust off my toga. I look pretty good in a toga, but a suit makes everyone invisible. Walk down a busy urban street in a toga and people know you're somebody special, but in a suit you're just another one of Them, unless you're another one of Us, and I don't know which is worse.

Thea is waiting for me in the bedroom closet. I jump back, not expecting to be accosted as I get dressed. *I thought you were in the basement with everyone else,* I say. Shrieks of noise echo up the stairs. Sally is chasing everyone and giving them paralyzing hugs. Thea sighs. *I told Sally my news,* she says.

And? I take down the hanger with the trusty blue serge.

And she congratulated me. And then Sam started to cry. My pants are tighter than I remember, almost too tight to wear. How can that be when I run around all day? I'm severely disappointed in myself, also I'm a little wistful about my toga — bet that wouldn't be too tight to wear. *Dad, I don't want to do it.* She hands me the source of her current joy and conflict, a little toy trumpet. *I don't want to be the trumpet girl anymore,* she says. *You can give it to Sam.*

I'd better explain. The twins' Grade One class is singing a song for the Winter Concert. We've been rehearsing it for weeks — except when I don't have time right now and when they forget where they put the script — and various children have been assigned to Important Duties. Sam was passed over, but Thea was picked to Hold Up A Trumpet — the trumpet I have in my hand — at a particularly apt moment in the song. *All eyes will be on me,* she told us in a breathless whisper, and Imogen said, *Wow.* I don't know if she was impressed or horrified. Her kindergarten class is singing the national anthem, but Imogen won't rehearse no matter how often I ask. Anyway Sam said, My *eyes won't be on you, sis!* and left the room, and now Thea wants to give up her chance at stardom. *Do you think these pants are too tight?* I ask her, a difficult decision for a father. Maybe if I wore a turtleneck outside the pants. *And will your giving up the trumpet make* Sam *feel better?* I ask.

She nods and says, *Well, sure,* but I know better than that and send her downstairs to fetch him while I try the turtleneck. I shiver when I check the mirror, somehow I've turned into Robert Goulet. Nothing wrong with that, I suppose — I could look like Winston Churchill, for instance — but it's not the image I have of myself.

Sam and Thea come in together, sit on the bed while I take off the turtleneck. I ask Sam if he would feel better if Thea gave him the trumpet. *Well, sure,* he says. *Give it here, Dad. Hey thanks, sis!* Thea bursts into tears.

Hmm. I take a regular button-down shirt from the closet. *Wait,* I say in my serious Dad voice, hard to do when my diaphragm is constricted by tight blue serge. Sam sits down again. *I want to judge wisely here,* I say, *and I don't think we have it right yet.*

Thea looks worried. *Dad, you can't cut the trumpet in half. Miss McQueen doesn't have another one.* The Bible studies are paying off, Torah or no Torah. I'm so surprised I break into a shout of laughter and the fastener at the top of my pants breaks apart and the pants fall to my knees, and of course the kids know this is not at all funny, so they don't explode into tidal waves of giggles, rolling on the bed and then falling onto the floor, their little faces contorted at the funniest thing they've seen in a month. Wait until their friends hear about Dad's pants falling down. And I think to myself, This never happens to Robert Goulet.

SALLY HOPES I'LL HAVE FUN at the office party. *Don't worry about us here. We'll have a great time.* I'm not worried about them, I'm worried about my half-hour streetcar ride downtown. Togas are comfortable and loose fitting but not designed for cold climates.

Ed and Elves

CHRISTMAS SHOPPERS DRAW BACK in horror, clutching their purchases and pressing their hands to their mouths. Sales clerks dressed as hardware elves or computer elves or Italian leather elves all stop what they're doing and stare out their decorated shop windows. You'd think they've never seen anyone chasing a runaway plastic go-kart through a mall before. With a two-year-old at the wheel. *Don't worry, Ed,* I call. *Daddy's coming.* The knee-high mechanical monster plows through tinsel and muffins and herald angels with an earnest and persuasive roar.

I don't often worry when I'm out with the kids because frankly I haven't time. Like painting and myth making, worrying requires leisure, but I'm worried now, we're approaching the Fountain Court. *Turn, Ed, turn the wheel,* I yell. I'm only a few feet behind him and, as he swerves, instinctively I jump and miss, sliding forward into a Salvation Army captain who loses his balance and falls, complete with tambourine and collection ball, into the fountain. Very impressive, but I haven't time to stop and stare. *Sorry about that.* I toss change at him and keep running,

LET ME BACK UP A BIT, it's ten evenings before Christmas and we're at the mall with everyone else, only they're buying sexy lingerie, antiques and save-the-rainforest bath beads, and we're buying gloves, diaper wipes and mints. And my wife wants to buy a nice crystal bowl for her artistic aunt, her other aunt gets a set of vice grips, I think. It's always a treat when she comes with us. The kids are all smiling and singing as we stroll through the echoing gift-wrapped department store. *We Three Kings of Orient* — Ed, *come back here.* He loves to play hide and seek in department stores. Thea drags him back to the stroller, which we use to carry our overcoats. Sam and Imogen are shadowing us from two aisles away, pretending to be detectives or Native Americans, I can't remember which. In the mall my wife ignores the YOU ARE HERE directory, which I like to check because I tend not to know WHERE I AM. Hand in hand with Thea and trailed conspicuously by the last two Mohicans, she heads into the *Ding Dong Merrily on High. You have Ed,* she calls over her shoulder, like the pilot handing over control of the plane to the co-pilot. *I have Ed,* I reply. We'll all meet up again outside the crystal store — *That's* outside *the store,* she reminds me. *Remember last time.* I check again and I still have Ed. He has climbed into the stroller and is waving his arms calling, *Faster faster.* I head for the YOU ARE HERE directory.

It's a difficult choice, left to the toystore and muffins, or right toward the pet shop and popcorn. *You want to see the fish and puppies?* I ask Ed. *Or the toys?* I like to give him a choice, it's a kind of control for him. All the books talk about it. *Telephones,* he yells. *Want telephones.* I blench, remembering the last time we visited the beautiful space-age phone center. Ed tried to do a Houdini with phone cords and couldn't get loose, in the end a very grim Bell employee had to get the scissors. *That's four hundred dollars' damage,* she told me. *Could have been worse, madam, we were going to look at fax machines,* but she wasn't mollified. Ed is upset when we pass by the telephones, calling me *You big bully,* his latest phrase. Shoppers stare while I smile fondly. Isn't he cute? And then around the bend, past belts, science experiments, shoes and chiming clocks, we see a display of miniature vehicles in fluorescent orange molded plastic.

We're both fascinated. My childhood was bereft of go-karts, also mini-putt, but that's a story for another time, so we stop. *Tell me about them. How fast do they go?* I ask the pimply youth in the elf costume. I'm wondering if I can scrunch into one. There's a little practice track and everything. Only eight kilometers an hour. I'm disappointed until Ed climbs in and turns a switch. *Hey, look out,* yells the youth as the machine jumps the track and roars away, scattering shoppers like confetti.

I'll bet you think you can run eight kilometers an hour, well you can't, not through a holiday crowd anyway. My movements are jerky — well, if the shoe fits — and my breathing is ragged. Apparently Ed's go-kart is good for twenty minutes because it's fully charged, kind of like Ed himself. In the background familiar carols tell of silence and peace. Ed makes a wide turn into our mall's huge cathedral-style center court, where eight hundred kids are lined up to see Santa. The court has recently been remodeled to illustrate the Holiday Spirit. There's a long gentle slope down through Toytown to Christmas Village, and the entire landscape is filled with pieces of recognizable Christmas tradition in tasteful papier-mâché. I notice security elves in attendance. About time they got into the act. Ed misses the line, thank heavens, but drives straight into the exhibit.

Everything seems to happen in slow motion. Ed starts to weave. He brushes against a candy cane, which totters but stays upright, and then he plows straight into Tiny Tim. There are gasps and screams, and then a great hush falls on the crowd — the go-kart is headed straight for a baby lamb. Nearby mothers cover their children's eyes. Somehow the go-kart buzzes right past. Everyone sighs in relief, and then groans as the little drummer boy gets smashed to pieces. Frosty's next. One of the security guys nearly catches Ed then, but he cuts left and a whole row of sugarplum fairies goes down like dominoes. I hear wailing from the kids and static from the walkie talkies, and Rudolph won't be leading any sleighs for a while. Ed reaches bottom and keeps going, but the machine misses a beat as it starts up the ramp to Santa's throne. We close in. Ed tries to climb again and again, but he's run out of time and juice. Reminds me of that scene in *The Great Escape*, only a little closer to the ground. I pull him out of the go-kart safe and sound, give him a big hug and ask him what the dickens he thought he was doing — coincidence because mall security asks me almost exactly the same question.

MY WIFE TAKES MY ARM as we stroll serenely toward our exit. It's a soft and seasonal picture now, *O Holy Night* echoing gently, Ed asleep in the stroller, Thea carrying the crystal bowl, Imogen and Sam crouched to ambush us by the cruisewear display, and the bells of the Salvation Army jingling in the background. *Daddy, why is that wet man shaking his fist at you?* Thea asks. I shrug and walk a little more quickly.

My Meeting

THINGS ARE SMOLDERING in the schoolyard. All the moms and dads are huddled in corners, talking very excitedly, stabbing their fingers at each other. Something mysterious has turned the playground into a powderkeg. I wonder what. Walking past a clutch of parents I wave and they nod and go back to their — it's not an argument, they're all on the same side — back to their concerted hissing. I overhear a symphony of reinforcing whispers. *Disgraceful ... last straw ... a school tradition ... last night my daughter brought home ...* and then someone says *Kwanzaa* — I may have heard that wrong — and they all go, *Aah.* They know what he's talking about, but I can't hang around and hear more because I have to console Eddie.

He and Immie and I are playing catch in the schoolyard while we wait for the Grade One class to get out. I suppose I shouldn't call the game "catch" since we aren't catching the ball, not ever, not even once, not even when it lands in our hands. What we are playing is "drop." Ed is crying because Immie's last throw hit him on the hood of his snowsuit and bounced straight up to land on the low roof overhanging the school doors. I hold my arms out from my sides in the universal All Gone gesture. Ed cries bitterly for three seconds and then sees Sam and Thea.

Sam waves at me, dumps his knapsack at my feet and races with his friend Michael to the Thing — that's the huge wooden play structure they built in the middle of the schoolyard. It's got a tube slide and a swaying bridge and a firefighter's pole and a hundred truck tires. The official name is the Fantasy Adventure Kingdom, but to most of us it's the Thing. I wish I'd had one when I was a kid. They can talk about falling educational standards all they want. There may be more switchblades in grade school than in my day, more needles, gangs, condoms, graffiti and cellular phones, but there are also more adventure playgrounds and fewer fights. Maybe because there are more parents. Where was I? Oh yes, Sam and Michael climbing on the Thing, Immie and Eddie giving up on the ball and kicking a block of ice around instead — some things don't change from generation to generation — and Thea and Rebecca skipping together and singing.

The nearest knot of moms hiss and draw themselves up like provoked swans. One of them — Michael's mom, who has never really spoken to me of her own accord before, I fancy she lumps me with dairy and refined sugar, things best avoided — beckons me over. *It's disgraceful, isn't it,* she says.

I've never seen any reason for wishy-washy support, even if I don't know what I'm supporting. *I agree wholeheartedly. Disgraceful is an understatement. If disgraceful were* all *it was, I'd be less concerned,* I say with a friendly smile. Maybe I've overdone it, she looks puzzled. I call to Sam to tell him we're going home soon. He waves. *O dreidl dreidl dreidl,* sing Thea and Rebecca. *I made you out of clay. O dreidl dreidl dreidl, Together we will play.* Charming and seasonal.

Michael's mom shakes her head. *Multiculturalism,* she says, doing her best to pronounce it like a four-letter word. I nod grimly. So does she. We're standing there beside the chain-link fence, nodding grimly at each other. I feel as if I've been accepted at last. I'm one of them. In a minute she'll invite me over for coffee. *So you're with us,* she says. I raise my clenched fist. *To the bitter end,* I say. The other moms are approaching. They hear this last remark and break into applause. I simper charmingly and look around for Eddie. *And we'll expect you at the meeting tomorrow?* says Michael's mom. Let's see, Immie is watching a ball-hockey game, Thea and Rebecca are playing that complicated pattycake that girls do — she's tried to teach me and I get as confused as I do during my wife's step exercise video — but where is Ed?

Meeting? I say, and then memory floods over me. *You mean the PTA meeting. Well I'd love to come of course, but my wife will be working late and Ed's been keeping us up these past few nights. He's getting used to not being in a crib. Anyway, with four small children I just wouldn't be able to …* I keep meaning to go to a PTA meeting, just to see, but I haven't yet. I've never been inside Toys Я Us either and the reason's the same. I'm afraid.

The school always arranges babysitting, Michael's mom says. *And we'll all be there.* She smiles encouragingly. You know, she has a nice smile, very fresh and clean, she should use it more often. *We'll save you a seat,* says one of the other moms. Peer acceptance at last, but I can't bask in it because I catch sight of Ed — fifty feet away and six feet in the air. Somehow he's managed to toddle across the schoolyard and climb halfway up the Thing. I take off at a dead run.

ONE MYSTERY IS SOLVED over dinner. The kids tell me about Kwanzaa, the African earth-friendly December festival. Sounds deep and tribal and convincing until I find out it's not even as old as I am, whereupon it loses some of its ancient luster and sounds as authentic as pizza or chow mein — well, those are popular too. An astounding concept though, the ready-made tradition. I wonder if it was like this two thousand years ago, old farts shaking their heads and talking about newfangled ideas that wouldn't last. Probably.

And then we all got in a circle and sang our dreidl song, says Thea. My wife doesn't know the dreidl song, so Sam and Thea teach her. *Didn't they have dreidl songs when you were a little girl, Mommy?* asks Thea.

My wife can't contain a smile. *Not at my school, honey. None of the priests knew them.*

I have a question, says Sam. *What's clay?*

*   *   *

THE KIDS ARE IN BED, and the two of us are sharing a moment, folding laundry in the living room. I've always liked folding laundry, it's precise and technical and at the same time it's very soft and tactile, very sensuous — even if you're sorting through blankies and footie pyjamas and baby-sized under-pants — and there's a nice smell to just-dried clothes. In our house it's kind of a barbecue odor, the drier has two settings, Off and Scorch. Anyway, there we are and it's getting late and the snow is falling gently and sparkling under the streetlights, and the radio is playing soft and soothing memories, and somewhere nearby a car is trying to start and, well, we look at each other and it's the same for both of us.

I drop the sheet I'm folding, take one — only one — step toward her, and Ed falls out of his new bed again. I recognize the compact little thud his body makes when it hits the floor upstairs. The overhead light flickers. Outside the car is still trying to start, but the engine just won't turn over. Ed begins to whimper. Last time he fell out of bed he needed a visit with Mom and Dad and a drink of water and a story and a cuddle and a lullaby before he went back to sleep. This time too.

THE PTA MEETING STARTS bang on seven o'clock. No time to wait for stragglers, we've all got to get up tomorrow and some of us still have our Kwanzaa shopping to do. We fill the sixth-grade classroom. I'm sitting at the back with Ed asleep in the stroller beside me. The PTA president is a little guy with a receding hairline and receding chin and, in between, a strong counterbalance in protruding eyeballs. He looks, on the whole, very convex. And nervous, *I'd like to thank you all for your, uh, enthusiastic turnout,* he begins in a throaty tenor. Not a good choice of words, *enthusiastic*. I'd have gone with *concerned* or *numerous*, or maybe just skipped the intro altogether. We aren't enthusiastic, we're grumpy and miffed and upset and fed up, but I suppose you can't thank people for a disgruntled turnout. I can't see our agenda, Ed is clutching it in his hands and I'm not going to risk waking him up to get it. Besides I may be joining him shortly. A couple of playground moms notice me. They actually smile and I experience a moment of group belonging and warmth. Maybe I will get to the Toys Я Us one of these days. Then the president shuffles through his notes, clears his throat and begins.

I've spent my life avoiding meetings, so I can't tell you if this one was typical or not. I try to pay attention, but somehow my focus keeps shifting to Ed. He looks so angelic when he's asleep with his arms spread wide and a little smile on his face, and there's a little dried crust of snot on his nose that moves in and out when he breathes — really quite hypnotic. I fumble in my pockets for a Kleenex and bring out the usual collection of cough drops, elastic bands, small plastic toys, fluff-stuck pennies, mittens, and envelopes with very important phone numbers on them but alas no names to tell me who I'll be calling — and finally a Kleenex from a previous ministration. Looks like it has almost as many miles on it as our car. The crust of snot is rippling bravely in the breeze, a flag of inconvenience, and I'm about to lean over and attack it with my Kleenex when I become aware that people are putting up their hands. Well I know they don't all have to go to the bathroom, they're voting on something. I raise my hand too, don't want to look like an idiot, and imagine my surprise when the president points his ruler at me. *Yes?* he says wearily. *Do you think the children should be learning songs about Hanukkah?*

Is that what we're talking about? I'm surprised. *Why sure. It's coming up to Christmastime, isn't it,* I say. *And let's consider that Christ himself would have celebrated Hanukkah. He'd probably have been an expert practitioner on the dreidl.*

All around me are open mouths. I feel like a mother bird

dropped in on a nest of starving chicks. *Don't you all think so?*
I say. *I do. Joseph wasn't just a good Jewish papa, he was a guy
who worked with his hands. He'd know about dreidls. And I
can't imagine Mary not letting her little boy fool around with
whatever toy was popular back then. And anyway, didn't one
of the metaphysical poets write about the world as a spinning
top? It'd be an appropriate plaything for the Messiah.* I smile
around, no one smiles back. I'm trying to remember the poem
and, as usual, all that's coming to mind is a recipe for chili con
carne that I saw on a bag of dried kidney beans.

Begin with two bags of beans, it said in small letters. I read
them after I got home with one bag. I substituted boldly, adding
ketchup and ripe olives, I think, or prunes, something that
would be the right color. Anyway it was a mistake and I had to
offer double desserts to get people even to let me put it on their
plates.

Mr. Scrimger? The president knows my name now, someone
must have told him. *Do you have anything to say to Mrs. Field?*

One of the playground moms is on her feet, an earnest lady
in a blue-jean dress and clunky boots, with a rock on her finger — I'm serious. I mean a rock. From here it looks like
granite — and another few rocks around her neck. No time
to admit I wasn't listening or to think. I open my mouth and
— *I just want to make sure we're paying enough attention to
the needs of the children,* I say. Sounds like an appropriate
comment at a PTA meeting and I make it firmly, the way I'd
ask the Toys Я Us clerk where the Barbies are. I expect to be
ignored or told to go to aisle five, but for some reason the
room dissolves in a flood of angry outbursts. People are
shouting and pounding their desks, and the president is calling for order. Michael's mom is on her feet, shaking her fist.
I take the opportunity to clean Ed's nose and look over at the
door to see Thea peering in. I wave and she makes her way
over to my chair. *How's the babysitting room?* I ask.

Boring. She rolls her eyes. *There's millions of kids and nothing much to do. This looks more exciting. Why is everyone so mad?*

I shrug my shoulders. *I honestly don't know,* I say.

I'M NOT THE MAIN EVENT though. The issue that has all the parents ready to explode is farther down the agenda, where the PTA is, for the first time in living memory, *not* hiring a Santa Claus to appear as a climax to the Winter Concert. *Every year since I went to this school myself there has been a Santa Claus at the Winter Concert. Of course we used to call it a Christmas Concert.* This is from an irate mom from the part of the playground where the senior grades hang out. Very fiery and Celtic-looking — easy to picture her ancestors at the Battle of the Boyne, and her distant descendants still remembering it.

I rise on a point of order. *Could we,* I ask, *defer this discussion for about two minutes?* Puzzled expressions clear up as I escort Thea to the door. *You're afraid I'll hear stuff I'm not supposed to hear, aren't you, Daddy?* she asks. *Bad words? Bathroom talk? Stuff like that?*

I give her a gentle shove down the hall. *Or worse,* I say — *chimney talk.* Her face clears up. Probably she's remembering the last time I tried to light a fire in our fireplace.

AND THEN, I TELL MY WIFE with a shiver — it's late at night, the sheets are cold to the touch — *everyone voted against the PTA board and called them names, and the board resigned, and we elected a new board with Amanda's mom as the president, and she promised to find us a Santa Claus, even though it's short notice. And then Ed sat up in the stroller and started to cry.*

Our bedroom faces north and the window takes a Zen attitude to weather — who can tell what is outside? it asks, and what is inside? My wife's exhalation is clearly visible before the breeze whips it away. We turn to each other for warmth, and maybe, just maybe, for something more — a little Kwanzaa cheer perhaps — but just at that moment the door opens and Thea is standing there with water dripping from the sleeve of her pyjamas. She's shivering even harder than I am. *Dad,* she whispers, *I've been trying and trying and trying but I can't turn off the tap in the bathroom.*

Canadian Christmas

YOU DON'T NOTICE YOUR KIDS growing up until you take it for granted — Thea tying her shoes, Immie getting dressed, Sam almost telling the time and Ed talking on the phone. Lunch is over and I'm on my knees in the sunshiny kitchen, not giving thanks for the rejuvenation of the freezer after its recent near-defrost experience, though that mightn't be a bad idea, but washing the floor. I thought I'd take the opportunity while my wife and the children walk down the street to pick a Christmas tree from the lot beside the fruit store. Should be a brief excursion, but if I remember correctly the War of the Spanish Succession started out as a brief excursion. When I took the kids tree shopping last year we had passionate arguments, name-calling, accusations, tears, temper, threats and finally treats. *See you in an hour or so,* my wife said. I think she was optimistic.

Yes, at ... eight o'clock? said Sam hopefully. Thea pointed out that he was looking at the wrong hand of the clock. Then she reminded him that each number is really five numbers, but Sam had already heard all this from me, he didn't have to take it from his sister. *Bye,* he called on his way out the door. Ed declined their invitation. There are lots of chances to pick a Christmas tree, but Dad washing the kitchen floor is an event on a different time scale — kind of like Halley's comet or a change in dynasty.

WHEN *DID* I LAST DO THIS? I wonder. I don't recognize half the stuff I'm scraping off. I'm happy to have Ed's help until I notice he's eating some of it, and I send him away with a stern lecture — I'm not too worried, it started out as food anyhow, which is more than you can say for a lot of the stuff he puts in his mouth. He's bouncing repentantly on the couch in the living room when the phone rings. He hits the ground running before I can get off my swollen knees — really, how did our grandmothers do it, taking the entire house apart, sterilizing it, and then putting it together again every week? I'm practically crippled after an hour.

Oh hi, Grandma. Ed is standing on a kitchen chair with the phone up to his ear — looks quite comfortable. My attention is momentarily distracted by — what *is* that? Looks like cheese but it's the consistency of high-impact plastic. I cannot tear it, not even with the pair of pliers I find under the radiator. I don't know whether to alert NASA or Prada. The stuff would make great shoes or luggage, and it would also be able to withstand the heat of re-entry into the earth's atmosphere. You could wear it, drive it, build with it, fly it, anything except eat it. The new miracle product, Vulcanized Velveeta. I hope the guys at Kraft know what they've got here.

I get most of the floor done while Ed is chatting to my mother. He doesn't call her a big bully because he's practicing a more appropriate phrase. *I want it,* he says at intervals into the phone, nodding enthusiastically, his eyes all lit up. Words to warm a grandmother's heart. What *it* is I can only guess. My mom gets all sorts of catalogs and has recently taken up knitting. I'm afraid of the offspring of her generosity and his enthusiasm, especially since he gets so hot.

I want that too, he says, *and that* — when he learns to dial
we're going to have to get a parental-control chip to block out
the home shopping channel. Then he says good-bye and
hangs up.

Hey! I say, up to my elbow in Mr. Clean — not an attractive image, is it? Ed goes back to bouncing on the sofa and
the phone doesn't ring again. When I phone my mom, there's
no answer. I poke my head into the living room. *Ed, did
Grandma want to talk to me?* He smiles and shakes his head.
Well, maybe she got what she wanted from him.

THE TREE SHOPPERS RETURN while I'm trying to chase Ed
upstairs for his nap. A single look at the three long faces tells
me that the Hundred Years War is still on. Immie has her
arms crossed in front of her, she's not admitting a thing. Sam
rolls his eyes. Thea is crying bitterly. *And now we'll never get
a tree. How can we have Christmas without a tree?*

My wife tries to calm her down. *Of course we'll get a tree,
honey. Don't you worry, there are plenty of trees out there.* I
try to calm her down too, *And if we don't get a tree we'll celebrate Kwanzaa instead,* but she's not comforted.

I leap over the top of the sofa and surprise Ed, whose shriek
of delight turns into a cry of protest when I carry him to the
stairs. He has to have a nap because he's going to be up late
tonight. *You know what time it is,* I say. Sam's eyes are glued
to the mantel clock. His lips move silently and then he says,
Ten-thirty! Poor fellow, that's what the dial says all right but the
clock has been broken since we got it. *Very good,* I tell him, carrying Ed upstairs and tucking him in. He doesn't say, *I want it,*
to me. *You big bully,* he says. I suppose I am but — *It's for your
own good,* I tell him. *You've got a big night ahead of you.*

*   *   *

THE KIDS ARE SUPPOSED TO REPORT to their classrooms at seven o'clock for the start of the Winter Concert. Sam is dressed and ready to go, belt buckled, teeth sparkling, hair burnished, parka zipped, boots laced, hat pulled down tight, and mitts on, by four-thirty. *Okay,* I say. *Now don't move for two hours.* He scowls thoughtfully behind his muffler. Sam is really working on this time thing. *How many Mississippis are there in two hours?* he asks. *Seven thousand,* I tell him, and his skinny little shoulders droop. I wrap presents, put through a couple of loads of laundry and lay out the tools I'll need to get the Christmas tree up, if we ever buy one — saws and adzes and spirit levels, bolts and guy wires and and old brace and bit in case I have to go through the floor. Thea and Sam rehearse their song a few dozen times and get it perfect. Ed is a rapt audience. He sits and watches them, and when Thea holds up the trumpet he holds up his hand too. Dinner is french toast — not a good idea because you can't eat french toast without syrup and you can't eat syrup without spilling. I'm still self-conscious about my clean floor so I spend most of the meal under the table, alternately yelling and wiping. Sam has removed his hat and mitts to eat, but he casts anxious glances at the two kitchen clocks. *It's six thirty-nine,* he says accusingly to me, like it's my fault. *Isn't it?* That's what the digital clock says. *Don't worry,* I tell him, *that clock is fast.* He thinks about that and spills some syrup. I wipe it up. I'm on the floor anyway because Ed has flung away the last two bites of his french toast so that he can lick the syrup from his plate. *How can a clock be* fast? says Sam. *It says six thirty-nine — there, it changed to six-forty. That's the time.* Thea licks her fork, smiles serenely and points at the other clock. *It's six-thirty,* she says. *See — the big hand is halfway around.* Sam shuts his eyes. He does that when he's upset. *The clocks say six-thirty* and *six-forty?* he says. *And ten-thirty,* I remind him, *don't forget the broken one on the mantel.* My wife gives me a dirty look. *It's six-thirty,* she tells Sam.

He waves his hand in frustration, knocking over his milk glass. *How can you be sure?* he quavers. She gives him the answer he needs — not *Because,* or *Eat your french toast,* which would have been my answers.

Don't worry, honey, she says. *You'll get it.*

Immie's dressed up too. She's wearing a suit jacket and pants and a white button-down shirt. She looks big-city tough, as if she should be hanging around a street corner in Spanish Harlem. She hasn't spoken in hours. I know she's nervous. *There's plenty of time,* I tell her. *Would you like to practice your part?* She shakes her head. A small piece of french toast slides off her fork onto the floor. I pick it up, wipe the table, then the floor. *Darling* — my wife smiles at me — *you're not eating anything. Don't you like french toast?*

TIME TO GO. They all get their faces and hands wiped. *Hang on,* Ed tells me seriously, runs away and comes back a moment later. *Do you have to go to the bathroom?* I ask him and he shakes his head. *Are you sure?* I believe him but I check the seat of his pants anyway. How does that saying go, Trust everyone, and cut the cards. *Okay, into your coat.*

It's a beautiful Saturday night, not too cold, a light wind and the moon riding high and full behind the clouds. The street is packed with families and the school is all lit up to welcome us. *Look,* Thea shouts, *it's Santa! Santa!* A large and shadowy figure peeks out from behind a tree and then lumbers across the lawn to open the back door of the gymnasium. The kids want to go after him but I hold them back. Some mysteries are best left undisturbed and that would include the area behind the tree where Santa was standing. We're right on time. The children look so proud and independent on their way to their classrooms. Immie turns at the kindergarten door and gives the tiniest wave. The halls are thronged so I keep tight hold of Eddie, even when we're sitting down on the floor in front of the front row because there aren't enough seats in the gymnasium.

All around me are parents — anxious parents, proud parents, hot and stuffy parents, enterprising parents perched atop the exercise bars with video cameras, parents with small children who keep escaping and being recaptured, and parents with babies who just keep sleeping. No one is carefree or completely comfortable — no one would rather be anywhere else in the world.

Good evening, everybody! Our principal has a booming voice and no notes, thank goodness. She stands in front of the curtain, shading her eyes from the glare of the school spotlight. *I would like to welcome you all to this year's Winter Concert.* She smiles around the gym. A hideous thought strikes me, and I lean over and whisper in my wife's ear. The principal asks us to rise and listen to a very special rendition of our national anthem. Chairs scrape, the curtain rises smoothly and my wife shakes her head. She doesn't know where Thea's trumpet is either. *Maybe she has it with her,* I whisper, but deep down we both know better.

Immie's teacher, an incredibly nice and patient young woman, blows into her pitchpipe and holds her hand up for attention. The audience quietens and the video recording lights go on. The junior-kindergarten class, two dozen well-dressed and wiggly little children being careful not to wave at their parents. Immie told us very earnestly that we were not to worry if she didn't wave, she wasn't supposed to — the whole class takes a deep breath.

The teacher's arm comes down. The kindergarteners know what that means. They open their lips to form the first words of the anthem. The hall is hushed, expectant, though of course it's impossible to stifle very little kids and I hear someone in the back saying she has to go to the bathroom. I'm holding Eddie so he can see.

ONLY GRADUALLY DOES IT DAWN on us that we are witnessing a very special performance indeed. The kindergarteners, in a collective panic, are not singing — no, that's not true, they're singing silently. They *look* good, the striving eager anxious little faces are perfect, they're following the teacher's waving arm, their mouths are opening and closing, and and and — no sound is coming out. Not a note, not a word, not a whisper. They are singing, but not out loud.

Seconds pass — ten, fifteen, twenty — and do you know what? I find myself singing. I don't think of myself as particularly patriotic, but there's something about your national anthem. And I'm not alone, lips are moving nearby, framing the words we all know so well. *With glowing hearts we see thee rise, the true north strong and free.* By the end of the anthem the entire audience is singing quietly. *O Canada, we stand on guard for thee.*

It is a completely magical moment. For a few, a very few heartbeats the country and the children are one, and we are proud of them both, and of ourselves for caring. No one laughs, though I notice a few smiles. My wife grabs my hand and holds tight. The class follows the teacher's moving hand. Immie makes a characteristic gesture, brushing the hair away from her face. Does she know? Do any of them? Can they understand why, when the teacher brings her hands up in a sweeping gesture of conclusion, the whole gymnasium erupts in a torrent of released emotion, cheering and laughter and, yes, I confess, tears. Most of them seem to take it all as their due, and so it is. One of the boys in the back row is punching his neighbour as the curtain falls.

*   *   *

HARD FOR THE REST OF THE CONCERT to live up to the opening number, and it doesn't, but some of it comes close. One of the Clarinet Club members introduces their second piece as *Black* ... and then she gets a fit of the giggles, and the girl beside her finishes for her, *Bottom Stomp,* she declaims in a loud voice, and then the whole Clarinet Club giggles so hard that the teacher has to come onstage to lead them. The next number is a medley from *South Pacific.* I tell you, there's a haunting emotional quality that a grade-school Clarinet Club can bring to *Gonna Wash That Man Right Out of My Hair* — I shiver when I hear it, it conjures up images of wailing spirits round the tombs of the undead, really quite chilling. Later on we all start clapping and stamping our feet in time to the Glee Club's stirring rendition of *Dreidl dreidl dreidl.* And then the curtain rises again, this time on a group of eager, smiling Grade Ones — and Thea.

She's on the end of the row and looks like a tragedy mask. Ed's been dozing but he perks up at once. *This is it!* he whispers loudly. Thea hears him. She gives us a halfhearted smile and then hides her face in her hands, which, I notice, are empty. Sam's hands are empty too. He waves enthusiastically. Telling Sam not to wave isn't enough, you have to convince him that it's important. I remember asking him to try to color inside the lines and he just shook his head and told me that the picture should be blue *here,* and *here* was outside the lines. Anyway I wave back, and then Miss McQueen hits a note on the piano and the song begins. All this time Ed is restless even for him. He fumbles in his clothes and struggles when I pick him up. *Do you have to go to the bathroom?* I ask. He shakes his head violently.

The song sounds pretty much the same as usual, but I can sense Thea's dread growing as they approach her bit of business in the second verse. Shortly before we get there I feel a familiar sense of loss. Looking down, I can't find Ed. My first thought is bathroom. I look around and am surprised to see people laughing. My wife darts forward, but Ed's already got one knee on the stage. He pulls himself up and totters forward. I suppose he could be more noticeable but I don't see how — maybe if he carried a drum major's baton — but he's not carrying a baton, he's carrying Thea's trumpet, and at *exactly* the right moment he holds it up. They train public school teachers well. Miss McQueen carries on and, at the end of the song, she brings Ed forward for his own bow. I apologize for wrecking her act but she tells me not to be silly.

The problem, she says, handing him down to me, *will be trying to duplicate the whole thing next year.*

AT THE END OF THE CONCERT the lights in the gymnasium go right out, and from the middle of the darkness comes the sound of sleighbells. We all go *OOH.* There's a crack of a whip and big jolly *HO HO HO* and then a couple of unexpected bumps. The lights go up to show Santa lying on his stomach on the stage. *Jeez, did that hurt,* he says levering himself upright, a big barrel-bodied guy with highly noticeable teeth. I can't believe it. It's Roy, the delivery guy from the Peruvian restaurant.

Happy Holidays! he calls. *HO HO HO. Season's Greetings!* hobbling to the front of the stage, dragging his sack after him. *Jeez Louise, my ankle's killing me,* he mutters, and then louder, *Have you all been good little boys and girls? Hey? Do you deserve some candy? I'll bet you do.* He reaches into his sack and starts to throw handfuls of candy into the crowd. Eddie grabs a piece. His eyes are like saucers, he's only a few feet away from Santa Claus. I wonder how calm I'd be if I were a few feet away from a grown-up superstar — Linda Evangelista, say, or Luciano Pavarotti or Donovan Bailey. Probably I'd just feel short or thin or slow.

I've got to go now, boys and girls. Got a few things to do before I'm ready for my big job next week, says Santa, sucking on his false teeth. *It's the preparation takes the time. Don't you find that?* This is the experienced renovator talking. *Jeez, I tell all my customers they'll get a great job if they'll just be ... patient.* He stands there for a second, lost in thought, then makes his way slowly offstage, favoring his ankle. *HO HO HO,* he calls over his shoulder. I can hear him echoing down the hall, fainter and fainter.

Couldn't the PTA get anyone else? my wife whispers.

I guess not, I say, but I have to admit I like the idea of a Santa Claus who rides a bike and offers to paint your school.

It's late when we get home. Even the clock on the mantel is telling the correct time. Everybody should be right now and then. Thea gives me a specially big hug when I tuck her into bed. *Only four more days,* she whispers. I nod. *Well, in case I forget to tell you, Merry Christmas, Daddy.*

Merry Christmas, I whisper back.

Tidy Up and Throw Away

CHRISTMAS MAY BE THE HIGH POINT of the year as far as my children are concerned but it's amazing how quickly they get over it. I was still trying to figure out how the camera flash worked when Imogen, from the middle of a pile of wrapping paper, asked if her birthday was coming soon. *Tomorrow!* I lied by four months, anything for a Kodak smile. I pointed the camera at her but instead of clicking and flashing it started to rewind itself, I hope we didn't untake all the pictures from Hallowe'en.

And now, two weeks later, it is as if the holiday had never been. The entire season seems nothing now but a fever dream from which we have awoken refreshed, and with a boxful of new toys and mittens. Routines re-establish themselves, the rhythms of life continue after this briefest of interruptions — flood and ebb, wax and wane and wax again, not something I've ever done to the floor.

Speaking of things lunar, I've got my friend with me today. I don't know how else to describe my very personal and very periodic urge to tidy the house. My voice and blood pressure go up, my eyebrows and tolerance go down and my sense of humor goes away. For a few hours in the month I become hell to live with for everyone I know, me included.

Look at this! I shout on entering the living room. *Look at this mess! Do you know what this looks like?* And of course the kids do know. They remember from last month, and anger is not a creative emotion, you tend to say the same thing over and over again. *It's a pigsty, that's what it is! A trackless desert of disorder, a lair of bestial.*

They're still young enough that they don't roll their eyes when I get on my hobbyhorse and start galloping around, partly because even they can see that the room *is* a mess. I'm not comfortable with objective judgments, but when a room has a big upright piano in it and you can't see the piano, that's a messy room.

Tidy everything up! I shout. *I want furniture right-side up. Skis and scuba tanks in the closet, cold cereal back in the boxes, stuffed animals on the beds, live animals outside, not like last time.* I hate sounding like this but I can't help it, and Midol doesn't do any good. I go on, *I want toys in boxes, cushions on the couch, iron lung in the basement, books in bookcases, clothes in the laundry pile, and all the string — where did we get all the string? — back where you found it. Yes, Ed?*

He looks like he doesn't know whether to cry or hit me, partly because his nose is all swollen with what might be sinusitis according to a panel of leading doctors who wrote the medical textbook I picked up at a lawnsale last year. They advise us to keep the condition under observation and consider seeing a doctor if symptoms persist. They advise this for everything from a broken leg to schizophrenia. I like the book because it tells me to do what I'd do anyway, makes me believe I'm naturally medical the way other people are naturally musical or naturally able to parallel park. Don't tell me it's practice, I've been practicing for years and I still usually end up parallel to a claims adjuster.

Does your face hurt, Ed? I ask. He nods. All week his nose has been getting wider and wider. Sounds like the sort of thing that might have happened to Pinocchio if he'd been brought to life by the Plaid Fairy instead of her blue sister. *I think we might have to take you to the doctor,* I say. *Right after we tidy up.*

Ed picks up a balloon and holds it tight. *Don't break it!* he says. *You —*

ALL OF MY MORAL ADVANTAGE goes out of me on an escaping sigh. Ed is recalling the Balloon Incident, a time a few months ago when it was just him and me in the basement. He was like a teeny wrecking ball, smashing toys, knocking over file boxes, flinging laundry in all directions. They say you can't talk sense to the wind or a cat, but you don't feel bad when you yell at the cat, you only feel stupid. I yelled at Ed and felt bad and so did he, so bad he immediately ran over to a box of toys and, with great effort, dumped it upside down. Then he sat down and glared at me. I stood still and glared at him. Impasse.

I was in the middle of laundry — an unnecessary comment, like saying that I was still breathing, I'm always in the middle of laundry, but dirty clothes were suddenly far from my mind. For ten seconds we stared at each other. *Put those toys away!* I said. You know what he said. *Yes!* I said. You know what he said. I went over to the box, turned it right-side up and put in a handful of toys, pointed to the rest of them. *Put them in the box,* I said. You know what he said. *Yes!* I said, and then lost the moral initiative when I added, *Or —* and couldn't think of anything. He didn't sneer exactly, he doesn't know how, but he dribbled a bit, offensively and unnecessarily, and, with less effort this time, upended the toybox again. I didn't send him to his room or lecture him or spank him or forgive him — those are all grown-up responses. No, I picked up a balloon, showed it to Ed and then broke it with a loud pop. Yellow balloon, picture of someone with a lot of hair on it, Einstein or Ronald McDonald or someone. *Pop!* And my brilliant stratagem worked. Ed stopped throwing toys around and began to cry.

Slowly, dejectedly, and with infinite care, he selected one toy from the pile, lifted it up to the box and with a sad little sigh plunked it in. And sat there on the basement floor. *Poo-poo head,* he muttered under his breath. I don't know where he got the phrase — devastatingly accurate, mind you. *Oh yeah,* I said. If he wanted to act like a two-year-old I could too. I picked up another balloon — we'd had them ever since our last trip to the museum or McDonald's and until this minute we'd all forgotten about them, but right now they were important bargaining chips. *Keep going!* I said. He whimpered when he saw the balloon, picked up two toys, dropped one, picked it up, dropped the other one, and burst into tears again. *If you don't pick up the toys,* I said, *I'll pop this balloon too. Now move!* Guess what, he picked up the toys. Guess what, I felt like an idiot. Some victories aren't worth winning — now, months later, he remembers the time that Dad acted like a poo-poo head.

Don't worry, I tell him. *Your balloons are safe, but you have to help the others tidy up.*

They're moaning and carrying on, something about Tidy-Up Slaves. *It's horrible,* says Sam, *the living room is the messiest room in the house.* Thea shakes her head, working steadily if not quickly. *No it isn't, the laundry room is the messiest.* Sam is about to debate the point but catches my eye and bends himself to work hurriedly.

I drift toward the kitchen but find my way unexpectedly blocked at the door. Imogen stands with her arms outspread, *What is the password?* she asks. *Cheese,* I tell her. That was the password last time. She shakes her head. I don't know how James Bond did it, in our house the passwords change as frequently as Ed's underpants. *Sesame,* I sing, *Sesame Mucho.* Imogen shakes her head. *The password is Pony Pals,* she says. *Okay, Pony Pals,* I say. She shakes her head. *I was lying,* she says.

Beep beep! Ed pushes her aside with his high chair, I hadn't even noticed that in the living room. She shrieks and runs away. *Thanks, Ed,* I tell him. The high chair is looking pretty ratty, the tray is cracked and a lot of the stuffing is coming out of the seat. Ed is almost big enough to go on to a phone book, and fortunately we live in a big city.

Back in the living room I help put small toys in boxes, amazed, as I always am, at the sheer volume of stuff we have accumulated without trying. In my nightmares my mind looks like this, full of useless data that I seem unable to get rid of. *What is this?* I ask, holding up a — hell, I don't know what it might be — an earplug, or the tip of a pool cue or a piece of rubberized asparagus.

It's a stegasaurus leg, Sam says, and I believe him. Kids know what every piece of every toy is and where they all came from, down to the day of the week and what they were wearing when we got it. *Don't you remember?* one of them will say. *We got that shield at Burger King last winter. We went there after taking Thea to the dentist. She got a yellow toothbrush and a sticker with Darth Vader's brother on it* — almost as scary as being able to remember the combination to my eighth-grade locker a quarter-century after I had to use it last, or the theme song to Saturday morning cartoons like —

> *Hercules, hero of song and story.*
> *Hercules, winner of ancient glory,*
> *With the strength of ten ordinary men*
> *Hmm hmm hmm*

Kindness in his eyes,
Hmm hmm hmm
Hercules, only the evil fear him.
Hercules, you can feel safe when near him.

HMM HMM HMM ... Damn now would you believe I'm upset that
I *can't* remember the theme song. I used to be able to do all the
verses. They say that Alzheimer's means never having to ... no,
darn it, they don't. I add the dinosaur leg to the toybox and take
a moment to consider Ed, whose nose is dripping an ugly color.
He rubs it and frowns, picks up a small plastic superhero
(Spiderman, Spiderman, Does whatever a spider can) and
places it inside the box. I feel his forehead, a meaningless gesture really since he's almost always hot. He's hot now. I try to
remember when his nose started to bother him. He seems happy
enough, but I don't think I am. I've seen enough sick kids to
know that something is rotten in the state of Denmark. We've
moved beyond my Wait And See medical text. Left to its own
devices Ed's nose will sort itself out about the same time as the
Balkans. It looks like antibiotic time in the old corral. I just hope
the drugs are more effective than a UN peacekeeping force.

THE LIVING ROOM ISN'T TIDY, but it's tidier. I can see the piano
over behind the basketball hoop and alpine tent. I free the
slaves and, without too much more ado, we pile into our
coats and boots and mitts and hats and stroller and set out
along the well-worn path to Dr. Imre's clinic, which seems to
be our home away from home at this time of year. My parents
go to Florida for the winter, we go to Dr. Imre's — it's south
too, but only a block, and then two blocks west. The place is
a bit like Florida, lots of white shoes and polyester and just
full of Canadians, the good thing is we don't have to phone
long distance to find out how the kids are doing.

I lift Ed from the stroller and find the way into the clinic blocked. *What's the password?* Imogen demands. I remember a warning I saw on a churchyard fence in Rosedale. *BEWARE OF THE GOD,* I intone in an awful voice, and Immie gives a little yip and moves aside.

Dr. Imre is his usual sarcastic self. *Always nice to see a regular customer. Hello, Eddie, will you be wanting the usual?* But the examination does not follow its regular pattern. The doctor doesn't say *Tsk tsk* and threaten to amputate. He frowns, blinks, and then gets frighteningly polite and calm. *How long has he been like this?* he asks me, and when I tell him he nods and writes rapidly in the file — not a prescription.

I want you to go to the hospital now, he says with a smile. *There's a specialist on call.*

I'm always worried when things go quickly at the doctor's. *What is it?* I ask. I move mechanically, nod and smile at the kids. The key is not to show fear. Everything is going to be fine, isn't it. Isn't it?

I'll call to tell them you're coming, he says.

The hospital is about ten blocks away. No point to a cab, even if I could find one. The neighborhood is a maze of one-way streets constructed like a fat man's arteries, not encouraging to traffic flow, and the main thoroughfare is thoroughly jammed. The stroller flies along. By a miracle all the homeowners on the way to the hospital have shoveled their little stretch of sidewalk. The older kids keep up as best they can without complaining. They know something's up. Despite my best intentions I must be leaking anxiety through my smile.

I'm running through negative medical scenarios in my own mind. For some reason cerebral meningitis keeps popping into my head. That's serious, I remember, even my team of leading physicians thinks so. *Don't worry, kids,* I say with a smile as meaningful as a weatherman's. They nod grimly, they're worried.

An ambulance is turning the corner with the siren blaring

so I speed up. I want to get to the Emergency Room ahead of the gunshot wound or heart attack or whatever it is — *My little boy has something wrong with his nose!* I call out as the automatic doors open. Those people are good. They have us rerouted upstairs before I get my Health Insurance Card out of my wallet.

A soft-spoken youngster with a wispy beard and a warm handshake greets us as we enter his fourth-floor office. *Hello hello,* he says to the kids, bending low to shake hands. *My name is Bob. How are you all today?* We all say we're fine, except Immie, who says that Bob is a dog's name. Bob laughs heartily and takes Ed from my arms and seats him on the examination table.

Did you hear from Dr. Imre? I ask. *He said he was going to call.*

Bob doesn't answer. *Tell me, Ed, do you like magic?* He's staring into Ed's nose as he says this, smiling pleasantly behind the magnifying flashlight. With his other hand he reaches into Ed's shirt and pulls out a bouquet of flowers. Ed stares and asks, *Am I better now?* I guess he thought that was what was wrong with him. Bob laughs and shakes his head, and Ed laughs too.

Actually it's odd, and I can't speak for Ed but I've started to feel better since we came in. I was a bit run down — stress and tension and the remains of my monthly indisposition — but I find myself smiling at Bob because he's so happy. The other kids are smiling too. It's almost uncomfortable, but none of us stops smiling.

What is it, doctor? I ask. *What is wrong with Ed?* He's putting away his flashlight and taking a small bottle from a locked case in the dispensary. Absentmindedly he offers me a deck of cards. *No thanks,* I say. Sam picks one. Bob looks me in the eyes. I'm used to being judged by my juniors. He doesn't put me off. No scrutiny is as tough as your children's —

especially if you've been found wanting in an important area of parental duty like Dessert Selection or Number of Bedtime Stories. *We're going to find out in a minute,* Bob says to me and *It's the seven of clubs,* to Sam. *Hey,* says Sam. *It is.*

The doctor has Ed lie down, drips a couple of drops of the liquid from the bottle into his poor swollen nose, and distracts everyone with a magic pencil that grows to twice its length, snaps and then somehow reforms itself. Ed can't move because there's money growing under his head and if he moves the money won't be there. He giggles and stays still. After a moment Bob takes out a pair of tweezers and, while Ed is still giggling, pokes sickeningly far up his nose with the tweezers and pulls out — a dripping thing. My heart turns over. *What is it?* I gasp. It's the size of my finger and it could be anything, even another dinosaur leg for all I know, except it's squishy. Ed's still giggling.

I think it's a piece of sponge, says Bob, writing a prescription that will clear up the residual infection. I have a vivid mental picture of Ed at mealtime, picking away at the soft spongy seat of his high chair.

Bob finds a quarter underneath Ed's pillow, and hands my wiggly little boy back to me. *He'll seem a bit hyper for an hour or so,* says Bob, *but that's the effect of the drug. Don't worry.* He pats Ed on the head, shakes hands with everyone again.

What drug? I ask, wondering about my insurance. *Cocaine,* Bob smiles enigmatically. *Opens up nasal cavities. That sponge just popped into view.* My tonsils pop into view at this point as my mouth falls open. *Oh,* I say.

Dr. Bob makes his exit, stopping when he reaches the door because Imogen is blocking his path. *What's the password?* she asks. He bends down to whisper in her ear. She stares at him. *How did you know?* He steps past her and disappears down the hallway.

*   *   *

REALITY REASSERTS ITSELF in the elevator. Thea wants to know if we can ride it up and down for a while and I say no. *Why?* she asks. *Because we have to get home,* I say. You know what she asks. *Because we have to have dinner,* I say. You know what she asks. *Because it's dinnertime and we still haven't tidied the house,* I say. You know what she asks. *Because I say so,* I say. At which point the world goes black and the elevator stops with a jerk.

Sam and Thea and Imogen look scared in the pale glow of the emergency lighting. I'm not scared. We're no more than twenty feet off the ground and we're together and everyone is safe and healthy. I was more scared on our way over here. Ed keeps giggling.

A City of Two Retailers

ONE OF THE MOST STRIKING THINGS about a great and teeming city — I'd be quicker to call it an asset or advantage if I knew for whom — is its contrasts. Mean streets and generous helpings, dark strangers and fairweather friends, those who smell their cottage cheese before buying and those who wait until they get home, thin women with thick hair and, yes, men with no hair, and Ashley's Fine China Shop and Roberto's Boxing Emporium and Skate Exchange. I took the children to both retail outlets the other day, we needed skates and table settings, ever have days like that? And the difference between the two places struck me like a razor-sharp knife, maybe the only item actually in stock and for sale at both establishments. I mean, I didn't see a Lalique crystal duck-call at Roberto's and I don't think Ashley's sells a .30-.30 repeating dinner service with telescopic sight. But both stores let me in and took my money and smiled. Maybe it was the children. Maybe the economy's in worse shape than we think.

*   *   *

ROBERTO'S FIRST. I find it in the Yellow Pages under Sporting Goods. It has a big ad and an address I recognize as way downtown. An asthmatic leprechaun answers the phone. I ask if they have secondhand children's skates. *Sure and we do,* he says, wheezing softly. *We've everything and all, that we do.* I hang up and ask Ashley's about my place setting, specifying credit, phone and sale reference numbers, feeling like a jet pilot plotting a course — *Roger, switchboard, I repeat one niner niner seven November,* and that's just the expiry date on my Visa card. *And there's ample parking under the Manulife Centre,* I'm told. I'm conscious of a faint and surprising echo, the guy at Roberto's mentioned the parking too. Only he hadn't said *ample.* He said there was *lots.*

I decide to hit the skate exchange first. There might not be time for both errands and I can't coop the kids in the car all afternoon with only a salad bowl and dinner plate to show for it — cruel and unusual punishment. We drive around the block a couple of times with all of them taking turns shouting, *There's a spot, Dad!* and me saying, *It's across four lanes of traffic,* or *That's the Hospital Emergency Entrance.* I take a spot right in front of the store. I suppose there is lots of parking if you aren't choosy about tickets — *Don't smash the door into the fire hydrant,* I tell them. A man is leaving Roberto's as we approach, a nice man, he holds the door open for us and turns away before spitting on the sidewalk.

Inside the store it's warm and dusty and full of — *Punching bags, Immie! Look at the punching bags!* Sam and Imogen immediately adopt their Gentleman Jim Corbett stances and dance over. *Keep your hands up,* I tell them. The skates are at the back, past the free weights and knives, darts and fish hooks and live grenades — not exactly childproof, but nobody seems too worried, certainly not Thea, who points out familiar apparatus from the Biker Barbie set she got for Christmas. Ed has to be pulled away from — well, from everything, but most especially the giant Swiss Army Knife display. I'm just in time to save him from getting his arm caught in the motorized bottle opener.

Getting fitted for our skates is quite an anticlimax. A young man with a bolt piercing the middle of his forehead is patient, knowledgeable and adept at dealing with laces which must by some law be longer than the child is high. I figure the kids will outgrow their skates while I'm still in the process of threading, looping, wrapping and tying. For the first time in my life skiing seems attractive. It may cost ten times as much, but at least the boots snap in. The final price is determined by Roberto himself, a wizened old party in one of the customer chairs who smiles benevolently when Ed drops a ten-pound weight on the floor and covers himself in lure spangles and camouflage cream. *What would Your Honor say to a hundred dollars, now?* he asks me, wheezing gently. *It's a fine price, so it is. Sure, you won't get a better deal in the city.*

I've noticed three or four customers spitting as they leave Roberto's — must be a local custom, a formal sealing of the bargain. Well, heck, I'm feeling sufficiently at home here at the survival store, even without my plaid flannel shirt, just another rod-and-gun and uppercut kind of guy, so, after shepherding the kids through the door, I turn aside and ... what I'm trying to explain is just how I happen to have a mouthful of phlegm when I see a familiar uniform in a familiar posture — *Please, officer, I was just about to move my — Oh, sorry about that.* Lands right on her boot. They talk about a spit shine, don't they, she stares at it, stares at me. I've felt more suave than I do right then, a perfect mood for visiting Ashley's. On the drive uptown I tell everyone not to touch *anything* when we get to the store, then I tell Sam and Thea to stop teasing each other and Ed to take his fingers out of

Imogen's nose. PLEASE TAKE TICKET says the machine at the underground lot. *No thanks,* I say, *I just got one.*

*   *   *

IMAGINE AN ENTIRE LANDSCAPE filled with precious objects, any of which could shatter into a million expensive pieces at the gentlest nudge. Shelf after shelf, room after room, rainbows of color, spiderwebs of delicate brilliance, an empire of incredibly breakable plunder and me at the head of a delegation of visiting Visigoths. We pile through the door together — good thing it doesn't revolve or we'd still be there — more like the Keystone Kops than the sack of Rome actually. Ed log-rolls forward toward the display table, Sam and Immie are back in their boxing stances and Thea's coat sweeps broadly and dangerously behind her.

Everyone STOP! I shout, the GI who discovers that his platoon has blundered into a minefield. We all freeze for a split second while I rescue an eggshell ornament from almost certain Humpty-Dumptydom, and then we are ourselves rescued by Celeste, a majestic, perfumed presence with a tolerant smile where I expected horrified expostulation. She must have trained in Ashley's Pamplona office. She accepts us as a matter of course, carrying a bowl of jujubes, which she places on a marble table beside a huge fishtank made of what looks to be bulletproof glass. *Help yourselves, children,* she says with genuine charm. I could kiss her except she's too tall.

No, the horror-stricken faces belong to the clientele, several of whom withdraw the hem of their garments in a marked manner. On being asked if she's with us, one poor lady — well, maybe not poor exactly — exhibits a peculiar blend of shocked disgust and nausea, an expression I recognize from high school. My dates often looked like that on the dance floor. I check to see if my fly is undone.

Celeste calculates the amount of jujubes to a nicety. I sign my Visa slip just as the last one disappears into Immie's mouth. Sam and Thea are standing at opposite ends of the fishtank while Ed bounces back and forth between them like a pinball. *Will there be anything else today?* Celeste asks as though she means it. I'm watching the fish follow Ed around the tank, those lure spangles must really work. *No,* I say, and I mean it too. We share a smile. *I've got two girls of my own,* she tells me in a low voice, sharing a guilty secret. *They're at figure skating this afternoon.* I can't help wondering where they got their skates.

Neighborhood Wash

OURS IS A FAMILY NEIGHBORHOOD with a main shopping street running down the middle of it. Some of the signs are in English — STOP, for instance, and NO PARKING and DELICATESSEN. Lots of delicatessens. And prowling up and down between them, day and night, winter and summer, but especially winter, in their black kerchiefs and elastic-sided boots, backed up by those collapsible bundle-buggies, there are Baba Police. Very embarrassing it is to be out on a walk, as we are this cloudy winter day, and suddenly find yourself obviously anathematized in a language you don't understand. *That boy is going to freeze to death!* she cries, a gnarled widow with a glittering eye, pointing at Sam's unzipped coat. *What kind of father are you? Don't you know it's thirty-seven degrees below zero with the windchill!* I may not be quoting word for word, but that is certainly the drift of her accusation, hobbling over on arthritic ankles and pinning Sam against the wall of a nearby apartment building while she does him up.

And the baby, look at the baby. With his face uncovered he'll freeze solid, like a block of ice he'll freeze, the little darling!
I always smile. You can't beat up a little old lady in a kerchief. She's one of those forces of nature. Besides I know that in ten minutes the boys will wriggle free of those horrible constricting winter clothes and get back to serious pneumonia research. *Thanks,* I tell her, *you're very kind,* but she's busy tying some kind of seafaring knot in Ed's parka hood and forcing a candy into his mouth. Then she stops dead, hands to her face, the picture of horror. *Angels and ministers of grace defend us!* or something like that, she cries. Across the street a little girl has lost one of her mitts.

We're on our way to the laundromat because our washing machine is undergoing a crisis of faith. Maybe it's been reading the religious leaflets that end up in the recycling basket. NONE ARE FREE FROM STAIN, they say, and WASHED IN THE BLOOD OF THE LAMB. Anyway, little black marks are starting to appear on everything I wash — further evidence of original sin, I guess. The repair service is sending round an appliance healer, but in the meantime cleanliness is not next to godliness — in fact it's two and a half blocks away.

Sam and Thea and Immie are enjoying a holiday away from school while their teachers get professionally developed. The twins are sliding into things — hydrants, paper boxes, telephone poles. I don't think it's a great game, but they do and they're the ones falling over and lying on the ground, so who am I to say. Imogen is beside me, licking snow off her glove. *Just make sure you know where the snow has been,* I tell her. She frowns up at me — *What do you mean? It's been in the sky,* she says. Eye contact isn't always enough with Ed, so I'm holding onto his — no, dammit, I'm holding onto the bag of dirty laundry and he's — *Come back, Ed!* — climbing a snowbank whose previous whereabouts are all too clear. It's the color of a schoolbus. I rescue him and we continue our march.

The gang of skinheads is hanging out in the next laneway, waving their arms and laughing, using I can guess what kind of words, even though I don't know them. *Careful, Sam,* I shout, dragging him out from under a parked car. They're recent additions to the neighborhood — forty or fifty teenagers who just appeared one day like the rash on Imogen that no one could understand, not even Mrs. Klesko, and her little Jerry has had every disease known to Western medicine and a few from the mysterious East as well — *He's out of danger!* she exclaims every couple of weeks, hauling down the quarantine flag from the front of their house. Immie didn't seem unhappy, so we never took her to the doctor, tried to avoid striped clothes because we didn't want her to clash, and after a few days the spots went away. The gang doesn't look as if they're going to go away, they're having too much fun terrorizing retailers and schoolyard moms by — well, by being there and looking like that. Big bad bald — it's scary all right. Mind you, Elmer Fudd looks like that too.

I've had dealings with them myself because they like to hang around the schoolyard near our house. You may say it's hard to get a gang of skinheads to move, but it's not. The key is to hold a child in your arms. Ed's best, he smiles and points at their tattoos and they move grudgingly out of the way so we can play hockey. But you can't actually get rid of them and you sure can't scare them. Or can you?

You there, yes you! The withered crone is addressing us, but the gang startles like a herd of deer at the approach of a wolf. They recognize the kerchiefed baba as a local figure of power, like a Dickensian beadle with a more sober uniform. Of course they can understand what she is saying. She has a cane and it takes her a long time to reach us, but she doesn't run out of things to say and as far as I can tell she doesn't repeat herself. The gang shivers and moves farther off, I notice. *It's a disgrace!* she calls to me, *that's what it is. Do you know what that child is doing?*

Sam is lying on the ground under a streetlamp, apparently stunned, but she's not pointing at him. Ed and Thea are wrestling for control of the stroller and Imogen is — *Eating an icicle, that's what she's doing. She'll make herself sick!* Or maybe, *She'll stab herself!* I can't tell which. The baba limps up to Immie, whirling her cane like a club. Immie drops her icicle. The baba turns in a flash, sets Sam on his feet and dusts him down, and straps Ed into the stroller, shouting at me all the time, how can I be so irresponsible. As the skinheads shuffle away I catch the leader's eye. He smiles sympathetically, a first. I wave, he nods and hurries after his group. By now the old lady is giving out candies. Her hand is all twisted up with arthritis but the kids don't seem to mind.

ELIZABETH'S COIN LAUNDRY is a happening kind of place. We fit right in with the rest of the clientele — an old man in a straight chair, snoring, and a young woman just out of a strait-jacket by the looks of things, spinning and talking to herself. Twelve machines, of which six are labeled OUT OF ORDER. I suppose you could say the place was half-working or half-broken, depending on whether you were an optimist or a pessimist. One of the supposedly working machines has a potted palm inside it, tipping the balance toward pessimism.

I don't waste my time looking for the latest *Tatler* or free cappuccino, just open the bags and dump the clothes, add the soap and coins, and stop Ed from climbing into the dryers, a full-time job in itself. *And what shall we do now?* I ask, settling down in a plastic chair molded to fit no part of human anatomy that I can work out. I can understand why the old man chose the straight chair. I can understand why the young woman is standing up.

I'm not a fabric-softener kind of guy. We've got about twenty minutes before the wash is done. *We could go down the street and get some smoked meat for lunch,* I say, *or we could play a game. Ed! NO!* Sam pulls him away from the dryer. I thank him. Imogen is taking careful steps down the center of the room, counting with her eyes closed. *Don't forget fifteen,* I tell her. She opens her eyes, stumbles, frowns at me accusingly. I tell her I'm sorry. Sam and Ed are assuming martial-arts poses, though Ed in the bottom half of his snowsuit is more reminiscent of a miniature Sumo wrestler than a Ninja warrior. They'll keep that up for a few minutes, or until Ed can't stand it any more and tackles Sam.

How about Water Fire Log? Thea asks. We're working on variations of the Scissors Paper Rock game. In this one the Fire burns the Log which floats on the Water which, of course, puts out the Fire. I'm happy to encourage cleverness unless it involves physical danger or making a mess, so I tell her sure. After a few rounds Thea wants to try another variation. We get as far as Chicken pecks Grit when one of our machines lights up and says *Tilt.* Wouldn't it be great if you got a free wash when that happened. It doesn't really say *Tilt,* it says *Unbalanced Load,* and I know how it feels. The kids crowd around as I lift the lid and squelch around inside. *Dad,* Sam whispers, *that lady is talking to herself.* Ed leans over so far his nose is practically touching the water. *Don't worry, Sam,* I say. *Lots of people talk to themselves. I do it too — of course you might not want to use me as a benchmark of sanity.* If Ed falls in, I'll have to rebalance the load again. I pull him back. *Dad, is she dangerous?* Sam asks. I close the lid and the wash starts again. The lady is standing in front of one of the broken dryers, shaking her head and haranguing the Unseen in a loud voice. I put my arm around Sam, sit him on my lap — boy, is it uncomfortable — so I can whisper in his ear. *She's not dangerous,* I say. *She just seems a little unbalanced to us, like the load of laundry.* Sam frowns. The lady takes the OUT OF ORDER sign off the dryer and hits the round glass door with her fist. The dryer starts up. I must remember which machine that is.

Do you understand, son? He thinks a bit, nods. *Now she's spinning again,* he says. *Like the wash. Does that mean she's okay?*

I open my mouth, close it. *She's fine,* I say at last. Ed has noticed the lady as well. He pushes a chair over to the dryer on the end, climbs up and bangs on the door. Nothing happens.

Look, says Thea, *there's a doggie outside the window. Oh Dad, isn't he cute? Isn't he? Hello, boy!* Thea wants a dog. Put like that it doesn't sound like much, she'd like a dog, so what, I'd like lower interest rates — but I don't think about interest rates all day long. I don't draw pictures of interest rates. I don't importune my bank for them, promising that it won't be any bother if they lower interest rates, that I'll feed the interest rates and take them for walks every day, that all my friends have lower interest rates, that the house *is* so big enough, the interest rates can sleep in the basement, or in my room, please please please.

Ed sees the dog too. He points and bounces up and down. *Duck,* he says.

Dog, says Thea. *Duck,* says Ed. *Dog,* says Thea.

Duck duck duck. Ed isn't taking *dog* for an answer. He knows what a dog is, of course. He can say Bow wow ... or St. Bernard, for that matter. But would an avalanche survivor be reassured to know that a St. Bernard duck was on the way?

Yes, that is a cute dog, I tell Thea. Her face brightens. Maybe I shouldn't give her hope like this. How would I like it if my bank talked encouragingly about interest rates and then slammed the door in my face — wait a minute, that's what they do. *I want one!* Eddie jumps off his chair and bounces over to me. *I want one.* He and Thea are firm allies on the dog issue. She slips her little hand in mine. *It would be protection for the house,* she whispers. I squeeze her hand, thinking, Just what we need, a watchduck.

*   *   *

THE MAGIC DRYER WORKS for me too. I hit it a couple of good ones and it starts. The young woman is still there, by the way, sunk in a corner, muttering to herself. I put the rest of our clothes in the next dryer, fumble around in my pocket for coins, and ...

NO! She leaps dramatically to her feet. She's taller than I thought, quite a striking person with her dark red hair, dead white skin, and eyes that aren't looking at anything I can see. I stop and smile at her. She points. *NO! NO!* I reach out to touch the dryer. *No?* I ask. She shakes her head. *No.*

I shrug, point to another dryer. *Okay?* But she's sunk back onto the floor. I feel mildly foolish, but I don't mind spending thirty seconds transferring clothes. It's not superstition so much as politeness. I don't want her to feel bad. While our clothes are drying, Imogen and I count our footsteps to twenty-nine without missing a single number, not even fifteen, Thea and Ed sit at the window, pointing out a whole flock of dogs, and Sam practices jumping over the stroller and landing on his back on the piled-up winter coats. The lady spins out the door without saying anything. We call good-bye but she doesn't answer.

We leave as a withered old lady is coming in. Her bundle-buggy is full of black clothes. She stares at us in dismay. *You thoughtless man,* or something, she says, *a good thing I happened by.* Baba Police are never off duty, she has everyone's hood done up before I can thank her.

THE LAUNDROMAT BURNS DOWN a week later. Thea and Sam are in school, but Ed and Immie and I are out strolling and we stop to watch for a moment. The local paper reports that the fire was caused by a short circuit in one of the units. I wonder which one. No I don't.

Spare the Rod

THE SUBJECT OF DISCIPLINE doesn't come up very often at our house. Bedtime, yes, and the difference between girls and boys and what's for breakfast and how big were the dinosaurs and why does Barbie's motorized scooter keep running into the wall — but discipline, well, maybe it's just that there's always something more interesting to talk about. *Eat your peas,* I tell them, *or* — or what? Or not, I guess. My usual response to misbehavior is evasion. *Stop pulling Thea's hair or — say, does anyone want a Lifesaver? Do you hear that noise in the closet? It sounds like monsters.* The kids don't want to get in trouble any more than I want to them to be there, we're all on the same side really. Besides, exploring the basement for monsters has to be more fun than pulling your sister's hair.

And what is misbehavior? Rules like NO SHOUTING or NO JUMPING ON THE FURNITURE are fun, but you can't take them seriously. If kids didn't shout and jump around they'd suddenly have eight waking hours to fill, all the time they're not eating and wrestling and slamming doors. And there are times when shouting is the right thing to do, such as when a two-year-old picks up something — *THAT IS NOT A BALLOON, PUT IT DOWN, ED* or *THERE'S ENOUGH WATER IN THE BATH.* So we have family rules, but none of them is strictly observed, not even by me. What we're really interested in is NOT BEING MEAN and TELLING THE TRUTH, great ideas until they come in conflict or you're trying to sell your house.

Anyway, there I am in the kitchen, spreading peanut butter with a lavish hand and trying to remember who takes it plain, who with jam, who with honey — peanut butter is for kids what whiskey is for adults, except that kids don't get mellow after two or three sandwiches — when I hear a sudden rise in the hullaballoo level in the living room. *Quiet!* I shout, folding Sam's sandwich, cutting Thea's and Imogen's in half and arranging Ed's in bite-sized throwable pieces. The storm still rages. *Lunch!* I call, that should calm everyone down. But it doesn't. I hear Ed. He's not in serious trouble. Someone would come and tell me, the way they did when he found the tape gun, *Dad, there's a mummy in the basement and it sounds like Ed!* — enough to get any parent's attention. I arrive on the scene just as he wrestles a plastic horse from Immie's grasp and hugs it to his body.

Oh dear. I put on my Judgment of Solomon face, expecting her to appeal to me, but she's been in kindergarten all year and learned some new tricks. Before I can stop her she picks up Barbie's coffee-table-sized convertible — honestly, that doll lives better than we do — and smashes it over Ed's head.

The shocked silence doesn't last long. Ed shakes himself free of pink plastic fragments and scampers to the kitchen, still clutching the horse. Sam stares in admiration at his little sister. *Ever cool!* he says. Immie looks as surprised as the rest of us. She tries a frown but underneath she's pretty pleased.

Thea meanwhile is doing a slow dissolve into tears. After all it's her car, she got it for Christmas from Grandma.

Solomon gives way to Judge Jeffreys — actually he's easier to do — the eyebrows come down and the voice is raised — *Get to your room this instant!* With a black cap I'd be perfect. I go over to mop Thea and lead her into lunch. Bits of pink chassis crunch under every footstep. No doll accessory comes with a three-month warranty — three minutes is more like it. I hope Barbie's insurance is paid up.

Ed's fine, drinking milk and reliving the episode with Sam. Thea brightens when I promise her an extra cookie, but now the boys feel hard done by and I reflect that, after all, Ed is the victim. *You can have an extra cookie too,* I tell him. *And me?* says Sam. I nod and head upstairs to talk to the accused. *Why does Sam get an extra cookie?* Thea calls after me. *I don't know,* I call back.

Immie is sitting on her bed looking angelic. *I'm sorry,* she says before I can open my mouth. *Why did you do it?* I remember my parents asking me the same question. I could never think of an answer, and neither can Immie. *What am I going to do with you?* My parents used to say that too, and I shrugged. So does Immie. If she was older I could take it out of her allowance or ground her, but she doesn't have any money and she's too young to go out by herself. I go on for a while sounding like an old record and feeling like a bully. When Immie reaches out and pats my hand, I stop talking because my mouth is suddenly busy smiling. I wish I were better at this. I'm probably hurting her in the long run, spoiling her, after all she did commit aggravated assault with a car, but I can't stay angry. I still remember Sam laughing at me when I was yelling at him once years ago, real sincere laughter. He'd never heard anything so funny. His little face screwed up in ecstasies of mirth and all my anger drained out like bathwater, leaving a little dirt ring that disappeared when I began to laugh myself. And that's a good memory.

So Immie and I go downstairs hand in hand, and Immie says she's sorry to Ed and to Thea and we all have another cookie. Before she goes to kindergarten, Immie helps me vacuum the living room and I ask Thea if there's a vehicle Barbie can use while we're getting her car replaced. She's already thought of this. She runs to get the weekly flier they keep delivering and I keep putting out to be recycled.

Oh, I say when I see the picture of the lovely pink ocean-going yacht — in the picture Barbie is at the helm and Ken is leaning over the side. Another difference between girls and boys.

SPRING CLASSIC

Fitting In

I'M STARING INTO THE MIRROR at my wife's face. She's standing behind me, putting on makeup while I shave off my two or three days' growth of — I don't know what to call what I wear on my face, it isn't really a beard, but it's too long to be any kind of shadow. I usually shave after a workout at the YMCA or if I'm invited to a party — that is, infrequently. Given my social and fitness schedule, I sometimes go for days and days getting hairier and hairier, kind of a slow-motion lycanthropy — and then my face starts to itch, and I reach for the shaving cream and wound-dressing kit. I wore a real beard a while back. Most guys try a beard at one point in their lives just to prove they can, the way most women will give stiletto heels a brief try — if you wear them for any length of time you're in danger of looking like an Orthodox rabbi or a streetwalker.

Beautiful, like satin — my wife likes to encourage my hygiene — *but why this morning? You just shaved a couple of days ago.* I blush beneath the rest of my shaving cream. My wife and I don't have a lot of secrets from each other, but I don't know how I can tell her I'm shaving because I'm going to be spending this lovely April morning with five or six other women.

Isn't that Immie's voice? I say. My wife frowns, does that thing with her lips to squish the lipstick, wipes most of it off on a Kleenex, and disappears. Immie's in her room. She doesn't sound insistent — more desolated, a puppy caught in a trap. Thea sticks her head into the bathroom to ask if she can watch TV before school. *Yes, but first find Ed,* I say, so she turns and hollers at the top of her lungs — *ED!!* surprising me so that the razor zigs instead of zagging. I reach for the toilet paper. *I could have done that,* I tell Thea with a fair amount of asperity, if that's the word I want, sounds like a trendy herb. *I know, Daddy. Why didn't you?*

I hear my wife's voice. *I've got him now,* she says. Imogen thanks her and runs down the stairs. My wife tosses a small, struggling body into the toilet. *First ant of the spring,* she says. *It was right in the doorway, holding poor Immie at bay.* I frown. I kind of like ants, maybe because they're industrious and group-centered, unlike me, I like nurses too, and sailors and Americans. *Should you be killing ants so early in the year?* I wonder. *Do you have a license? Are they even in season yet?* My wife would like to make a witty reply but she's running behind, so she blows me a kiss and scoots.

Ed slides down the stairs from the third floor on his stomach just as I finish the scraping part of my shaving ritual. Now all that's left is the stanching of the blood. *Yes?* he says. *What is it — is Cindy here?* Cindy is the babysitter whose morning lecture schedule is going to make my rendezvous possible. *Hi, Ed,* I tell him. *I just wondered where you were.* He stares at me seriously. *I am here,* he says.

Sam wanders into the bathroom to brush his teeth, something he does every time he bites anything, even his nails. He's become very interested in dental health since Geoffrey down the street got a cavity filled and explained the whole process in vivid detail. *Gross!* he comments as I start to peel off the little dottles of Kleenex that are holding my face together — this from the little boy who eats glycerine-candy bugs and watches the dismemberment channel.

Wait'll you hit puberty, I tell him, wincing. Good thing I don't wear cologne or I'd be in agony with all that raw skin. The doorbell rings and I'm still in my pyjamas. *That'll be Cindy — tell her to come on in,* I say to Ed, who stands at the top of the stairs and bellows, *CINDY!!*

I stare at him. *I could have done that,* I say.

As I WALK DOWN THE STREET under a sun that feels warm for the first time this year, under trees that are ready to burst into leaf, past brown soggy grass and carefully tended tulips, I'm filled with the excitement and fear of conditional acceptance. It all takes me back to school, where I managed to *not quite* belong to quite a number of groups — even groups I thought I belonged to would move dates without telling me so that I would be the one who showed up at the wrong address on the wrong night with the wrong utensils. *Oh, didn't you know?* someone would say. *Didn't someone phone you?* And they would all giggle away their embarrassment and I would go home with my boutonniere and bowling shoes and accordion. Maybe that's why my heart is beating so quickly as I walk up the steps to Angelina's house for coffee.

What if it isn't today?

But it is. *Come on in,* Angelina says, very friendly, leading me to the kitchen. *You know everyone* — and for an agreeable change I *do* know everyone, there's Trinley's mom and Douglas's mom and James's mom and Amanda's mom — I've seen them hanging around the playground together ever since Sam and Thea were in kindergarten. *Hello hello hello,* I say, taking an empty seat and a slice of nut bread, and surprising a look of sympathy around the room — not pity for the outsider but, *Your poor face, whatever happened?* I don't want to go into embarrassing detail, so I tell them I was attacked by an idiot with a razor, and they gasp and shake their heads and take polite nibbles of nut bread. They don't seem to like it but I do, my slice is already gone. Nut bread is great stuff but hard to eat without making a mess, there are crumbs all over me and my chair. I brush them off absentmindedly and get ready to discuss what it's really like to bring up kids and how awful men are and I don't know what movie stars are coming to, how could anyone find *her* attractive with her great big — in short, shop talk.

I like to read the headlines of the supermarket magazines and watch promos for daytime TV shows. I figure I'm pretty well prepared as long as we don't get too technical about soap operas. But I don't want to lead off. I'm just a rookie. There's a pause while we get our coffee poured and then Margery starts in — that's Amanda's mom, the current president of the PTA, the Chair, she calls herself, non-sexist, although I think she's being a bit upholsterocentric. What about those pieces of furniture you *can't* sit on — anyway, she introduces the topic of the morning, which turns out to be Extra-Curricular Activities.

I'm disappointed. I was hoping for a long discussion of the girl with two heads who can sing a duet by herself, I can't remember if that was *Geraldo* or the *Star,* caught my eye, I tell you. The moms have a lot to say about hockey and gymnastics and doll making and choir practice — their kids seem to live for the moment every day of the week. I'm tired just listening to Trinley's whirlwind schedule. If she were my kid I just know she'd never make it to Advanced Découpage on time with the right scissors. I express some of my incredulous admiration, and Trinley's mom giggles charmingly and tells me it's easy with — get ready — the Kids' Pocket Organizer.

I stare around the room. All the other moms are nodding, their kids have them too. I marvel at the idea of six-year-olds telling each other to have my mom call your mom and we must do juice sometime. I wonder if the devices are waterproof or if they short out every time they end up in the laundry — which would probably be a pretty regular occurrence at our place. Also I wonder whether our kids are missing out because they do not have to juggle, for example, clarinet, soccer, Cub Scouts, Junior Achievement, debating (another great concept, debating for first-graders, *Did not, Mr. Speaker — Did so, Mr. Speaker — DID NOT, Mr. Speaker)*, Chess Club, Mineral Club and karate. No wonder I never see Douglas after school. All Sam and Thea have is art lessons on Tuesday afternoons. The rest of their Pocket Organizer would be empty unless they wanted to remind themselves to Slam Doors or Complain About Bedtime. And these activities don't seem to require any mechanical prompting at all.

Amanda's mom has a tendency to hold onto the floor. I guess she's used to it, being a chair, but she's sipping her coffee now and I see a chance to change the subject. *There's a team of cryogenics specialists in California who claim to have thawed the two-hundred-year-old body of Marie Antoinette,* I say. You'd think this would be a great conversational icebreaker, that ideas and opinions would start to flow like a river in springtime. Nope. *At least they think it was Marie Antoinette. It might have been Sara Lee. In any case the headline was "Let 'Em Eat Some More Cake."*

Douglas's mom is staring at me. Angelina looks out the window. There's a fine show of early flowers in her neat back garden. I'd comment on them but they're not tulips or daffodils and I don't want to offend her by saying, *Those purple things look great.* Heigh ho, I don't seem to be making a good impression, as the dental student said.

I hope they don't think I'm being sarcastic because I'm not. Marie Antoinette is my kind of news story. I'm no information gourmet. I don't know anything about tribal significance in Burundi, I couldn't tell you the name of our own Minister of Agriculture or the winner of this year's Nobel Prize for Chemistry — or any other year's for that matter. I know the Dow Jones and the Bank Rate fluctuate on a regular basis and lots of people get excited about it — but I don't. On the other hand — *Did you read about the alphabet diet, I say, where you eat things that begin with the same letter all day long, beginning with apples and antipasto — one woman lost forty pounds on X and Z alone.*

Amanda's mom breaks an embarrassed silence with an amused snort, then the other moms start to giggle. None of them will look in my direction. I don't think they're laughing *with* me. It appears that time and marriage and family have not made a communal animal out of me — once more I have come to the wrong house on the wrong day with the wrong kind of shoes. Oh well, at least there's lots of nut bread.

I MEET STEVE ON THE WAY HOME. He's Erin's dad, a big bear of a guy with a loud hello, a mighty handyman before the Lord. He's working nights this week, he tells me, gives him a chance to catch up on all the little jobs around the house that his family has been bugging him about. *If I get any spare time, maybe you and I could have a go at your porch, he tells me. Sure looks like it could do with a fix-up.* I smile and say I was thinking of hiring someone to fix it.

What? Steve's upset, his jaw falls open. *You don't need any help on a job like that, he insists. Saw off the end, replace some of the tongue-and-groove and rehang the railing, it'll look like new.* He slaps me encouragingly on the back. *Don't worry if your saw doesn't have depth settings. It's a really easy job. All it takes is confidence.*

We're outside the house now. Imogen is standing in the front window. She points at me excitedly, knocks on the window, waves and then topples backwards out of sight. Looks scary but she's done it before, usually she lands on the couch. *All it takes is confidence, and a saw,* I tell Steve. He swallows quickly but he's getting used to me by now. *You don't have a saw?* he says. *Well, look, I'll lend you mine. And an extension cord — the saw is electric. You knew that, didn't you?* I have to smile. *Didn't you?*

The porch does look as if it's about to fall down. I tell Steve I'll think about his offer, but in my mind I'm back with the supermarket tabloids. Last week one of the headlines read, *Aliens Fixed My House!*

Where are those aliens when you need them?

My Recipe for Meatloaf

DAD, COULD YOU PLAY — I don't hear the rest. My head is in the refrigerator. I grab meat and onions and resurface — *because you never have time.* I put my ingredients on the counter, what else do I need? Celery salt, pepper. *Never have time for what?* I ask Immie and Eddie. *Time to play Attack Dollhouse,* they say in unison. They're standing side by side with matching accusatory expressions while I'm thinking there's something nice about *Dad, can you play,* it feels so much friendlier and more inclusive than *Dad, can you lend,* which is what it'll be in ten years' time — unless it's *Dad, can you remember.* And I'm thinking, garlic, where's the garlic. *You promised you would play,* says Ed.

I locate garlic that doesn't feel too fresh. Mind you, neither do I. It is four o'clock. The meatloaf has to be in the oven in half an hour or it won't be ready to eat until we're all brushing our teeth. I remind them that I played Emergency Room with them just that morning. I was an accident victim with contusions and delusions and they were Dr. Hook and Dr. Slice, and when they were finished they put all their tools in the sterilizer and we shot a few holes of golf together — all around the living room, with plastic clubs and balls and plastic cups for the holes. It wasn't as easy as it sounds, our living-room floor is not exactly level, in fact you can always tell which guests do their sit-ups regularly because they're the ones who don't need help getting off the couch. The game got a little ugly when Immie went into a victory dance after holing a long putt, and Ed bit her finger and she whacked him. We had a chorus of apologies, and Immie needed a Band-Aid and Ed didn't need a Band-Aid but got one anyway, and when Ed got a hole-in-one he stopped dead, stared at Immie, stared at me, and then said, in a very quiet voice, *Oh, good.*

I explain that for the next half-hour or so I'll be busy cooking, and Immie's face lights up — *What's for dinner?* she asks and I tell her, adding that I'll be able to play after I've put it in the oven. She thinks that over, nods. *And what is the French word for antlers?* I say I don't know. *I wish I could have antlers,* she says. I take crackers out of one cupboard and the big metal mixing bowl out of another. I ask Ed if he wishes he had antlers too. *I wish I could play Attack Dollhouse,* he says.

Eggs, oil, herbs, leftover barbecue sauce from the spareribs we had last week, mustard, Worcestershire and soy sauce. Frying pan and loaf pan. Something's missing, what is it? Eggs — no, I've got those. Thea stomps into the kitchen. *Dad, you have to play with me,* she says. Again I prefer *You have to play* to *You have to bail* or *You have to identify* or perhaps *You have to snap out of it,* but I can't now, the sun is almost gone. I turn the dial on top of the stove to 350 degrees. The oven will follow in its own good time. Now I'm committed, once the oven is on there's no backing down, they probably felt like this at Oak Ridge, Tennessee, when they finally succeeded in making the heavy water. I work fast and precisely now, chopping a large onion and throwing it in the frying pan, breaking one (no, two) eggs into the bowl on top of the sleeve of cracker crumbs and two pounds of ground beef and pork, adding thyme and savory, mustard and Worcestershire, salt and pepper, and some of the reddish stuff in the jar with no name. I generally add whatever's on the countertop to the blend, it saves time picking and discarding — though you do have to draw the line. Some recipes say to put in carrot peelings and cabbage leaves, but don't do it. You don't really notice them but you know they're there, vegetables, lurking inside the meatloaf like zombies in a suburban cemetery, gonna come and get you in the middle of the night.

I still haven't got my hands dirty yet, and that's just as well because Ed shows up with a deck of cards fanned out in his two hands — Dr. Bob made a deep impression on him. He doesn't have the doctor's dexterity quite yet. In fact Ed's fan slips as often and almost as far as Josephine Baker's. *Pick a card,* he says. I laughed the first time he did it, and it's still a good game. I pick a card and then he walks away and does it to someone else. The deck is getting easier and easier for him to deal with, next time we play bridge with the Sagals we're all going to be confused, instead of just me.

Cy and Heloise are our neighbors to the west, an older couple who love to tell us how much they paid for their house in 1961 and their car in 1966 and his coat in 1958 and — well, you get the picture. I once worked out that two of our monthly mortgage payments would net out their entire lives, down to the stray dog they picked up in 1987. A devoted couple, kind of charming to be with, considering I spend the evening asking what is trump and being gloated at. Ed drifts away and I finish browning the onions and add them to the big bowl, then plunge my hands into the swamp of meat and mush and start squeezing. It'll only take a moment, sixty counted seconds and then I can wash off and deal with any emergency, but just for that moment I'm vulnerable to sudden attack, and that's when I remember the missing ingredient.

Sam wanders in — *Help,* I say, *you're a lifesaver, Sam. Can you go to the fridge and bring me the milk?* Milk is an important part of my meatloaf. It's not something you can ignore like, say, *bouquet garni,* which as you probably know is like *je ne sais quoi* — you add it if you have any and go straight on if you don't. My mom always used cigarette ash as her *bouquet garni* — she was way ahead of the craze for grilling and smoking everything. I don't smoke so I use ketchup, it seems to do about the same thing. Anyway, my point is that I need milk and I need it now, the stuff in the bowl is becoming sticky. Sticky is bad. Adding milk will make it — sorry to use such technical cooking terms — guckier, which is what I want. I ask Sam to pour some milk into the bowl — *Not so much! There, thank you, Sam. That was kind of you and kind of stupid of me.* The mix has gone straight past gucky to goopy.

Can I help you squish it up? he asks. *Sure,* I say, even Escoffier had to start somewhere. *But remember to wash your hands first, and roll up your sleeves.* That sounds wrong. *No, no, roll up your sleeves first, then wash your hands.* Oh well. He pulls up a chair and digs in as Immie and Thea and Ed arrive to announce that they want to help too. What do the Mormons say? — the family that cooks together ends up ordering in pizza. I make room for them all and notice — *Sam, you are wearing pyjamas.* He looks sheepish, ironic, since, *I'm a wolf,* he explains, *and they sleep during the day.* So they do.

No getting around it, we're going to need some more crackers. I heave my hands out of the meatloaf primeval, a big evolutionary step for them. Next thing you know they'll be wearing gloves and starting fires. I wash thoroughly, even my wrists and the bottom of my sleeves, which I guess I didn't roll up far enough.

The box is empty. *Who's been eating the crackers?* I bellow, startling them all. *You had some last night,* Thea remembers. *I know that. Who* else *had some?* I don't know if I actually glower at her, it's not something I practice in the mirror, but I try to glower. *It was after dinner, Daddy. You were sitting there.* She points with a goopy finger. *Careful,* I say, and she smiles. I'm going to have to work on my glower but not now, because I have to find something to thicken up my meatloaf mix. Do I have breadcrumbs lying around to feed the mice? I do not. I don't even have any bread. I was going to go out after supper and buy some to make the kids' sandwiches tomorrow. I scan the shelves, calm and collected. I have a few minutes before the oven gets to the right temperature. Let's see what we can substitute. Ketchup, for once, won't work, but there's always my other standby. No, not Oreo cookies — I don't want to waste them — but cold cereal.

PEOPLE ARE ALWAYS TELLING ME I should lock the door. *You never know who you'll be letting in,* they say, and the answer is, no, I don't, but I know who I'll be locking out. Me. I've always maintained that there's no burglary deterrent like a stroller and a couple of tricycles on the porch. No one, not the most demented of degenerate, drooling, drug-crazed, psychopathic junk-bond salesmen, is going to suspect you of having anything in the way of liquid assets. And what kind of gang is going to bother to trash a place like ours — how will they know which rooms they've already done? We do get more than our share of nice teenagers with chocolate bars to sell, but a digital alarm system is more expensive and you can't eat it — and, as I say, I'd probably just end up making it hard for me to get in.

Take now, for instance. The doorbell rings and I can see it's the guy who reads the gas meter. *Come in!* I call. No way I'm leaving four kids with their hands in meatloaf. He walks past us with his eyes averted. I don't blame him, in a job like his you see too much of other people's private lives. *Thanks for stopping by,* Thea calls after him. She's a good hostess. He doesn't reply, he's already out the door. Thank heavens I don't have to lock up after him.

Now comes an important decision — Corn Flakes or Shreddies? I'd like oatmeal but we don't have any. I used the last of it in a manic-depressive chocolate cake — darn thing jumped and giggled all over the place while I was making it up, and then wouldn't lift its head out of the pan when it came out of the oven, no matter how nicely I asked. It's that repressed Quaker background, I suppose, though I don't know that Froot Loops would have been a saner choice. Right now I decide on Corn Flakes because there are more of them. Within seconds the oven announces that it has climbed to 375 degrees above sea level, and the mix attains a state of perfect guckiness. On the command *Out hands!* the children remove themselves from the mixing bowl. I transfer the contents to a loaf pan and pop it into the oven.

Ed is first under the tap because, while all kids are conductors of sticky and messy materials, Ed is a perfect conductor. Ever wonder how the honey or Magic Marker is conveyed to the rug and the furniture? I tell you, it's *through* the kids. Ed is amazing, he's like copper wire, he can reach for a jam-filled donut with his right hand and *instantly* discover jam on the tablecloth under his left hand. I myself have seen this. When he finished the donut there was no place in the room I could *positively* say was free of jam, and I'm including inside the heating ducts.

I clean off as much of the meatloaf mix as I can see, but there's still an hour and a half before we can eat it. *I know what we can play,* Sam says to Thea. *How about superanimals? I want to have the claws of an eagle* and *a gorilla's arms for swinging away through the trees.*

This is a great game, the kids get to build their own animal from spare parts. *I have a cheetah's speed and chipmunk cheeks for storing my food,* says Thea, makes an interesting picture, I have to say. Immie wants to have gills for swimming and a skunk's tail. *And what about you, Daddy?* they all ask. I'm already thinking about vegetables. Meatloaf should have mashed potatoes and gravy and canned carrots, but I don't have any. All I can remember seeing in the fridge is some wilted bok choy and a half-jar of pimento-stuffed olives — sounds like a recipe for a stir-fried martini. Hmm. *I will assume the fierceness of a half-price-sale shopper,* I tell them, *the gall of a divorce lawyer and the instinctive camouflage of a junior partner at a full board meeting.* That ought to scare them. *But first I will play Attack Dollhouse because I promised.* Well, not right away — first I have to wash the bok choy and clear away the mess, including a cookie sheet I can't remember taking out. I wonder who did it and when and for what.

By the time I get to the living room the children have collected an array of spring-loaded Ninja darts and Bat missiles and the great siege catapult that goes with Sam's medieval castle set. For some reason we don't like to trash the castle, but Thea's multiroomed plastic mansion is always fair game. In fact, Attack Dollhouse is our favorite full-participation activity right now. All the children contribute their small toys to the defending army, giving it a scary but somewhat incongruous appearance. There's GI Joe on the stairs, and a couple of transforming robots on the balcony, SAS Barbie guards the front door, while Batman and Dopey the Dwarf patrol the roof. Franklin the Turtle is getting along very well with his Teenage Mutant cousins, and Barney and his firetruck provide an interesting counterpoint to the denizens of Jurassic Park watching from the garage roof. I love the inclusiveness. I think an army that has a place for Daffy Duck and the Little Mermaid and the Incredible Hulk is a good army. I confess to some misgivings when Robin Hood and Bambi are left within bowshot of each other, but that may be my own cynicism. And I'm so glad for Ken. It must be a relief to have other guys to talk to, even if they have capes and superpowers and all you have is a smile and a tennis racket.

Ed launches the assault, bringing down Snow White with a long-distance catapult. Thea topples a T-Rex, Immie's lob shot brings down a Zee-Bot, and soon the missiles are flying fast and furious. *What's wrong, Imogen?* She's wincing and favoring her hand. *My finger hurts where Ed bit it this morning,* she tells me. I ask her where her Band-Aid is, noticing that Ed isn't wearing his either. *I think I left it in the meatloaf,* she answers. Ed nods. He thinks so too.

A COOKIE SHEET should be placed under the loaf pan to catch the spatters. Drain the meatloaf and serve in slices, either hot or cold — or try to forget the whole thing and order pizza. The French for antlers is *bois* (pl.).

Virtual Fear

I'm having a nightmare. A small and ghostly presence has invaded my room. It fixes me with pale luminous eyes before reaching out a long and skinny hand to shake my shoulder. *No no no,* I say. *Not me, take her, take her!* My wife sleeps on the far side of the bed. *Please,* I say, *you don't want me, you want your mom.* Not heroic maybe but it's hard to be heroic when you're half-asleep. Also I remember all this from last night. Anyway, there's no avoiding your fate. The specter has come for me. *Dad!* says Sam, *I'm scared.* Well, I'm a sensitive guy, and what can you respond to a statement like that from a little kid you love dearly? *So what,* I tell him. He pulls the covers off me. I reach for them and encounter his muscular little arm, flesh all stretched taut and quivering — reminds me of no part of myself, except sometimes my forehead. He pulls on my hand. *Dad, you have to come now. I'm really scared. Dad, there's a cyborg in my room.*

I'm not asleep anymore but I'm still horizontal, fighting the long retreat. *No there isn't,* I say. Uselessly. I know this whole incident will be over sooner if I get up and deal with it, but I'm too tired. I know that the front porch needs all sorts of work done to it, and the roof needs shingles and the lawn needs fertilizer and I'm not dealing with any of these problems either — let's face it, I'm fighting the long retreat on a lot of fronts here. *There aren't any cyborgs,* I say.

Actually I don't know that there aren't any cyborgs, how can I when I don't even know what they are, but it's the sort of thing I'm expected to say. I remember drawing comfort from my parents' assurances that there weren't any ghosts. *There are so cyborgs, and there's one in my room now.* Somehow I don't find this compelling. Now if Sam had any sense, he could get me up in a minute by saying that there was water in his room, or money, or termites or real-estate agents, or any of those other ugly, boring, grown-up material things. But cyborgs ... My breathing stretches luxuriously, my mind is fuzzing over like the skin on cooling soup, and I'm off to dreamland when Sam grabs me again. *Dad, you just have to get up now!* And he's right, I do. Cool night air working on an exposed bladder. *All right, all right,* I say.

Once I'm actually up, there's no comic dozing, no fits and starts of winkin and blinkin before I can return to the land of nod. If I'm awake in the middle of the night, I'm ready for action. *How about something to eat?* I ask Sam, who stares at me. How can I eat at a time like this. It was the same when my wife was nursing him. I was working at a restaurant at the time and always tried to get home for the midnight feed. Maybe it was the power of suggestion, but I always ended up ravenous. She'd yawn herself to bed while I made a sandwich and hung out with the babies for a while. Sam and I wander downstairs for a cookie and a glass of milk. *Got to be properly fueled to deal with cyborgs,* I tell him. Whatever they are.

Cookie in hand and milk on the table, it is time to face the facts. *Tell me about it, Sam,* I say. It's best to confront your fear, say the words out loud — *I'll have to pay the repair people.* There I've said it. Does it make me feel any better? I guess it depends on how much I have to pay. *Come on, son, you can tell me. What are these cyborgs going to do to you?*

He shakes his head. *Nothing,* he replies with his mouth full of coconut cream. I nod approvingly. *I'm afraid,* he says, *of what they're going to do to* you, *Dad.* Oh.

Remind me, I tell him, *exactly what these cyborgs look like.* He does, in grisly detail. They're bad guys with major weaponry built right into every appendage.

And I just know they're going to strangle you in your sleep, Dad. I see the picture in my mind. It's awful!

I try to smile heartily. *Don't you worry, son, it'll take more than a seven-foot heavily armed being made of steel and circuits and rippling muscle to get rid of your old man,* I tell him. Though not much more, especially if it catches me when I'm asleep or bending over a stove or in some similarly vulnerable position. *Cyborgs,* I say, dismissively. *I've eaten tougher things for breakfast. Remember that President's Choice whole-grain cereal we tried — Memories of Scott's Cottony Softness?* Sam mumbles his cookie with a doubtful yawn.

He's been concerned about death and dying for a little while now — part of his age group, a lot of seven- and eight-year-olds end up sounding like Dr. Kübler-Ross. *I'll be so sad when you die, Daddy,* he said the other day, tears coursing down his cheeks, quite affecting — *How do you think* I'll *feel?* I asked, but he just shook his head. My little Sam, give him and his buddies ten years and they'll all be sounding like Dr. Kevorkian. I carry him up to bed, he's so tired he can't stay awake even to be afraid. *Don't worry, honey,* I tell him. *Everything's going to be all right.* Then I go to bed and dream.

In my dream I have somehow turned into Cyborg Dad. I have a Kleenex dispenser on the end of one arm and an automatic sandwich-maker in the other, the top of my head unscrews to reveal a frisbee launcher/bicycle pump, my voice box is a tape recorder set to cry *Don't slam the door! You'll have someone's eye out with that! Take it out of your mouth, ED!* and *There there, honey, tell me all about it,* every few seconds. The cyborg version of myself is ubiquitous, totally reliable, soft, smiling, and able to find things, programmed to make instant fair decisions, park close to the entrance, and shop for bargains which I take full advantage of with the coupon replicator which is located in my — well, this was a dream, I must have got confused by the concept of replication — anyway, I saved a lot of money.

SAM IS BRIGHT AND FRESH in the morning, unlike me and Thea. *What's wrong, honey?* I ask her because she's usually the cheerleading type — turns cartwheels on her way to the breakfast table and shrieks loud enough to break glass when the Rice Krispies start snapping and crackling. *I'm afraid, Daddy,* she says.

You're talking about cyborgs, aren't you, I say sympathetically. She stares. *No. I'm afraid about — throwing up.* Oh. Does this mean that she's worried about something else and is translating the worry to a feeling of nausea, a reference she can understand — triangularizing, they call it, unless I'm thinking of navigation. *Do you have a stomach ache?* I ask. She shakes her head. I'm *not going to throw up,* she says.

Not her too. *Are you worried about* me *throwing up?* I ask. But she shakes her head again. Good. *Are you sure it isn't really about cyborgs?* I say. *Or dying, or the house burning down in a whoosh of white flame?* She stares, swallows, shakes her head very doubtfully this time. *Or lightning striking? I used to worry about that when I was your age. Or earthquakes or atomic war or killer deadly insects or scorpions or anything like that?* She bites her lip, frowning. I'm only trying to be helpful, I can't understand all these white faces. Even Ed is a bit wide-eyed and I didn't think he was afraid of anything.

Promise you won't laugh, says Thea — how could she think her old man, her biggest fan, could so far forget himself as to laugh at any deep concern of hers, what kind of insensitive, mean, emotionally starved pinhead — *the way you did last time,* she says.

I promise, I say. *What are you afraid of?* She hems and haws and finally, *I'm afraid that Barbie is going to throw up all over me,* she says.

I clasp my hands in front of me. *Go on,* I say, and then I can't help myself — the smile that I've been holding back with iron self-control bursts out. *Daddy, stop that. You promised!* I'm not laughing, I swear I'm not, but I'm having trouble keeping a straight face. I hide behind a sip of coffee. Mind you, Bulimic Barbie would be a realistic-concept doll showing kids how tough it is to be that perfect. Thank heavens for the support she gets from her therapist, Dr. Ken, and doesn't he look handsome in a goatee? My coffee goes down the wrong way and I choke. They don't have any inhibitions about laughing at Daddy's distress. Kids are so heartless. *Eat your breakfasts,* I manage to gasp, *or you'll be late for school.*

I MEET REBECCA'S MOM on my way to the park with Immie and Ed. They're in the twin stroller and I'm pushing as fast as I can because that's the way they like to go. *Faster,* they shriek, *faster faster faster.* And I'm puffing and panting in the spring sunshine and they're waving their hands and laughing and then we're overtaken by a smooth-striding runner in a spandex bodystocking — *Oh hi there!* I gasp.

Her narrowed eyes sweep over me as if I'm a speck on her front walk, then she remembers who I am and slows her pace to mine. *Hello* — she calls me by name, very embarrassing because I've never known hers and I can't address her as Rebecca's mom. *Isn't it a lovely day to be outside?* she says. She's not sweating or breathing hard. Her chest rises and falls as smoothly as her feet. *This is my favorite time of year.* She smiles. I nod wordlessly and push Ed, who has climbed to his feet, back down into the stroller. *These first few hours of spring, sudden warmth after months of barren cold, must be the most precious we can ever know. When I heard the forecast I canceled all my morning appointments.* I shake my head in admiring agreement. I'm not up to prolonged conversation. Also I can't help thinking, doesn't this woman ever lighten up? — even her time off is significant. *On days like this I could run forever,* she says. Not me, I can run for another two minutes and then I'm going to faint right here on the sidewalk.

The park gates raise their stern wrought-iron heads at the end of the block. The light changes to yellow, and Rebecca's mom's nostrils quiver — like a war horse saying Ha Ha among the trumpets, she speeds away from us and crosses the busy street at a charging gallop, seconds in front of the traffic. At once I slow down and begin, wrackingly, to cough. It takes me a minute to get my breath back and, when I do, the light is red again. I don't mind. I wait, a patient screw, content to clip-clop my way through the rest of the day.

DINNER IS MACARONI AND CHEESE. Thea frowns worriedly at it. *Don't worry,* I tell her. *Macaroni and cheese is very easy to digest. No one ever throws it up, not even babies — see, Ed has a big smile on his face.*

Thea studies him carefully for signs of incipient nausea. *He isn't actually eating the macaroni and cheese, Dad,* she comments. *He's just squishing it up into a ball.* An observant girl, Thea, and that's not all he's doing. *Take that elbow noodle out of your nose, Ed!* I say. Dessert is popular and bought from a store. We finally finished the Royal Irish Constabulary chocolate-chip cookies I made last week, black on the outside and tan on the inside. Smiles spread like umbrellas in a sudden downpour when I bring out the familiar light blue bag with chocolate-covered marshmallow puffs inside it. I make up a plateful and can't resist a little arithmetic lesson. You've got to strike while the iron is handy.

How many cookies on the plate? I ask. *And how many of you? So how many cookies each?* They all arrive at the same answer at the same time. *Not enough!* they cry with their mouths full. And they're right, I suppose. I put out some more cookies. *I have four cookies here,* I say, *and there are four children — Sam, come back!* I run after him, but he says he has to go to the bathroom. So there are only three children when I return to the kitchen table — but there are no cookies left. I'm not really surprised. I sit down beside Ed and take a cookie out of the bag for myself. Time enough for another lesson tomorrow.

IT'S MIDNIGHT AND I'M STARTING to yawn. I put down my pen, check on the kids, crawl into bed beside my sleeping wife and float gently down into dreamland in a spiral, one of the millions of soft spring maple keys currently covering our lawn. One of these days I'm going to have to rake them, but not tomorrow. Or the next day. Or ...

Sam waits until I'm well and truly asleep to wake me up. *Do you notice anything different about me?* he asks. I don't, maybe because my eyes are closed. *I was kidnapped by aliens, and taken to camp,* he says. I open my eyes. We've talked about going to camp this coming summer. I used to go to camp. That's where I didn't learn to tie knots and light fires and sail and paddle a canoe. It's a lack of experience no child should be without. Where else can you go and have so much lore pass right over your head?

Did you get any merit badges? I ask Sam, whose teeth are chattering. He wants to sleep in our room. *I'm afraid the aliens will get me again!* he says. I tell him there are no aliens in our house, and his face wrinkles up, he wants to believe me but — *How can you be SURE?* he asks. Kids must envy our certainty, just as we envy their health and appetite. I carry Sam into the hall. *How about sleeping in the girls' room?* I say. *Would that make you feel better?* He nods, we ferry some blankets and pillows, and I get ready to go back to sleep for a few hours. *Good night, son,* I call not softly enough because I wake up Thea, who immediately starts to whimper.

He's too close, she says about Sam. *I don't want him so close. I'm afraid he's going to throw up on me.* I tell her not to worry, he won't throw up. *Yes, he will.* I shake my head and she bursts out — *How can you be SURE?* I give her a kiss. *Because I'm your dad,* I say, *and dads know these things.* She sighs and snuggles into her comforter. Back in bed I think about her, warm and rosy in the middle of her sleep. Much better than worrying about the unpainted house. I'm asleep before I know it, dreaming happily about stacks of clean, folded laundry.

Fear Itself

OUR NEIGHBORHOOD SHOP WINDOWS and telephone poles are full of seasonal advertisements — snow shoveling, chimney repair, and lost cats curl up at the edges, wither, and fall like leaves, only to be renewed by babysitting services and lawn-sales. This afternoon I find out about an open house, a new palmist, used baby clothes, and a Quality Workman who specializes in Porches Repaired and Houses Painted — I stop. I've already interviewed two contractors about the front porch — fine, upstanding, confident men in leather tool belts, expensive men from the Yellow Pages, one of them with a plastic helmet on his head and a set of blueprints under his arm. The sign I'm staring at is hand-lettered in sloppy block capitals. The phone number is local. Hard to imagine this guy with a cellular phone.

The children are all with me. Sam is away ahead and calls back to us, like a lookout from the masthead — *I see one.* At once all thoughts of home improvement flee my mind. I urge Thea and the stroller forward. *Good afternoon!* I call to the

Sagals, who are sitting on their front porch watching — well, they must be watching us, there isn't much else happening at the moment. They wave.

I can hear it now, the grinding wheels of the streetcar as it climbs the hill to our stop, which is, alas, across the street. The pavement is wide and busy, and the nearest traffic light is several blocks away. I wish we weren't going uptown because the downtown streetcar stops on our side of the big street. But there is nothing particular for us if we go downtown — nothing except the lake, and we've been to the lake already this week, and today is the twins' art lesson with Miss Vaal. If we don't get there on time, Sam and Thea will miss out on their chance to be Georgia O'Keeffe or Titian or whoever. Miss Vaal says they have definite potential, she stared me right in the eye when she said it after their first lesson, tapping me on the arm with her blood-red fingernail, *Definite potential,* so we hover on the sidewalk while the southbound traffic flies past us and the streetcar grinds closer and closer.

The parked car directly in front of us pulls out and gives us a chance by attempting a U-turn in the face of oncoming traffic. (I will remark parenthetically that our main street is famous for its frequent U-turns, stately ballets can be witnessed quite regularly at even minor intersections, two or three cars all U-turning in perfect order and good fellowship, letting each other in and raising their hats to each other, for we are a polite and hat-wearing neighborhood, even if we can't make up our mind where we are going.) I take advantage of the U-turn to get the kids out into the middle of the street, lagging behind the car like a careful halfback following his blocking, and get to the streetcar stop just in time.

What is it? I ask Ed, who is struggling and grunting to himself in the back seat of the stroller. I stop searching for the tokens I put in my coat pocket — but which pocket? The streetcar pulls up and the kids dash inside, except for Ed, whose sweater is caught on a protruding piece of the stroller. He's stuck. I can't get him out quickly and I can't collapse the stroller with him inside, so I try to combine the two operations, folding the stroller slightly and carrying it onto the streetcar with Ed's head and feet sticking out of the front end. *Hey!* he says, and rightly too. *Sorry,* I tell him.

The driver doesn't know me. He frowns and asks how many of those kids are mine. *As far as I know, all of them,* I say. *They look like me, don't you think?* He stares, not as wide as old Mrs. Willan when she made the same comment — *Don't the children take after their father?* and my mother replied, *Why not? He wasn't just farting, you know* — my mother is not one to mince words when she can use them whole. *It's usually one adult, three children and an infant,* I tell the driver, who nods. At length I discover which pocket it is that I have put my tokens in — it's the right front pocket of my other coat. I pay cash.

Thea won't sit with us. She chooses a seat nearby, beside a huge young man with no hair and a bloodstained sweatshirt. Maybe it's animal blood. Or maybe he cut himself shaving his head. I unravel Ed and pry him out of the stroller. *Who wants a mint?* I ask and get takers all around, including the bald young man. His hands are clean. He can have a mint.

That has to last all the way to art class, I begin, but Ed has already crunched right through his. *More, please,* he says. I shake my head.

MISS VAAL BELIEVES that the visual arts offer an outlet for the emotion that we need to express in order to be fully human. Her classes last a half-hour. The little ones and I do some comparison fruit shopping, exercising our scientific intellects while Sam and Thea express their emotions. We decide that California strawberries drop faster than grapes and squish easier and create more fuss with the help. *Are you buying those berries?* the irate fruiterer shouts at me. Ed has one in his mouth. Immie bursts into tears. *There there,* I tell her, *he's mad at me, not you.* Ed's face clears up like a suddenly sunny day. *They're good!* he says. Breakthrough. I still remember the first time he ate tuna salad. Strawberries are good for him, who cares what they cost or where they come from. I buy them on the spot, calming the proprietor, but Immie is still crying. *There's a bug on them,* she says. I can't see the bug, I cast a look in Ed's direction. Maybe it wasn't the berries he liked. Bugs I can find him at home for free, there's a little ant party that meets every night under the sink in the bathroom, very convivial, I ask them to turn out the light when they're done.

Sam is waiting for us on the front porch of Miss Vaal's studio, with the look he has on his face when I send him to his room — a kind of joy that is at once fierce and calm, very easy to picture that look on the face of a French aristocrat on his way to the guillotine or an early Christian on his way to the Colosseum. *Did you enjoy your art class today?* I ask neutrally. He knows he hasn't done anything wrong but I don't — not yet anyway. He nods without speaking. It's up to Thea to break the news. She comes out bubbling with joy and achievement — *Here's an elephant I made out of clay, Daddy, and a picture of a bug, and Sam got kicked out of the class for not doing what Miss Vaal told him.* Thea shows her bug picture to Immie, who screams and hides behind me, and Sam explains.

Like every explanation I get, it is delivered from at least two sides at once — Sam beside me as we are walking toward the crosswalk, and Thea from in front of the stroller, amplifying her brother's point, occasionally introducing conflicting testimony. Imogen wants to tell me about some art she did once, last month I think, and Ed insists on drawing my attention to a puppy that is barking inside a parked car. I thank him, nod to Immie and bend over to hear Sam more clearly. I'm not all attention, but I'd say I am more than half attention, a much higher percentage than usual.

The *point d'appui,* as the French say, is, it appears, the Bingo Hopper, a rounded inked stamp usually used to highlight *Under-the-N-78* in church basements. Sam has fallen in love with it. Some artists use a square-cut brush, others prefer a point, still others show a real preference for the palette knife. Some artists understand almost instinctively how oil paints are layered to produce a depth of color, others respond to the immediacy of acrylics or the transparency that can be achieved with egg tempera. This commitment to a specific medium can become a temporary fixation. I felt that way myself about sour-cream-and-bacon-flavored potato chips — not compulsive exactly, but interested in *every* facet of their character, how they went with diet cola, with late-night TV, with gloves, crystal bowls and serial music, how I *felt* about them when I was looking at the sunset or thinking about my wife or sorting dirty laundry. Sam was similarly attracted to the Bingo Hopper as a vehicle for transmitting his ideas, using it almost exclusively for several Blue projects and then, when Miss Vaal suggested he try another medium — Thea thinks it was the spangled glue gun, Sam himself says it was *That dumb string painting* — anyway, he said, *No.* Pretty bluntly. And proceeded to execute another four or five paintings with the Bingo Hopper in, I think, Red. He shows me one while we are waiting for the streetcar and I must say it seems a perfectly respectable art form, somewhere between Piet Mondrian and a satellite weather map. I can't understand the controversy, but Sam is *persona non grata* until he apologizes, says Thea.

I did apologize, says Sam. I tell him that's good. *There's some gum,* says Ed. *Did not,* says Thea. *See, Daddy. Right there on the sidewalk,* says Ed, leaning out of the stroller to point. I tell him I see the gum. *I did so. I said, Sorry, Miss*

Vaal, but I have to use the Bingo Hopper. Sam flushes, recalling the moment of conflict. *Daddy.* Immie tugs at my coat. *And then you pushed her,* says Thea. *I did not,* says Sam. *Did so.* Ed falls out of the stroller. *Daddy,* says Immie. I ask her what I can do for her. *I didn't push her. I just took back the Hopper,* says Sam. *Look at the gum, Dad!* says Ed. He's on all fours on the sidewalk. I pick him up. *You pushed her and she fell down,* Thea says. *She tripped,* Sam replies. *Did not,* Thea says. *Did so.* Sam's mouth opens wide as he takes a deep breath, *Did so did so did so did so.* Ed takes a step forward. Immie climbs shakily to her feet in the back seat of the stroller. I support her. Thea pushes Sam, who pushes her back. I tell them to be nice. Ed tries unsuccessfully to lift his foot. Immie bawls in my ear, *DADDY, THE STREETCAR JUST WENT PAST US AND I HAVE TO GO TO THE BATHROOM!*

Ed's foot is stuck to the pavement. Thea and Sam are standing nose to nose, saying, *Did so Did not Did so.* I can't help myself, I start to giggle. The streetcar disappears in the distance. Ed finally delivers his foot from the sidewalk, but it's still attached by a sticky pink umbilical cord. I giggle harder. Immie is hopping up and down in the stroller. Thea and Sam struggle briefly together before falling over. I'm laughing hard enough to hurt. I turn around just in time to spot a taxi. I gesture hysterically and the cabdriver slows, looks us over and then shakes his head and speeds away. I can't say I blame him. On top of everything I'd have to ask him to wait outside the house while I found enough money to pay him. A familiar-looking van pulls up to the curb beside us. It shouldn't be parking here, it's a streetcar stop. The window rolls down. *Need a lift?* my wife asks.

I PHONE THE NUMBER on the telephone pole and get an answering machine. *I'm out on an important job right now. Leave your name and number and I'll get back to you real soon,* says a familiar voice. I'm a little discouraged. Our porch isn't an important job. I'm impressed, though, it's nine o'clock at night and this contractor is still at work. I leave a message and go downstairs for another chapter in the neverending laundry, pausing a moment because the house is, due to some incredible freak in the weather or Earth's gravitational field, QUIET. I can't hear a pin drop because our basement floor is covered in dirty laundry, but I can hear Godzilla drop when I pick up a pile of clothes with the monster hidden inside it. I make a note of his whereabouts, because Ed is sure to ask me if I've seen him, and then I drift upstairs with a vague idea in mind, just a gray formless notion on the edge of the desert horizon, a small cloud of an idea that may disappear with a puff of wind or may, just perhaps, with a bit of luck and encouragement, mean a rare and refreshing moment of rain.

As it happens my wife is having a similar idea. We lock up the house, turn off the downstairs lights and check the children. My wife runs a bath with bubbles that smell of soothing balsam and then, with the smile that always lifts my heart, suggests that I join her in the tub. In one convulsive movement I add to the pile of dirty laundry on the bathroom floor and jump in. Men, we're all the same, we'll do anything to get clean. My wife is still undoing her robe. There's a hook for it on the back of the door. I'm soaking in heat and bubbles and anticipation, and she's standing with her head close to the wood with a look of surprise and dismay on her face. I ask what the problem is.

SHH! Do you hear it? I can hear a regular crunching sound. Houses make all kinds of weird noises and this isn't too intrusive. *What do you think* — I begin, and then with an eagle's swiftness she stoops to crush a small struggling body between her fingertips. She throws it in the wastebasket — an ant. I listen again — the crunching sound is louder. Can it be

... can it? I climb out of the bath a lot more deliberately than I climbed in, and put my head against the door, recoiling almost immediately. The crunching is coming from inside the wood, a loud insistent sound, like a fat man eating a buffet-sized caesar salad. My wife shudders and almost instinctively belts her robe tighter. *I'm going to bed,* she says.

Not me. I'm too scared.

Fear Gets a Hit

THE TRANSITION FROM PHILE TO PHOBE is a swift slide down a slippery slope from the broad plateau of tolerance and mild, good-natured approval to the depths of fear and loathing. And you can't climb back up. Hard to believe I used to like ants but now, shivering in the bathroom under my artful but not thermal layer of soap bubbles, I am consumed by terror. My wife is in the bedroom. *Now we know where all the ants are coming from,* she calls. *I guess we'll have to get rid of the door.* I don't say anything. *Are you all right?* she asks with, I don't believe it, a yawn. *Are you coming to bed?* I open my mouth but no sound emerges. There's a purity to fear — it purges you of fatigue, anger, hunger, love and common sense — and germs. I had a spring sniffle but now my nostrils are clear of everything except fear. *Well, good night,* my wife calls. I take a deep breath.

It's no good telling myself the ants are smaller than I am or part of nature's rich bounty or much-punished souls bound upon the Wheel of Things with many lives to go before they qualify for platinum credit cards. I can't diminish the hungry little beggars or the threat they pose to MY HOUSE, the place I live in — actually it's not, technically speaking, MY house. Despite all the monthly mortgage payments I'll bet the bank still owns everything except the cracks in the plaster and the grouting in the bathroom. Prompted by an insane impulse, the same one that forces Sam to watch horror TV shows where green slime takes over the world, I put my ear to the door and THERE THEY ARE again, loud and insistent. I pound on the bathroom door and — they stop.

Silence.

I choke so hard I almost swallow my tongue. *They're listening to me. They know I'm here.* Oh God. Now I'm really scared. In my mind the ants are not only strong-jawed and ferocious, but somehow bigger than I am. It's like I'm a child in the dark listening to his imagination — and I can't run crying to Mom and Dad, or to the bank manager, even though it's her house. Last time I tried that she had two of the huskier tellers show me to the door.

I can't stand it. I have to get the infested door out of the house. Not sometime, not tomorrow — now. I run downstairs to get my tools, remembering halfway down that I am wearing nothing but a frown and some soap film, and return to what I am already thinking of in my mind as THEIR room — the bathroom. I put my clothes back on and run down to the back entryway, where everyone's coats and boots are. That's where I keep my tool box — actually it's a running-shoe box with a hammer and pliers and roll of gray duct tape inside.

On the floor beside the tools is a recycling box full of newspapers, envelopes, coupons and slips of paper with important phone number scrawled on them. In the Emergency Command Center of my brain, the small part that is still functioning, a bell goes off, prompting me to hunt through the box. I rescue a coupon for a new Chinese food place that might be worth trying and a picture of a tree, I think — Thea is going through a long and thin period, everything she draws looks like the credits of a Cinemascope movie. Miss Vaal called it Mannerism and frowned when I asked if it was Good Mannerism or Bad Mannerism — I like it when the painter remembers to say thank you — before I find what I'm looking for, the flyer that came this morning while I was playing badminton in the front yard with Immie and Eddie.

I AM SMITTEN WITH A MEMORY of the morning, the three of us cavorting in the warmth of the reviving year, waving to neighbors and the postman and teenage gangs and moms with tots, commiserating with the people who couldn't find parking spots, fending off Ed's attacks — he plays badminton as a contact sport. Life for Ed is a contact sport, he tends to play the man rather than the ball, and it doesn't even matter particularly which man — anyway, there we were on the front lawn, Immie hit the bird into the air for a change, and Ed knocked her down and she cried and I picked her up and made Ed apologize, and then hit the bird in the air to show Ed all was forgiven and he ignored the bird and charged me, laughing maniacally and waving his racket. A time of sunshine and innocence, will I ever feel like that again? I even smiled at the young man delivering flyers.

I just opened it before throwing it in the recycling box to make sure it wasn't advertising half-price pizza for a limited time only — those coupons I keep in a secret place until they expire, then I try to use them. *I just opened it* — that's what Pandora said.

DO YOU HAVE *THEM*? the flyer asks coyly. I smiled this morning, but now, reading carefully in the harsh glare of our kitchen light at midnight, now I realize — we do. I frown and read on.

DO YOU KNOW WHAT *THEY* CAN DO TO YOUR HOUSE? As I read, my frown deepens until my eyebrows make a scenic gorge down to my nose, my mouth opens wider and wider until it looks like a railway tunnel, and the thin choking sound that emerges would be the Simplon Express coming about a mile away. The clock ticks loudly overhead. I hear a streetcar rumble by — thunder on the right was considered by the ancients to be a most unlucky omen. I keep reading.

About halfway down I come to the bit where you CHECK YOUR HOUSE FOR THESE WARNING SIGNS, and of course it's like reading a medical textbook to discover if your occasional dizziness and chronic shortness of height are significant, and finding out that you have erysipelas eyestrain and an ectopic pregnancy — and that's just on one page. I recognize *all* the warning signs of incipient infestation, creaky boards, unexplained piles of sawdust, little banners saying Welcome, Out-of-Town Ants, Valet Parking in Rear, also something they describe as *a sticky substance adhering to the walls and floor in unexpected places* — I always thought it was Ed, but according to this flyer it's carpenter ants, unless it's silverfish, termites, cheesemites, dynamites, or the dreaded boring beetle (sounds like an uncle of mine, but you can't just move across the room from the boring beetle). INSECT DAMAGE CAN RENDER YOUR HOME WORTHLESS! warns the flyer, and I believe them — after all, they have a 1-800 number.

Heart in mouth and hammer in hand, I tap the door off its hinges. *I'm going for a little walk,* I call quietly, grunting under the weight of solid hardwood, aluminum fittings, and a million or two mortal enemies. *I may be gone for a long time.* Captain Oates got sympathy for this kind of self-sacrifice. I get a snore. Actually it doesn't take more than a couple of minutes before the door is leaning up against the metal fence at the edge of our property. I was going to place it on the porch but the porch is made of wood. Pleased that I am able to think of this, I go to bed and dream that my uncle has six legs.

STOLEN? MY WIFE ASKS the next morning. I nod my head. The door is gone from our front lawn. Ours is an opportunistic neighborhood, and someone may have made a bad acquisition. *Is there any way we can warn whoever took it?* she asks. She has this hyperactive workaholic kind of conscience, mine is more of a late riser.

Maybe we could offer the opposite of a reward for whoever has it. She frowns at me. She knows I don't mean it. It's an interesting concept though, *I wonder how you'd word the posters,* I say. *How about* — RISK *FOR ANYONE WITH INFORMATION PERTAINING TO A MISSING DOOR. What do you think? Would you notice that?* But she's already left to get dressed.

I can't find the flyer from last night. I search for a few minutes and find a card reminding me about a dentist appointment for later in the month, then I give up and pour myself another cup of coffee. To heck with the 1-800 number. Somehow the urgency has gone from the situation now that I can no longer see the door. It's out of my sight. Let someone else go out of his mind. My conscience needs its beauty sleep.

THE CONTRACTOR PHONES after lunch. *I saw your ad on a telephone pole outside my house,* I say.

He grunts and asks, surprisingly, if I remember which pole. *I want to know how my marketing strategy is doing,* he says. *Someone told me the poles on east–west streets are more effective than the ones on the north–south streets. People walk slower going east to west.*

I give him our street address, and he says, *Uh huh, I thought so.* In the background I can hear an amplified voice and a lot of vague echoing noise. I ask if he'll stop by and make an estimate on the porch. He pauses and then asks if I could tell him what I want done.

I can't remember what Steve said. *I want it fixed,* I say. *And painted. Oh yes, and we need a new bathroom door.*

He pauses for a moment. There's a roar in the background. *Two hundred and fifty dollars,* he says.

What? I can't believe he's prepared to make his offer so low. The others have all come in around two thousand. One contractor wanted three thousand, and he was going to need clearance from the city water and gas inspectors.

All right — two hundred even. He has to shout because the background noise is so loud. *But I won't be making much profit.* I wonder how he can make an estimate over a pay phone located on — I recognize the noise now — a subway platform. *Don't you want to see the porch?* I shout, but he has to go. He slams down the phone just as the conductor blows his whistle and the doors close.

THEA IS PLAYING *FRÈRE JACQUES* on the piano, and Immie and Ed are attaching orange strips of paper to the dollhouse when Sam comes home from Benson's house. *Dad, can I have a mataglapulator?* he calls even before he takes off his shoes. Could I have heard him right? *What is it?* I ask, chopping carrots with the speed and precision of a — *Damn,* I stare at the missing tip of my thumb, then start to hop up and down. Sam comes into the kitchen, shaking his head. *Mom says you should always be careful of knives,* he says. Amazing how restrained other people can be about your suffering. *And your mom is right,* I say shortly.

I wonder if my temper is because of my wound or because Thea has been making the same mistake consistently for the last ten minutes.

FRÈRE JACQUES, *Frère Jacques,*
Dormez-plotz? *Dormez*-plotz?

I thought I'd just blotted it out of my mind. I walk over to
the piano and show her. She thanks me politely.

TURNS OUT THE MATAGAPULATOR is a toy, *Does it make a noise*
or a mess? I ask. Sam ponders. *Ready, Daddy!* call Immie
and Eddie. *Coming!* I answer, opening the drawer where we
keep Band-Aids and finding a Band-Aid — how's that for
incredible. Sam follows me to the living room, where the dollhouse is now festooned in orange. Immie and Ed are both
wearing their plastic firefighter helmets. Quickly I attach
some strands of black construction paper to the roof. *Perfect,*
I say, *now who's going to call 911?* The fire trucks are parked
around the corner of the chesterfield.

The megalopulator — I'm having trouble hearing Sam over
Immie's version of a wailing siren — *makes a mess and a*
noise, he decides. *I was playing with it at Benson's. It's brand*
new. Of course it is. Benson plays only with new toys. I've met
him only a couple of times but I've heard all about him. He's a
recent arrival to the neighborhood but has already achieved
legendary status because he can't walk very well and — this has
been confirmed by several of Sam's friends — he has *every* toy
ever seen in stores or on TV. Even those toys that require special derricks to move them around — plastic Rolls-Royces with
working engines, miniature atomic rockets, backyard dredgers,
life-sized stuffed elephants — toys you can't imagine anyone
buying — Benson has them. He lives at two houses, Sam tells
me, because his parents are divorced. That's just a cover story,
though, I figure he needs two houses to keep all his toys. We've
invited him over to our place but he always says no. *Benson is*
so shy, his mom explains. Too bad, he might enjoy playing

Burning Dollhouse, complete with dinosaur pets trapped inside and sirens wailing and Five-Alarm Barbie looking very fetching indeed in her grimy overalls and sparkly eye shadow, with Ken suffering from smoke inhalation over her shoulder, and live background music to enhance the effect. *Sonnez les matines, sonnez les matines, Din dan* plotz.

THE DOORBELL RINGS. With a smile still on my face, I open the door and see — *Roy, how are you?* He smiles back, showing his piano-key dentures.

I thought it was you, he says. *Jeez, sure is damp. Say, if I'm going to fix your porch I'm going to need some money. I got costs, you know — labor and tools and wood and my land- lord hasn't paid the fuel company again, so I was thinking, if maybe you had — fifty bucks, I could get started on your porch tomorrow. Probably have it done for the weekend.*

I shiver, not the damp, maybe it's the sight of Roy's bike chained to the fence where I left the bathroom door last night. And my thumb hurts under the bandage. *So, can I have the mopoligulator?* Sam calls from the living room. *I don't think so,* I call back. Roy's smile shrinks a bit. *So how about twenty bucks?* he says.

The piano stops and my shoulders start to unknot. Funny how you don't know how you feel about something until you stop feeling it. I didn't even know I had a headache and now it's gone. I figure twenty bucks is a reasonable investment. *Please,* calls Sam. *You see, this afternoon I broke Benson's.* Oh.

Thea materializes beside me, introduces herself to Roy, asks how he's doing, and slips her hand around my waist. *What's for dinner?* she asks.

Bloody carrots, says Sam.

Police Picnic

THE NEXT FEW DAYS it pours rain — very good for the dandelions in our front lawn and the maple keys sprouting in our eavestroughs but not much good for porch repair. Roy drops by to apologize, and incidentally to borrow another twenty dollars. Saturday isn't much brighter, but at least the rain has stopped, so the kids and I pile out of the house so that my wife can prepare for an important interview next week. We head instinctively for Copernicus Street because that's where the neighborhood goes on Saturdays.

Sam is running on in front, Immie holding my hand and Thea pushing Ed's stroller into things — *Sorry, missus, and you too, Rover.* She's polite, is Thea, but determined. *Don't help me, Daddy, I know I can do it.*

Rover and the lady limp off, I call for Sam to wait up, he waves to show he's heard me but keeps running. Oh well, he can't get into too much trouble, the sidewalks are covered in people buying fresh fruit and smoked sausage. Ed makes another escape attempt, his fourth or fifth in a block. This time he swings his whole body out of the stroller, hangs by his hands for a second and lets go, landing on his toes just like you're supposed to, then losing his balance and being run over by his own back wheels — how humiliating. He hangs his head and allows himself to be hoisted back in. Thea promptly runs him into a mailbox and he cheers up.

Sam runs back with a worried look — *What is it, son?* I ask, but he just shakes his head and grabs my free hand. We walk on together for a few more minutes. Thea manages to just miss three shoppers in a row before pushing Ed off the curb and into oncoming — *Hang on!* — but fortunately slow-moving traffic. *How about if Daddy pushes and Thea helps?* I suggest, but she promises to take extra extra-special care. *I'm hungry,* Immie tells me. It's been twenty minutes since snack-time, so I guess she has a point. *Me too, Me too,* call the twins, and *Hands up!* — that's Ed, he likes to play bank robbers.

I put up my hands and then — *Oh hello,* I say to one of our distinctive neighbors. He's been around the area longer than we have, a wandering prophet with his belongings in a bundle-buggy. He looks the part too — hair out to here and beard down to there, kindly, glazed eyes. He doesn't ask, but people give him things — bags of apples, cigarettes. My wife made him lunch when he spent a couple of nights on our front lawn. Sam is holding my hand tight. The man points at Sam and says something I don't understand. *Oh yes,* I say, *he's with me.* The man nods, reaches into his living mane of gray hair, pulls out a jelly bean. And offers it to Sam.

A nice gesture, but I don't know whether to smile or gag. Sam shrinks back against me and I say, gently, *Thank you, but we couldn't.* Keeping my eye on Ed, who probably could. The man frowns and picks a bit of something — lint maybe — off the candy. It's a black jelly bean — at least it is now. I can't help wondering if it always was. I say thank you, tell Sam to say thank you, seat Ed firmly in the stroller and suggest a visit to the park. The man smiles, puts the jelly bean back for safe keeping and moves slowly, deliberately, up the street.

But I'm hungry, says Immie. Sam shakes his head vigorously. *I'm not,* he says with a shudder. *I don't think I'll ever be hungry again.* Thea is thoughtful. *I can see what they mean about never taking candy from strangers,* she says, pushing the stroller into a fire hydrant and eliciting a startled yelp from — can it be Rover? No, he's the wrong color, but now he has the same wounded foreleg. I like animals. I take control of the stroller.

WHEN WE GET TO THE PARK we see police cars and emergency vehicles burbling and squeaking away, lights flashing, a loud-speaker saying something unintelligible. But this is not a crime scene — at least not yet. There's a sack race or something in the middle of a nearby field — everyone seems to be falling down anyway. Tables are filled with hot dogs and cans of pop. People are lined up with paper plates, family groups mostly, though right ahead of us is a kid by himself, ten years old or so, and grinning from ear to ear.

Hi, he calls to us, *Hi.* We tell him hi. *A party!* says Immie, skipping up and down. Ed claps, he likes parties too. *Is it your birthday?* Immie asks the kid who is trotting energetically along beside us. *My birthday is coming up. I will have a party on my birthday.* The kid shakes his head. *Hi,* he says again. His mom comes up with a smile to tell us we're just in time for lunch. The kids' faces all brighten.

Sorry, I tell her, *we're not* — but she won't let me finish. *Don't worry about missing the games,* she says. *I know how difficult it can be. Come on, Harold, let's help this poor man.* And before I know quite how it happens, we're all sitting down at a picnic table. Harold and his mom bring us hot dogs, pop, donuts and smiles. *Gee thanks,* we all say, especially me when I realize that I've left my wallet at home.

IT'S A GREAT PICNIC. I've never seen so many friendly people. Police officers wander around with trays of food and drink and sympathetic expressions. *Have some more,* they all say. *Have another donut, another pop.* There are police cars to climb around in, and horses to pat on the nose. Everyone smiles until Ed points his hot dog and says, *Hands up!* — then they all look scared and put their hands up, even the guy with the gold braid on his uniform.

A mom approaches our happy, crumb-strewn table and asks with almost tearful sympathy which of our children is special. I say all of them and she sniffs and walks away — and only then do I begin to suspect where we are. I stare around, and now of course it's obvious. Harold for once in his life is not the odd one out. There is something tragic and heartwarming about all the kids in the park today except mine.

I pack us in record time. I don't know if I'm more embarrassed about gatecrashing or not noticing. The kids aren't embarrassed. When I tell Sam to put his arm inside his shirt he stares at me and asks, *Why, Dad?* And I don't have an answer. *Take a goody bag,* a woman tells us on our way out. *NO!* I cry, *You don't understand. I can't possibly. My children don't* — but she insists.

Maybe you know someone who would like a treat, she says.

And you know, I think I do. I just hope there's room in his hair to keep it all.

Neverending Laundry

I DON'T GET UP WITH ED at six o'clock any more, and I don't miss it, but it's kind of sad to realize that we no longer have a baby. A new era has dawned and I still don't have any spare time. I'm yawning and brushing my teeth when Thea bursts into the bathroom, holding a shirt like Exhibit A.

This is the only thing left in my dresser, she says. *How can I get dressed when there's nothing to wear?* Children are naturally choosy about their clothing because it's one of the few things they can control. I read that somewhere, and it makes sense as long as their father is up to date with the laundry. *Dad!* a shout from across the hall. *I don't have any* — something, socks, I'll bet, Sam's always running out of socks. *Try the dining room,* I call, I'm pretty sure I saw some there the day before yesterday. *Under the piano,* I add, spitting confidently.

Now let's see what we can find in the basement, I tell Thea. She rolls her eyes. I pause briefly on my way to put on coffee, gather toys, put toast in the toaster, pick up the morning paper, observing that it is warm outside and, apparently, Tuesday. Thea calls, *Dad, I'm waiting!* There's a picture of a cute child in her father's baseball cap on the front page, easy to keep your kid's clothes clean when you make six or seven million dollars a year. I'll bet that brilliant white shirt still has the store tags on it. On a whim I check the dining room, empty except for a dirty glass and a novel with a lurid cover. I pick them up, glance at the book—*Dad!*—hastily put it back and carry the glass to the kitchen, butter the popped-up toast and head downstairs.

SOME PEOPLE ARE GOOD at laundry — those fresh-faced moms on TV who rumple their children's hair and smile knowingly at us from behind their cups of never-spilled coffee. I take a more desperate approach. Dirty clothes are vermin. They live in hiding, they take hours to extirpate, and then they come back again. They even move on you — not exactly scuttling into corners when the lights come up, but I'll swear I've left a perfectly tidy bedroom and ducked back no more than a moment later to discover a veritable nest of soiled pyjamas in the middle of the floor. Made my skin crawl, I tell you.

Our washer has only two cycles now — CLEAN BUT SMALLER and GENTLY SHRED. The repairman told us not to expect much from our old machine. *Really, you want to get a new one,* he said, and I told him that, really, I wanted to get someone to do the laundry for me.

I caution Thea to stand a safe distance away while I investigate. The dryer door is open. I take a quick look inside, it's empty except for — *Imogen, what are you doing in there!* I haul her out and speak as sternly as I can. *You know you aren't supposed to climb into the dryer, not even for hide and seek. And where's Ed?* The washer isn't moving, usually you can approach it if it isn't moving. I reach inside and pull something out.

Not Ed. Turns out I'm in the WRINKLE cycle. My hand is on something only a contortionist could wear, though she'd look great in it. *Is this yours?* I ask Thea but she's gone upstairs to show her disappointment to someone else. I grab a pair of damp, twisted socks for Sam, hide everything else back in the machine, and almost faint when I see an animated laundry basket out of the corner of my eye. It's about a foot off the ground, brimful of dirty clothes and moving steadily toward me. For just a second it's Fate with a malignant load of unfulfilled duties, then I hear Ed's voice from underneath the basket. He's reciting to himself. He continues down the length of the room. Honestly, the load is as heavy as he is — wasn't there an ancient Greek who carried a calf every day while it got bigger?

Drastic times call for drastic measures, he says in slow measured tones. *We have nothing to fear but fear itself.* I ask Ed if he's okay. He puts down his load and folds his arms across his chest. *I will return,* he says, and then turns on twinkling heels to run for the stairs.

I've got to keep the kids away from the history channel. *Come on, Immie,* I say. *There's buttered toast for breakfast.* We go upstairs hand in hand to find the rest of the family sitting around the kitchen table with smiles on their faces.

Look, Daddy, Thea shouts. *Mom's awake! And look at the outfits she brought us back from her conference!* She holds hers up. Sam and Ed already have theirs on. Immie whoops and runs to sit on my wife's lap.

Very nice, I say, but inside my heart is sinking. We've solved the problem of what to wear today but in the long run it's just more stuff to get dirty.

What's That Big White Thing?

APRIL IS THE FASTEST MONTH, at least this one is. There's been so much to do — news to digest, implications to consider, advice to ignore, forms to fill in, decisions to put off, subdivisions to drive through, decisions to put off a little longer and then be forced to take, hugs and handshakes to exchange and finally, as the sun rises on this Sunday morning, an announcement to make to children who haven't seen much of their parents during the past few weeks. Hard to avoid it much longer, the real-estate agent is pounding the FOR SALE sign into our front lawn.

Dad dad dad! I awake from a dream of Arctic wastes to find that Thea has pulled off the covers. *Dad, there's a woman on our front lawn with a sign!*

I pull the covers back up. *Don't believe what the sign says,* I mutter sleepily. *The world will not end tomorrow. It's the same sign she had last year.*

Thea shakes me. *It's not her, Dad. It's another woman. The sign says FOR SALE. Is it true, Dad? Is our house for sale? Are we moving?*

Moving can be a traumatic experience for kids. All the books say so. My wife and I have had several chats about the best way to break the news. Gently, we both agree. *Yes,* I say, and roll over. Thea scampers down the hall shrieking, *Hey, guess what!,* and the next thing I know Ed is standing beside me with his hands on his hips. He doesn't care about any signs. He's hungry for breakfast.

WE MOVED HOUSE when I was nine years old, packed everything in boxes and watched the moving men lift our world onto the big truck and carry it away to a new neighborhood. It was an effortless process on my part. My friends were all at the new hamburger store so I didn't even wave good-bye. I missed the old place for exactly a week, then I went to a new school and fell in love with Connie Bailey, she used to give her kilt a little flip as she walked, just for me, I thought. I can't understand Sam's attitude.

I'm not moving, he says, clutching the downstairs newel post like a lifeline. I sit down beside him on the stairs, explaining about Mom's new job, how if we stay here she'll have to drive seven hours to work and seven hours back and we'll never see her. *I don't care,* he says. I explain about the new house. It'll be bigger, with a bigger yard, and he'll have his own room instead of sharing with Ed. *I don't care,* he says. I nudge him and lean over to mention the possibility of meeting girls in kilts at his new place, but he shakes his head — probably right. Connie, she was such a flirt, I'll never forget how heartbroken I was when I saw her riding behind Paul Gezink, with bubble gum I had bought her still in her mouth. I show Sam a picture of the new house we've promised to buy if we ever sell this one, but he won't look.

Excuse me. Thea squeezes past us on the staircase. She is carrying her overnight bag. She places it with care in the front hall and turns to me, hands on hips. *I'm packed. When are we moving?* she asks. Sam bursts into tears. Twins — identical attitudes to life. *I'm never leaving this place,* Sam sobs. *I've lived here all my life! You can't drag me away from everything I've ever known!* He's going to be a lot of fun when it comes time for the old folks' home. Thea shakes her head. *Well, Sam, we're all going to miss you. Maybe you can come to visit us sometime in the new place. Tell me again about the pink room that will be mine, Daddy,* she says. I give Sam a sympathetic pat on the shoulder and stand up. Time for my daily call to Roy.

HE ARRIVED ONE EVENING on his bicycle, with a load of wood on his shoulder and a power saw in the front carrier. *Got a cup of coffee?* he asked. *Keep out the chill while I'm working.* A little late in the day for work I thought, but he didn't, he set up a transistor radio and plied his saw energetically for a couple of hours removing bits and pieces of rotten wood and leaving us with half a porch and no railing. *I'll be back by three o'clock tomorrow afternoon to put in the new wood,* he said, *and have the porch done by the weekend.* Then he vanished into the night with another twenty of my dollars.

I haven't seen him since, though I talk to him almost every day. He never picks up his own phone, preferring to filter the outside world through his answering machine. He generally calls around three in the afternoon, often from a pay phone. *Jeez, I'm sorry,* he said just yesterday, *but this other job is taking a lot of time because my supplier won't deliver the right kind of concrete. I'm real picky about concrete. You use the*

*wrong stuff and you got problems — just like anything else,
right?* In the background I heard the clink of glasses. *Now
look, I'll be there tomorrow for sure at — two-thirty,* he said.
He never says, First thing in the morning, and he never says
something vague like, After lunch. He's always precise about
his times, and he's never here at the time specified, or any
other time. Still, it's comforting to know precisely what time
he won't be showing up. It drove my wife crazy for a while,
now she's resigned to it, and always asks what time Roy didn't
get to work today.

THERE IS A STRANGE NOISE coming from the basement. It distracts me, and my message to Roy is more abrupt than usual.
I hope he doesn't mind. The noise is an eldritch shrieking,
the ghost of an unfinished load of laundry maybe, doomed to
tumble around and around the Earth until it can meet with a
pure white soul — the Drying Dutchman. Not much chance
of salvation at our place, I fear.

The noise is coming from a toy in Imogen's hand, a siren
or something. I'm sure I've never seen it before. Do they
breed in the darkness, toys, roiling around yeastily inside
their castles and gas stations and magic mountains so that
kids can come down in the morning and play with something
brand new? I consider the situation with the critical eye of
one who will soon be putting everything we own into boxes.

Immie tugs on my shirt to get my attention. *Are we really
moving?* she asks me. I nod. *And will Mommy be moving
with us?*

I frown at my stupidity. Of course it never occurred to me,
the kids probably think we're getting divorced. Every time
you turn around, kids' TV is explaining about how your dad
still loves you even though he's driving a sports car and hanging out with girls that look like your big sister, or how your

mom still loves you even though she's moved across town and started hanging out with girls that look like your big brother. I bend down so I can talk head to head.

Don't worry, I tell Immie, *we'll all be together. Even Sam will be with us, though he doesn't think so right now. Do you want to see a picture of our new house?* I pull the real-estate snapshot out of my pocket, *There, what do you think?*

Immie gazes for a long time, biting her lip, finally pointing to the middle of the photograph. *Daddy, what's that big white thing?* she asks. I have to smile. City kids. *That, my dear, is a garage door.*

Her eyes open wide as saucers. *And will there be a treasure inside?*

I hate to disillusion her. *Not according to our auto insurance company,* I say.

I SEND THE KIDS OUTSIDE to play while I tidy the kitchen and decide not to start the dishwasher because there's room for another side plate. I hate waste, it's one of the governing principles in my life, thriftiness is next to godliness. I wonder what I'd do if I had to choose between a Good action and one that saved a whole lot of closet space.

When I get outside I find that our front walk has turned into one of those great Training Room scenes, the kind James Bond walks through casually while in the background people are rolling around in agony or falling ten stories onto a mat. Ed is industriously dribbling a basketball — no that's not it, the basketball is staying still and Ed is bouncing up and down. I guess the ball is dribbling him. On either side of him Thea and Immie are banging hockey sticks on the ground, they'd be getting ready for a faceoff, only they're ten feet apart. Sam is practicing Ninja kicks against the FOR SALE sign. I'm sympathetic to his feelings and I'm glad he's able to express himself, but, *The real estate agency has plenty more of those signs,* I tell him, *so it won't do you any good to wreck it.*

We decide to play ball hockey. It's a game we can all take part in and there are nets in the schoolyard. Teams are easy — everyone against everyone — but for some reason Imogen is getting upset. A few minutes into the game she sinks to her knees and begins to wail.

What is it? Are you hurt? What's wrong? I ask her, and she turns her tear-stained face to mine and cries, *I'm not winning!*

I'm impressed that she can even tell. *Who* is *winning?* I ask. I really don't know. By my reckoning no one has scored yet. Ed has knocked everyone to the ground at least once, but he's not interested in the ball. Sam and Thea have spent most of the time determining which team they will be playing for — we had those discussions in my day too, though the teams we considered were not from the Sun Belt. I stand in front of one of the nets, blocking the very occasional shot and smiling as I listen to the familiar cadences, cherishing even more the sound of wooden hockey sticks trailing along asphalt, the sound of winter when I was a child. I half-expect my mom to call me in to lunch.

I'm distracted by the behavior of a young couple across the street who stop and stare at the sign on our front lawn. They look up to the roof — oh how I wish I had got it repaired! — and down again at the porch that Roy will not be coming to work on in a few hours. They talk excitedly to each other, a nice couple with a new blue stroller. She takes out a pad and writes down the phone number on the FOR SALE sign. And suddenly I don't want to sell the house. Not to them, not to anyone. I remember the day we moved in, giving my vastly pregnant wife a piggyback over the threshold and then collapsing in the front hall. I remember furnishing the living room from the Goodwill store around the corner, I remember bringing the children home from the hospital, I remember — everything. I want to take down the sign and rip up our purchase agreement and forget about a garage and a family room and a big backyard — who needs these things when you have a neighborhood with a Christian Science donut shop and a Thing in the playground?

I'm so lost in thought that I don't see Ed until he's right on top of me, and then I can't dodge in time. I go down and the net is open and Imogen has a free shot from three feet away. With fire in her eyes she winds up and lets fly, wide.

I'M LEAFING THROUGH the stack of real-estate magazines on my bedside table, partly from force of habit, mostly from the masochistic urge to comparison shop after buying, so that you know *exactly* how much you could have saved if you'd only waited. *Large friendly family house, fireplaces, bright and sunny, close to schools and shopping* — a nicely spaced ad, it catches my eye.

Hey, this one sounds good, I say to my wife. *Wonder where it is?*

She cuddles over to my side of the bed. *That's our house,* she says.

I thought I had the Out Of Town section. I'm obscurely disappointed. It sounded like a nice place, maybe even nicer than the place with the garage door — *I was kind of hoping we could live there,* I say.

We do, she whispers in my ear. And so we do, for now. *How's Roy this evening?* she asks.

I think back to his phone call. *Very positive,* I say.

And what time isn't he coming tomorrow? she asks.

Eleven or eleven-fifteen — early for him.

My wife has the last word. *Early for him to be late,* she says.

 **SUMMER RUN-OFF**

When You Pay for Roy

AND SO THE DAYS and the afternoon shadows lengthen, the sun rises higher in the sky and the birds return, even if the grass doesn't, and Imogen blows out five candles on her birthday cake and starts counting down the hours until her next one — and all the while our house is unsold and our porch unfinished. Oh, there's been progress of a sort along both fronts, but it's not the sort of progress you can measure with human instruments. Prospective buyers are nibbling at our house and Roy is nibbling at our porch.

His sense of time is on a geological scale. He is not a careless fisherman in the stream of hours, or a mystic contemplating All Time as Now, and Now is Quitting Time — it's more studied than that, and more leisurely. There's something in the painstaking, unhurried contemplation of a distant goal that reminds you of being pursued by a glacier. A few days ago he finally finished putting down the floor and began the railing. Heloise Sagal was out sweeping her front walk, she beckoned me over. *Do you think Roy will be finished by Christmas?* she asked.

You know him? I said. She laughed. *Everyone knows Roy. He grew up here. Went to St. Vincent's school — my sister taught him in Grade Five.* I tried to picture Roy completing a homework assignment on time, and couldn't. *He's not charging very much,* I told Heloise, who shook her head as Roy, having finished a coffee, cigarette and Twinkie, bent to the task, taking a work from break. *Of course he isn't,* she said — *or you wouldn't be hiring him, yes?* I nodded my head. She bent closer, as if he could hear from fifty feet away. As if he'd try to. *The problem,* she whispered, *is that when you pay for Roy, you get Roy.*

There's a lesson for your life book. Heloise nodded sagely and went back to her broom.

THEA COMES HOME from school today with a message *From the Office of* Rebecca's mom, whose name, I discover with quickly passing interest, is Herodias — quickly passing because the note is about Thea and Rebecca going to the Wonderland amusement park this weekend, where the rides are — *So scary that people die, even teenagers. Please can I go, Dad?* Thea says. *Please, Dad. Please,* smiling up at me and taking my arm and batting her eyelashes. I open my mouth to say I don't think she's old enough, but she steps right in and says, *Oh thank you, Daddy. I knew I could count on you. Rebecca said you were too stuffy, but I knew my daddy.*

My mouth hangs open like a broken trunk door. *Stuffy?* I say. *There's nothing stuffy about being concerned for the welfare of your children,* I say, but I'm talking to the air — or rather to Roy, who has poked his head inside to ask if he can borrow a cup of our coffee. *It's way better than that stuff down at the Seven-11,* he says.

*   *   *

DAD, CAN I WATCH A SHOW *that's recommended for mature audiences?* Sam asks from the living room. I don't know, Sam is pretty mature for six, but somehow I don't think ... *What's it called?* I ask from the kitchen, where Ed and I are making rice. I might let Sam get away with Beach Volleyball or *Titus Andronicus,* but I don't want him to scare himself again. We've almost put the killer cyborgs behind us thanks to a brilliant idea by Miss Vaal, the art teacher.

Last week she suggested that her students try to draw the thing they are most afraid of. Sam's *Cyborg* 1996 (Felt Pen and Bingo Hopper on Construction Paper) is indeed a fearsome creation. *And that,* he told me, pointing to a large lumpy object at the top of the picture, *is a huge meteorite that is about to fall on the cyborg and crush him.* Sam's smile spoke volumes and I gave him a big hug.

Thea's picture was different — a little girl teetering on top of a big mountain. *Is that you?* I asked when she showed it to me. The girl is smiling and has a spoon in her hand. Thea nodded. *I started out drawing a big mountain and me falling off, and then I thought it would be better if the mountain was ice cream, and then I thought I would get myself a spoon so I could eat up all the ice cream.* It all sounded incredibly healthy to me, and not just because ice cream is full of calcium. I gave Thea a hug too.

Ed has got tired of counting the grains in a cupful of rice and pours it into the pot. *What's the show called?* I ask Sam again. There's a pause and then, faintly, I hear something about monsters and outer space and a chainsaw. *It's on at eight o'clock tonight,* says Sam. Well, that's one decision I don't have to make. *Eight o'clock is too late,* I tell him. *You're supposed to be in bed at eight o'clock.* Ed and I carry the pot of rice over to the stove. Dinner in forty-five minutes.

Sam comes into the kitchen, pouting. *Oh, Dad, please? Please? All my friends will be watching.*

I restrain myself, with an effort, from saying *And if all your friends were going to jump in the lake* — funny how clichés want to come home to roost. *No,* I say. Ed at my side adds, *And that's final.* Sam withdraws to sulk and I wash the rice strainer.

Dad, can I have some? Ed is holding his science experiment — that's what he calls it, an empty apple-juice jar into which he has been putting all sorts of things over the past few days, toothpaste and sand and dead flies and several kinds of juice — and now dish detergent. I squeeze a little into the top of the jar, and he laboriously tightens the cap and stares at the revolting cloudy green liquid. I'd like to keep it somewhere safe and up high, out of reach of children, but what's the point of an experiment you can't carry around with you and shake every now and then. I have made him promise by the most sacred of childhood oaths that he will not drink the contents of his experiment.

MOMMY, GUESS WHAT? My wife is just in the door, happy to shed her executive-commuter face for her guess-what face. Thea can't wait for her to guess, though. *I'm going to the amusement park with Rebecca. Isn't that great!* I'm hoping my wife will have some objection, but all she says is *Great!*

I cough. *You don't think she's too young?* I say. My wife shakes her head. *Won't you be going too?* she says. I open my mouth wide, but before I can protest I'm struck by a familiar smell. I check the rice — overdone.

Family dinner tonight. All of us around the big table with our heads bowed. Roast chicken and rice for everyone except Ed, who has frozen vegetables and cheese, and Sam, who would rather have a bread-and-butter sandwich than rice, and Immie, who finds that chicken gets between her teeth. *It gets between my teeth too,* says Sam, grinning wide. His mouth these days resembles an inner-city landscape — two huge permanent incisors stand like housing projects in a wasteland of blood and molars. Everything gets between Sam's teeth — he seems to be swallowing his food whole. Thea sits very straight and stares down at her plate while we wait for Immie to say grace.

In the name of the Father and the Son ... she begins, and Ed, as he usually does, asks me if I am the father and he is the son. I shake my head. Immie clears her throat and begins again. *In the name of the Father ...* and Sam asks if he can go to the bathroom. I shake my head again. *In the name of the ...* she pauses, stares around the table as if daring us to speak, *Father,* she says deliberately, *and the Son, and ...* the telephone rings. Thea jumps up from the table with a clatter of cutlery. Imogen bursts into tears. Thea has the receiver to her ear. *No, we're not eating,* she says, with technical accuracy. I pat Imogen on the shoulder. Sam says *Amen* loudly and picks up his sandwich.

It's for you, Mom. Thea brandishes the instrument like a cheerleader's baton.

Ed taps me on the arm. *Can I eat yet?* he asks. I tell him to go ahead before mold starts growing on the food. Imogen pushes her plate away. *I'm not hungry,* she sobs. Thea slides neatly back into her seat and picks up a chicken leg. *The lady said there was exciting news,* she says. *Try a little chicken,* I say to Immie.

My wife is waving her arm for silence and writing on the pad I can never find when I'm on the phone. I end up writing important numbers with my finger in the crumbs and grease of the tabletop. *When do they want to see the house?* my wife asks.

WE SEEM TO BE ONE OF THOSE wallflowers at the real-estate dance. Clean and quiet, a *nice* house, people say on the way out, signing false names in the book and disappearing forever. This is the first time anyone's wanted a private viewing. *Should I bake something?* I wonder. A magazine article says that the smell of fresh-baked cookies is a great selling feature. It doesn't say anything about burned cookies. My wife suggests taking down some of the cobwebs and finishing off the laundry, but the people are coming tomorrow afternoon, not next week. I don't know if there's time. *And leave the new bathroom door open,* I remind her. Roy hung it upside down and slightly crooked so that it has a tendency to close and lock itself. He's going to fix it as soon as he gets the proper hardware back from his landlord's brother, who also has several of Roy's best paintbrushes and a ladder but is waiting for Roy to pay the landlord a questionable utility bill, which Roy has already arranged to work off over the next month as long as he gets some air conditioning in time for summer — the problem with asking Roy a question is that you're liable to get one of Roy's answers. Anyway, the door remains virtually usable, and if we sell the house the new owners can worry about it.

My wife is giving Imogen her bath, and Thea and Sam are yelling at each other when the doorbell rings. I wander downstairs and open the door to Steve the barbecuer, who stands there strangely hesitant, his hands behind his back. He asks how I am. *Right as rain and ready to fall,* I tell him. *Won't you come in?* He shakes his head. He just happened to be passing by the house, he says, and he couldn't help noticing that the porch wasn't finished yet. He wonders if *he* could do ... well, do anything to help.

Poor Steve, it's killing him that a simple job is taking so long to complete. I smile sincerely up at him. *What a great and generous offer. I'd love to take you up on it,* I say. *But Roy has gone home with all his tools. I don't have anything that you need.*

Steve nods and then, with an embarrassed grin, brings a power saw out from behind his back. A horrible instrument, like a shark with an extension cord. *Could you ... do you mind if I just put in a few minutes?*

I hope he's not worried about my reaction. *Go to it,* I say. *And thanks. The nearest outlet is in the kitchen. Help yourself to whatever you can find.* I hear shrieks and thumps and my wife's voice asking what is going on. I go back upstairs.

THEA AND SAM HAVE GOT PAST the finger-pointing, voices-raised stage and the door-slamming stage. They're both whimpering piteously, Thea on her bed and Sam, it's his turn now, in the bath. I can't reach Sam because he has slammed the bathroom door, and of course it's locked. *Remember to wash behind your ears,* I call through the keyhole.

Thea's story is heartwrenching and predictable. *Sam scared me!* she cries. I ask her how. *I was telling him about going to Wonderland with Rebecca and how much fun we would have on the roller coaster and ... and he said ...* she pauses to sob. I ask what he said. Thea's face screws up. *He said that I'd fall off the big mountain and die!*

I go back to the hall. My wife is frowning at the bathroom door.

Sam, why did you scare Thea? I call. His voice is muffled. *She was bragging,* he says. *All about how she's going to Wonderland and I'm not. She was teasing me and being mean.* He pulls the plug in the bath. *Remember to dry thoroughly,* my wife says.

The sound of a power saw fills the air. Immie and Eddie run downstairs to find out what's going on. *Don't touch the cord,* I call. My wife asks if she can borrow my library card for a minute.

It wasn't nice to scare your sister, I call to Sam, while my wife fiddles the plastic rectangle into the opening between the door and the jamb. A credit card is stronger but it's too thick. *You know what it's like to be scared.*

My wife sighs with relief, the door opens and there's Sam,

nodding vigorously, a towel around his waist. *I know how bad it feels,* he says. *That's why I did it.* My wife hands back the library card, Sam moves with dignity to his room and I return to Thea. She hasn't moved.

I'm scared of the mountain, she says. *I want to go to Wonderland but I'm scared.*

I think back to the picture she drew in art class. A big mountain. *What about if you brought a spoon,* I say.

She shakes her head. *What about if I brought my daddy?* she says.

ED WON'T GO TO BED without his science experiment on the night table beside him. I go downstairs without arguing because there's no winning a battle of wills with a two-year-old. He has way more time than I do and nothing left to lose now that the sentence of bedtime has been carried out. I find the jar in the kitchen with the top off. *Ed!* I run back up, my mind moving even faster than my legs. Toxic, ambulance, hospital, stomach pump, exploratory post mortem, my own fault. *Ed, did you drink any of this?*

He shakes his head, holding up his little finger. *Remember,* he says, *pinky swear!* I check with the other kids. Thea is playing with parka-clad dolls who are pulling a sled through a paper snowstorm — Barbie of the Antarctic. Imogen is looking at a picturebook with Sam. No one knows anything about Ed's experiment. Strange.

The saw has stopped. I hear my wife's voice from the front hall. *Steve! What's wrong? Let me take your glass. You look awful. Come in and lie down. Can I get you something more to drink?* I hear Steve's anguished refusal and the thud as something, the glass I guess, hits the floor and mercifully doesn't break. The door slams. I wonder how much he drank. I wonder if he'll ever forgive us.

I Am a Mustard Rod

YES, THERE IS A MOUNTAIN in Wonderland, about a mile high, with a roller coaster that climbs and loops and winds its way to the top. The whole snow-capped edifice is made of confidence-inspiring plastic, there's even a plastic gorge for the roller coaster to plummet into, complete with waterfall and plastic boulders to smash our broken bodies on. The water's real, I know, because I can feel it on my cheek. I am on the roller coaster with Thea and Rebecca, who are screaming like lunatics, hair and hands waving wildly, and Rebecca's mother, Herodias, who sits in splendid calm with an amused smile on her face. She's dressed rather severely for an amusement park, in office stuff that fits and does all the way up — impressive but not really suitable. It occurs to me — not during the ride, I'm too preoccupied then, but earlier, when she picked us up in her very clean, very black, very German sedan — that she doesn't have much in the way of *fun*wear. Or perhaps *fun* at all. She's not condescending but she's sure a long way away. Probably she's just shy — not like me, I'm ill. Which of the Seven Ages of Man was the one where your stomach rolls in a fine frenzy from earth to heaven? That's me. I feel like a flea on a tango dancer. I'm trying to smile for Thea's sake, and, let me tell you, even smiling is hard. Pagliacci has to smile with a breaking heart, I'm smiling through the waves of nausea that seem about to swamp this frail craft, my body. *Isn't it great!* screams Thea, her hair streaming in front of her because we are currently going backwards at Mach 8. *Great!* I agree with a smile. Barf, clown, barf.

BEFORE WE LEFT this morning my wife took me aside for a moment. *You're doing a beautiful thing,* she whispered in my ear. *This will be a special day for you and Thea. I almost wish I was going.* My wife possesses the internal constitution of an astronaut and an inbuilt aversion to what she calls needlessly exciting forms of travel — tramp steamers and roller coasters and biplanes and bungee cords — while I, on the other hand, have the soul of a boy adventurer and an excuse-me stomach — one of those ironies O. Henry would have made a big deal about.

You'll have a good time, she said. *Thea has been bragging to all the other little girls about how her dad is the best dad, and not in the least stuffy.* Really? I could feel a little smile tugging at the corners of my mouth, right beside a shaving cut. My wife smiled back, gave me a kiss. *I'll stay here and wait for Roy to tell us why he won't be finishing up today,* she said.

All that's left is the end of the painting, four or five hours' work, but Roy's been waiting and waiting for the perfect day. Yesterday he called and told me it couldn't be that day because the forecast was calling for rain. *Roy,* I said, *it's three o'clock in the afternoon. It's been sunny since six o'clock this morning. All the kids are sunburned.* But he sighed and said you had to get the wood really dry before painting. *I'll give you a call tomorrow — jeez, this weather is just ruining my schedule. I've got three or four more jobs lined up after yours.* I can't remember a drier month. We haven't had more than a sprinkle of rain. If I'm his priority I'd hate to be the low job on Roy's list.

ALL BAD THINGS come to an end — difficult to believe sometimes, but I know it's true because I'm not in gym class with Mr. Godfrey any more, swinging helplessly upside down just inches from a purple, contorted face shouting, *What do you mean your leg is stuck* inside *the ring? What's it doing inside the ring? No one puts their leg inside the ring, Scrimger! Jesus Christmas, why'd you* do *such a thing?* I thought that day in Grade Ten would never end and it did, and so does our roller-coaster ride. We didn't even have to call the fire department like poor Mr. Godfrey. I wonder if he still has nightmares about that incident too.

You're feeling faint, aren't you. It's not a question. Herodias watches me like a hawk, ready to make an executive decision if she has to. *I'll take the girls on the next ride by myself,* she says. *You stay on the ground, all right.* That's not a question either.

Daddy, what'll we do next? Thea doesn't doubt my powers. I may be as white and shaken as a piña colada, but until I fall down dead or start to bark at the moon I am Dad, the omniscient, omnipotent dispenser of funds for milkshakes, T-shirts, games and rides — there are a few things they don't charge for at these amusement parks, but not too many. Wastebaskets are free, I think.

I don't know, I say. *What would you girls like to do next?*

Crowds swirl around us and music falls like a rainstorm from overhead loudspeakers. Thea and Rebecca are standing shake to shake. They stop, stare at each other and shrug at the same instant. They don't know either.

Nature abhors a vacuum even more than I do — maybe that's why it's so dirty outside — and Herodias, herself a force of nature, steps into the decision void with alacrity. *Lunch is next,* she says, pointing. *Over there.*

HOT DOGS FOR EVERYBODY, Cokes for the three of them, and a cup of coffee for me. *Keep the change,* I tell the teenager with the tattoos and the dead eyes who works behind the counter, only it turns out that what I thought was the whole meal was just the bill for my coffee and I have to hunt through my wallet some more.

There's no point in going to an amusement park to save money — if you want to save money, don't come. Collect limited-edition postage stamps instead, or Old Masters or *incunabula.* Mind you, your kids aren't very excited when you show them the new fifteenth-century commentary on St. Paul. *Great, an old book we can't read,* they say, and go back to watching the intergalactic evil channel. Whereas, my *Who wants to play miniature golf?* elicits instant screams of delight from Thea, even though she has her mouth full of hot dog. Rebecca's scream is cut off when her mom frowns and takes a wet napkin from her bag to wipe a minuscule mustard stain from her shirt.

Herodias herself is spotless. How on earth does she do it? When I eat a hot dog my shirt seems to act as a mustard rod, in fact, if I'm out in public I'll often attract condiments from nearby hot dogs as well as my own. Once I collected a daub of special sauce from at least four tables away. I was just sitting there with my coffee and cherry pie and, *wham,* out of the sesame-seed blue. That was unusual, probably an atmospheric freak. I attract lint as well, but they make lint brushes. I don't know that anyone's come out with a mustard brush yet.

I lower my eyes guiltily. Sure enough there's a broad yellow streak going down my front, and a splash of red nearby — those plastic ketchup packets are booby traps. Best to treat them like unexploded bombs, immerse them in water and then open them with pliers. *You have ketchup on your forehead, Daddy,* Thea tells me. I probably do too. I wipe myself. *Now it's all smeary. There's some mustard too.* Rebecca is watching, jigging from foot to foot, her eyes dancing with mirth. I wipe harder. She and Thea start to giggle. *What? What is it?* But they keep giggling. I don't know what's so funny about someone whose face is a different color from yours, or even two different colors, but they can't stop laughing now. And you know what? Out of the corner of my eye I catch Herodias in a teeny-weeny grin. Her usual smile is powerful and impressive — makes you want to buy a nuclear reactor from her or elect her to high office. Now she's grinning like she's actually amused. I guess there's just something about a man wearing condiments.

In the bathroom mirror I look crazed and colorful — one of those weak, cynical Somerset Maugham characters going slowly native under a sun that never sets.

LIFE IMITATES ART, they say, and so does miniature golf. The first hole, for instance, is cut in the shape of the Mona Lisa, the painting reproduced in full color on top of the astroturf. You have to sink the ball in the middle of her famous smile. I feel apologetic as I take my stance on the lightly clasped hands and bounce my shot off her forehead, but that kind of sensitivity goes away. By about hole fourteen I hardly notice that I'm standing on Van Gogh's corn-cob pipe. All I'm thinking about is, will the putt go into his ear, or not? Despite the classic course, my golf is kind of post-modern. I line up my putts and test which way the wind is blowing, clean my putter, take a few practice swings and then miss. Everybody beats me — the girls with giggles, and Herodias with a smile that turns austere whenever I call her Hero. *Everyone should have a sandwich in their life,* I tell her. She says she doesn't mind, but I think she does, a bit.

She doesn't mind taking the girls on the Whip Cracker ride either, and I sure don't. I feel faint just watching from down below with a bag of peanuts, and I notice that both girls are a lot quieter after this ride than they were after the roller coaster. We have an ugly generational experience outside the booth that sells cotton candy, voices raised in petition and denial, protest and entreaty. *No, you can't! The stuff is horrible, gets everywhere. I'll be washing it out of my hair for days. Please, Dad, please don't buy any!*

Hero and I look at each other. *But cotton candy is part of the amusement-park experience,* she says. I chime in. *My father always bought us cotton candy at the National Exhibition,* I say. I was kind of looking forward to it, to be honest. The girls shake their heads in unison but they let us buy one stick, to share, and we promise to wash up after we've finished.

The ride home is subdued. Thea and Rebecca are yawning in the back of the car, and Herodias is reassembling her personality behind the wheel. I notice her sitting taller as we get nearer to our neighborhood. Her jaw moves forward, her nostrils flare. She has the impressive look again. The air conditioner is set at a comfortable twenty-two degrees, but it seems much chillier.

Thanks so much, I tell her, leaning in to wave good-bye. *I enjoyed most of the day very much.* The front of my T-shirt is still colorful. For a second her chiseled features seem to soften, then she zips up the window and drives away.

THE FRONT PORCH looks exactly the way it did when we left. Roy would be conspicuous by his presence, but he's not there.

I guess the day lacks that final degree of pure heat and dryness, that Sahara quality prized by all really good exterior painters. *I can hardly wait to tell Sam about the mountain roller coaster,* Thea says. *It was so cool. He'll be so upset!* I'm afraid she's right. *Try not to rub it in,* I tell her. *You don't want Sam to feel bad.* She stares at me almost pityingly. *Sorry,* I say, *of course you do. But I don't want him to feel bad. Remember how you felt when he went to the Santa Claus Parade and you had to stay home because you were too sick?* Incredibly bad example. *Yes, and do you remember how he rubbed it in, Daddy? About the hot chocolate and the bag of caramel corn? And the toys Santa gave out? Remember? And all I got was stupid chicken soup and a stupid video I didn't even like!* There are real tears in her eyes and her chin is quivering. I am astonished and dismayed at her ability to conjure present heat from long-dead embers of envy and wrath. And at my own stupidity. We walk in silence around to the back door. *Hello!* I call, but the house is empty. The note on the kitchen table reads —

Real-estate office called to say there is a good
offer for the house. Details tonight. Gone to pick
up dry cleaning and pizza for dinner. Back soon.
Love.

Thea can read a few words. One of them is — *Pizza?* she complains. *I hate pizza!*

I STARE WILDLY AROUND at the kitchen, the little fingermarks on the doorframes, the pile of newspapers on the radiator, the messy countertop, the pictures of smiling blob figures and lopsided houses that are stuck all over the fridge, the cupboard doors that don't hang straight, the chandelier I found at a lawnsale for five dollars and paid an electrician's ransom to install, the oven that alternately undercooks and chars, the wretched linoleum I spent so many hours wiping and never actually got clean. Our kitchen. I'm going to miss it.

Someone wants to buy our house, I tell Thea.

Her emotional yo-yo does an Around The World and returns to her hand. *Yippee!* she shrieks. Dinner could be cooked cabbage for all she cares. She starts to skip around me, singing, *We're moving! We're moving! And I'm going to have a pink bedroom!*

Thea's face beams up into mine with such delight and confidence in the future that I can't help smiling back at her. When she knocks over a plastic cup half-empty of grape juice — only pessimists spill half-full cups — I don't get angry. I don't even feel like getting angry. I point out to Thea that the purple stain on the floor is exactly the shape and color of Barney the dinosaur but a bit smaller, and she laughs and so do I, and the phone rings.

Mr. Scrimger? I just want to tell you that we received your deposit check today. An elderly fussy voice, doesn't sound like she's from the City Parking Authority or the Insurance Office, and I can't remember writing any other checks recently. *Good,* I say.

We'll expect you on the fifteenth, she says. *I gave your wife directions to the cottage.* Now I know who she is. *The 115 highway will take you all the way over to Waterbury,* she says. *You can get on the 115 from the exit right after the Wonderland amusement park.*

Thanks, I tell her.

That big plastic mountain is a sickening sight but it makes a good landmark.

Sickening? She should see it from close up.

Cultural Outing

IT'S FOUR O'CLOCK on a bright summer afternoon and I'll bet the subway is crowded and noisy and dirty and hot. We're in a minivan with broken air conditioning — no real difference except for seatbelts and sunlight glinting blindingly off all the other windshields. *Watch out, Daddy,* calls Thea, sitting in the front seat playing with her miniature pet shop, each piece of which seems to have been custom-fitted to Ed's mouth.

WHAT, I say, braking, swerving, rechecking the mirror. Have I run over, failed to stop, executed an illegal — *WHAT IS IT?* Thea is frowning at her funny daddy. *Watch out for my kitty. I can't find her.* Oh.

Are we at the museum yet? Sam asks from the middle seat. He's hunched in discontent. Time in transit passes like a prison sentence for him, physically confined and forced to sit near his sister, he might as well be in school. *Soon,* I tell him, the parent's mantra, taking advantage of an opening in traffic to make a slightly messy left turn, sparing a second to look over my shoulder for Imogen, who should be sitting in the very back. She's disappeared but I'm not worried, I'm pretty sure I packed her this time.

And what do you want to see first at the museum — mummies or dinosaurs? I ask, funny how times don't change, isn't it. What did you want to see when they took you to the museum? The traffic light is red, so I stop, just like my driving instructor taught me.

Aren't we there yet? I shake my head — *No, Sam. Soon —* only the car behind me honks. A limousine, I ignore it, probably late for a press conference, and then I hear another honk from farther back. *Daddy, have you seen my kitty?* I pat her knee. *No, honey, but I'm sure he's here somewhere and when we —*

Motorcycle! shrieks Immie, sitting up suddenly, her uncombed hair making her look like a science experiment. It's a policeman — I immediately do up my seatbelt — who stops right beside us and motions us on. Gleaming uniform, flashing lights, urgent gestures while the cars behind us honk in chorus. I point at my chest the way you do, meaning, Me? You're talking to Me? And then I see the card on the front of the motorcycle. There's one on the limo too, of course, we're in the middle of a funeral cortège. *O my God,* I say, ever the *bon mot,* and stamp on the accelerator so we take off smoothly and respectfully like a bank heist.

Thea is giggling about something in the front seat — *Stop that!* I tell her. *Try to look serious.* Immie pops up again and starts to wave. *Sit still!* I cry. *They'll think we're making fun.* But it is a pretty funny situation, and when an old man on the corner takes off his hat and stares respectfully, I have to look away. At the first opportunity I duck out of line and cut down a side street with an unobtrusive squeal of brakes. I take the next turn and the next, dodging through traffic like a pinball to shake any pursuing mourners.

Did the mummies used to be real people? asks Sam. *And*

will their faces all be rotted away? Soon, I tell him, *soon.* He sighs deeply. *I'm hot,* says Ed, mumbling a bit. *Me too!* we all say together.

NOW I'M LOST in a downtown neighborhood not my own. After a few tense minutes Thea asks a pertinent question, *Why are all the cars pointing toward us, Daddy?* I take the next turning, and then the next, because I have no other choice. They don't seem to want drivers with initiative in this part of town. Several turns later I find a major street — not the one I was expecting but at least I know which direction it's going to take me, if only someone will let me turn onto it. Time passes, pressure from other waiting motorists builds behind me so that I feel like the cork in a dropped champagne bottle, and still they won't let me in — the purblind, selfish burrowing animals, eyes glued to each other's taillights. No wait, a kindly police officer holds up a gloved hand so I can get into the stream of traffic. *Thank you,* I call to him, waving. He frowns at me and I feel guilty. You know, he looks familiar, must be a standard police type.

Five minutes later Immie shrieks, *Gum!* the way someone else would say *Fire!* and it has the same galvanic effect. Many voices calling urgently, *Daddy, can we, I want, You promised, How come she gets, Not fair.* I ignore them all because I know where we are now, iron gates in a sober spiked fence, well-tended lawns, beautiful shade trees, rows and rows of tombstones. Not the museum. How'd we end up here? I don't want to go in but the policeman stands there waving us on, and I really don't see any chance of escape.

Can we see the rotted-away dead people now? asks Sam. Funny he should say that. I hand out gum while I'm trying to park, and somehow get boxed in between the lead limousine and the hearse, and then I have to stop. Thea leans over and beeps the horn to say Hi, the way we do at Grandma's. Sam's already out of the van. I try to look bereaved as I follow. I wonder if we'll stand out in our flip-flop sandals and Day-Glo T-shirts. Thea's frowning, trying to pull her kitty out of Ed's mouth. Sam confronts me angrily — *Dad, this isn't the museum.* I ruffle his hair affectionately. *Next time*, I tell him, *we'll go by subway.*

Kick Today

IT'S THE FIRST WEEK of summer holidays, a time for short pants and no worries. Moving day seems as far removed as snow and civic elections. It's afternoon again, feels like it's been afternoon all week long, dusty and golden and infinite. We finish our snack and dash out — *Don't slam the door, Sam* — into the dappled sunshine of our street to play a hide-and-seek game called Kick The Can, very popular because you get to — well, you can guess what you get to do.

I don't know how *you* play Kick The Can. This is our way. I'm it because I'm the only one who can count high enough. When I reach eleven infinity million and six hundred and eighty-eighty and four fingers (Ed's contribution), I say, *Ready or not, here I come!* and they all emerge from their hiding places screaming like banshees and I chase them in the direction of a can carefully selected out of our recycling box for its size and resonance — apple juice today — a can they proceed to kick in an orderly and dignified manner. Ed gets excited, runs after the can, tackles it, carries it away, puts it down and kicks it onto the road. I don't catch anyone, so I'm it again. We applaud every kick.

It's a noticeable game. By the time we've played three or four rounds, half the neighborhood has joined, including kids on bikes and skateboards, kids on crutches, kids in diapers, cool kids with long hair, short hair, no hair and clothes baggy enough to move in a different direction from the kid inside. I feel like a Scoutmaster — *Hi, what's your name? Of course you can play. Ed, leave Benson alone,* raising my voice to shout, *ALL RIGHT EVERYONE, HERE WE GO AGAIN!* Visiting moms smile wanly and maneuver their charges out of the energy vortex, but every now and then one will get swept in, one like Benson or Chris with his asthma. *I'm so worried,* his mom calls to me in the middle of counting. *He really can't tolerate mold.*

I nod sympathetically but I can't move because Ed has twined himself about my feet like a serpent and I've only reached seven hundred thousand and forty-five. I figure we'll find Chris when he starts to sneeze.

READY OR NOT, HERE I COME! I unwind Ed, and the two of us charge off together as the other kids emerge from behind pillars and trees and mailboxes, a sustained multi-voiced shriek rising from the street like steam from an uncovered pot. I lunge and miss a kid on a bike, grab for someone else and get a jacket with I'll swear no kid inside, miss Thea, miss Immie — behind me I can hear clatter and cheering — practically kill myself to miss a chubby stranger with a big smile, chase after someone whose name I forget, a giggling rawhide slip of a thing runs faster than I do, run some more and miss Chris, who's racing along merrily, no sign that he's asthmatic. I, on the other hand, am wheezing like a punctured accordion. I look round to see that all is well and can't find Ed.

I shrug it off, Ed gets lost a few times every day, I worry if we're in the museum or the mall, not so much if we're in the shoe store. But Ed isn't the only lost lamb. Benson's mom is searching the crowd frantically — and Benson is hard to miss.

It turns out we find Ed first, which isn't surprising because he's carrying Benson's crutch — *Where did you get that?* I ask him. He puts it down carefully.

Benson's mom has hysterics. *Help! Help!* she cries. *Someone call the police. My little boy is getting into trouble* — which of course isn't true, he's not getting anywhere. *There there,* I say. We all spread out but we can't find Benson right away, not even with all the kids helping.

Omigod, his mom keeps saying, *I can't remember what he was wearing and it's the first thing the police will ask. Do you remember what he was wearing?* I shake my head. I don't see that it matters what Benson was wearing. A six-year-old in a double leg brace is going to be noticed, especially as he can't walk without the crutch his mom is twisting in her hands.

WHAT'S ED UP TO NOW? He has a plan, circles cautiously around the crowd to grab the can but, instead of kicking it, he picks it up and trots purposefully toward our backyard. I follow at a distance. Ed looks over his shoulder before diving through the hedge. When I catch up to him he's placing the can with some care near our back porch. I stop. A lame little boy in a candy-striped T-shirt is crawling from his hiding place under our porch — you'd think his mom would remember a candy-striped shirt.

Ed stands respectfully back because it's Benson's turn. He's never kicked before. He has every toy known to humankind, including a brand new matagapulator to replace the one Sam broke, but he's never kicked the can before.

Slowly, his face twisted with effort, Benson hooks his hands on the stairs to pull himself up to a kind of crouch. He's right beside the can now. His left leg goes back, slowly

slowly, then forward just enough to topple the can. It falls without a sound onto our uncut grass. Benson's face is wet with sweat. He smiles when the can falls. And sinks back onto the ground himself. Standing beside him, with all the solemnity of his nearly three years, Ed begins to applaud.

Sam comes up then, asks me what's wrong. *Do you have a stuffy nose, Dad?* I clear my throat and look around for Benson's mom.

Cottage Life

1. Getting There

IT IS THE DAY, fabled from my own childhood — a day of mythic properties symbolic of freedom and adventure, the hunger for new places, new faces, new kinds of — *Dad, when are we going to be there?* Yes, it's the start of the family vacation, no day quite like it, not even the last day of school, which kids and teachers celebrated a couple of weeks ago while parents stood in the schoolyard with grim smiles on their faces, like polite children listening to classical music and secretly wishing the radio would blow up. Amanda's mom shook my hand and whispered, *Two more months.* I was able to give her the correct code response. *See you in September,* I said.

This year we're renting a cottage on a small northern lake with panoramic views and the smell of fresh growing things all around us for a change, not just in the back of the refrigerator. I'm as enthusiastic as Sam but I can control myself, after all, I know it's only nine o'clock in the morning and I'm the one loading the van. *Soon,* I reply, trying to close the trunk around our assortment of linens, kids' clothes, stuffed animals, beach toys, theodolite, mixmaster, sunblock, coils of rope, tent pegs, sleeping bags, to say nothing of the high chair, stroller, astrolabe and other larger pieces of equipment. And as soon as I think I'm finished, someone shows up with another bag that has to go in. I believe in packing carefully, in fact I'm the one who insists on the medical bag being handy because — well, what would happen if someone got hurt while we were pulling away from the house and the Band-Aids were in the back, underneath the oxygen tanks and crampons? Not a pretty picture, is it. But if we aren't on our way soon, the neighbors will think we're moving today.

Here, Daddy. Thea hands me a familiar pink plastic traveling case, the fourth or fifth one so far. I shake my head. *I don't think we need Stepford Barbie,* I say — besides, I never cared for what happens to poor Ken. Sam and Immie are already wearing their bathing suits, goggles and flippers. I figure they might be in a position to use them within four or five hours. In a sense they're right to wear them now though. The ritual of packing the car always plays in brilliant sunshine, don't you remember? I do. I remember the sun rising with terrible beauty over the hood of the family station wagon, Dad shaking his head as he tried to find the catch that would flatten the rear seat and increase our carrying capacity. It was always a glorious morning, and we always spent it in front of the house. The brilliant weather continued until we were in sight of our destination, whereupon the wind picked up and the sky clouded over very suddenly, and the minute I touched the water it began, always, to rain.

Meanwhile it is baking hot and Ed is in his element. This

is a time of lifting, his favorite activity under heaven. Thea, Immie, even Sam, tire of watching Dad rearrange things and swear, but Ed stays right in there, his face next to mine, contorted with effort as mine is, reaching as I do to pull, push, pummel various squishy parcels into spaces they were never supposed to fit. *Hold this,* I tell him, and his whole body swells with pride as he clasps the barometer to himself, or an air mattress or concertina. *I have an idea,* he says every few minutes. *How about we put that — here!* And he pushes another stuffed animal under the seat. Already we have bears with hats, dogs with spots, and kittens with tattersall vests, in addition to lizards and lions, ducks and donkeys, elk and their ilk. I wonder if Noah's parents had to put up with this.

Finally everything is loaded except Sam's caber. It blew down in the last storm and he's been dragging it around, with difficulty, ever since. *Couldn't you tie it to the roof?* my wife offers with her hands full of emergency cookies and juice boxes. Easy for her, she never failed Boy Scouts the way I did — even my shoelaces unravel. While the rest of my troop were making lean-tos and figuring altitude with a wristwatch and bent paperclip, I stayed behind to work on correct sock maintenance. The only badge I got was for cleaning my fingernails and turning a somersault—not much good if you have to survive in the wild. *No,* I say.

Not that I don't enjoy the outdoors. I'm looking forward to our cottage. Most days the closest I get to the smell of pine trees is my underarm deodorant. I hope I have the right set of directions. Last year we ended up at a factory furniture outlet. Wouldn't you know it? The one time in my life I ever found a parking spot near the door and I had to turn right around. I start the engine. I can't see anyone because of the mounds of luggage, but I hear enough voices. *Are we ready to go?* I call, and they answer together, *I don't have my seatbelt on,* so I climb all over, lashing people in and then they start to giggle. *Daddy,* says Thea, *you've put a seatbelt on Wolfie* — he's a little dog that belongs to Tim the bodybuilder across the street. The kids throw tennis balls for Wolfie, and Tim lifts our van out of snowbanks, it's a symbiotic relationship. *Arf!* says Wolfie from somewhere back there.

Hi, Mom, the kids cry as my wife climbs in. *Guess what Dad did?* She says she can't guess, asks me if we're ready to go. *Not quite,* I say.

2. Blind Date with a Cottage

WE'RE BOUNCING DOWN a typical cottage road — small rocks and dirt strewn at random on top of potholed limestone. I picture an early resident going forth with sackfuls of the stuff, Johnny Gravelseed, determined to improve the roadways. Inspiring, don't you think? The kids have stopped asking when we're going to be there because they know we're just going to lie to them. I'm peering through a dime-sized clear space near the top of the windshield—the rest is a paste of dust and bugs, impervious to my wiper blades—while my wife frowns at the written directions in her hand. *Left at the big rock,* she tells me, *then look for three larch trees in a row. At the top of one of them is a bittern's nest.* You'd think we were searching for the legendary lost crown of King Arthur, but we're not. We just want to find, after two and a half hours on the road with a vanful of children, toys, hard-cooked eggs, licorice allsorts (and wasn't *that* a mistake), the quaint rambling picturesque cottage we've rented for the next two weeks.

More cryptic instructions. I turn left at a battered signpost with a dozen family names on it. Can they all be for the same place? There must be a strong oral tradition to flesh out these bare bones of ownership —

The MacIntyres, Tyrone and Kate, who summered here 'til
   sixty-eight,
Entailed the lakefront lot upon their second — no their
   third son Don,
A thankless wretch who never mowed, or cleared his stretch of
   snowy road,
He sold to strangers in the fall, yclept Elizabeth and Paul,
They rent to anyone at all.

— and meanwhile the forest primeval is scraping our paint-work and the road primeval is ruining our suspension and this small crawling insect is determined to make a nest in my ear.

When, despite my best efforts, we run right into a tureen-sized hole, the kids wake up from their trance and immediately open their *Are we there yet?* mouths as if no time has passed at all. I'm sure it was like that at Sleeping Beauty's castle. I ignore them because my wife is pointing at the opaque windshield. I bring us to a skidding halt. I don't know what I expect to see — grazing dinosaurs, shrunken heads on poles, a bottomless pit. *I think,* she says softly, *that sign says THE WATSONS.* I feel a little anticlimactic. *Oh yes,* I say. *And are the Holmeses staying next door?* She shakes her head. *We are.* Obediently I turn aside. We bump down a goat track for a few hundred yards and then — *Good heavens,* I say.

A RENTED COTTAGE is like a blind date. You don't know what you're getting until it's too late and you're stuck for the evening. They're not as big as they sound over the phone, just like your date, and they're in worse shape, and full of so many annoying habits that, after ten minutes, you're thinking, When can I go home? On the other hand, you're probably not quite what you were pretending to be either, a tall, well-behaved family with a swimmer's build and wavy golden hair, you love exotic cooking and romantic walks and you never bounce on the furniture or slam doors, do you? Disappointment is a two-way street with plenty of traffic in each direction, and if you want to get off you have to signal clearly. Or something.

Isn't it a lovely view! my wife exclaims, sighing romantically as we stand in the front room surrounded by children burrowing in our luggage. Of course it's a great view, we're three hundred feet above the lake. Good thing we brought our alpine gear or we'll never get to the beach. *Too bad it's clouded over, but I'm happy to get away from the —*

SPIDER! shrieks Imogen, emerging from her nest. My wife and I look at each other — the look you get when your blind date starts demonstrating card tricks — meanwhile the children are lined up against the far wall shivering. Some of this is just surface hysteria. Thea collects bugs back home, and Ed isn't really afraid of anything except nutritious foods, but Immie and Sam are genuinely terrified. *Oh no,* they say to each other, shaking their heads. *Oh no oh no oh no.* I know better than to try reason. *I'll take care of it,* I say, tossing aside a paddle, three shirts and a lariat, and uncovering a good-sized spider in the act of bearing away — you'd swear she was going to try it on — a Barbie shoe. So that's where they go. *Don't hurt it.* My wife likes spiders, but the kids have a different opinion. *Stamp on it. Crush it. We want to see guts!* It's a way of controlling the situation, very natural and therapeutic too, but I don't see how we're going to reach a consensus. *How about if I stomp on the spider without hurting her,* I say, *and then take her outside.* In fact the spider vanishes before I can pick her up. *Got her!* I lie, carrying an empty handkerchief to the door and throwing it out. Crisis averted for now, the children and I put on our raincoats against the drizzle and go outside to look at the view from our cliff. Ed is drawn to the edge the way a moth is drawn to the flame, only faster and more insistently. *Don't go near the edge.* I hold him with his face next to mine but his legs are still moving. When my wife joins us, she has this funny look on her face — not funny ha ha. *There's a wasp's nest somewhere in the bathroom,* she tells me in a low voice. I blink. I'm on a blind date with Charles Manson.

3. Step by Step

OUR COTTAGE IS CONVENIENTLY SITUATED on a bluff. From the back door it's just a hop, skip, jump and plummet to the beautiful private beach. Or you can take the stairs, as we plan to do this lovely afternoon, complete with our towels, sunblock — *Stand back, Ed!* — plastic buckets, spare tires, sieves, mining equipment, beach umbrella, frisbees, kitchen utensils, and Surfer Barbie's pink dune-buggy; also footballs, basketballs, beach balls — *Stand back, Ed!* — and insect repellant, and thermoses in case we get thirsty. We won't get thirsty, I know that, because we won't be down long enough to get thirsty, but I also know that if we didn't bring the thermoses we'd get thirsty before we got to the bottom of the — *Ed! Stand away from the edge of the bluff.* His little legs keep moving even after I pick him up and carry him away. Like a compass needle to true north, Ed is drawn to the edge of the cliff, he doesn't know why or how, can't stop his feet from moving closer, closer, ever closer, willpower gone, hearing gone, nothing but the cliff, the cliff, the cliff. I can hardly wait until he discovers girls.

I stare at all the necessary equipment. *Are you sure we need to bring the skeleton people and the dinosaurs?* I ask, but of course we do. *The dinosaurs are going to dig up the skeleton bones just like they showed us at the museum.* I'm starting to think it might be easier to bring the beach up to us, bucket by bucket, than to bring all of us to it. The way I figure it, we can establish base camp about halfway down the slope, pick up our Sherpas there, and get down to the beach in time for lunch. Unless someone has to go to the bathroom.

The only way to get down is steps. Think of those steps, the famous ones that the faithful are supposed to climb on their knees. That's our way down. Only the faithful get off lightly, they don't have to go up and down carrying blankets, towels, and dumptrucks all full of sand, and Ken in a total body cast. If only there was a funicular. But I don't think even we would have rented a cottage that advertised cable-car access to the beach.

Mom will join us in an hour or so, after she's finished working. She's going to bring the snack. That sounds great, I tell her, my voice muffled from under the inflatable canoe. A scene like that needs a dog, but we don't have one. We have everything else, though, or wait — we don't have a bathing suit for Imogen. *Honey, where's your suit?* I ask. She went through a long period where getting dressed wasn't a question of what to wear but yes or no. *I am a kitten,* she informs us, *and kittens don't wear bathing suits.* She's getting too old for this, I suppose, but on the other hand who else is going to be climbing down the hundreds of steps to the beach? I can't believe we're going to be greeted by a crowd of disapproving oldsters, and anyway they would all die on the way back up. *Oh,* I say. Firmly.

Sam comes running out of the house, screaming, *They're after me!* You'd think he was Al Capone. *They don't care about you, Sam,* I tell him. *They're only bees. If you leave them alone they'll leave you alone.* He looks over his shoulder doubtfully. *Did you remember to wash your hands?* I ask. *Yes,* he lies. I can't blame him. The buzzing in the bathroom is kind of disturbing, especially if you're trying to work out whether it's coming from underneath where you're sitting, if you follow me.

Well, let's go! I say, leading the way to the rickety staircase. I go first because I don't want to fall on anyone. Elephants lead the way down the hill for the same reason. After a dozen steps downward, I look back. We're strung out like a baggage train. Thea has already left the staircase to hunt for flowers. *Come back! We've got to keep together!* If only we'd brought the ropes, I think to myself. Another dozen steps and another look back, Thea is hopping down, Sam is swinging on the railing, Imogen is picking her way with the care of a Jain priest anxious not to step by accident on another living thing, and Ed is sitting down to examine the sole of his foot. I'm afraid to think how many lives he's set himself back. *Come on! Don't stop! We've got to keep moving!* Now I feel like Scott of the Kawarthas leading my doomed expedition to the South Beach. To sleep is to die! Another couple of dozen steps and I'm starting to feel the load on my shoulders. I turn around just in time to see Thea stumble and sit down suddenly, knocking Sam's feet out from under him so that he sits down too. They both start to laugh, thank heavens. *Stop playing games!* I have to yell because they're too far away to hear. *And come on!*

A dozen more steps. Behind me, stretching up the hill like pulled taffy, are my children. Imogen stands still, shivering patiently while Thea wraps her in a towel. Sam is seeing how many steps he can jump down without falling — not four, it appears — and Ed is favoring one foot. I hope he hasn't picked up a splinter. The beach beckons.

It's hard to measure distance on a slope. I figure we're about halfway down.

4. With Baited Breath

DADDY, WHY IS RAIN CALLED RAIN? Thea's eighty-ninth or ninetieth question of the morning and it's only snacktime. *It's an old Iroquois word meaning Clear stuff that falls from the sky and ruins your picnic,* I tell her, sick of saying *I don't know.* Snack this morning is Chelsea buns, a recent discovery for us. Our cottage is near a picturesque village that specializes in Chelsea buns — maybe most cottages are, when they're not near picturesque villages that specialize in collectibles or pure maple syrup. Those long winter evenings must really stretch out. Anyway, I'm not complaining, I like Chelsea buns, especially when they're fresh from the oven and not offered in the same establishment as our village's other specialty, which is bait.

I've never thought seriously about bait, but there are obviously lots of people who do. Shop after shop down our main street, and that's what they all sell. Snacks and bait, novelties and bait, real estate and bait, stamps and bait, ice cream and bait, hair cuts and bait. I never see any on the shelves either. I suppose they must be sold out. *And can we have a fire tonight?* At last a question I can answer meaningfully. *No,* I say. Across the street is our restaurant's competition. FRESH CHELSEA BUNS it says in the window in huge letters, AND LIVE BAIT. I'm sure the buns are great over there, but we're over here because a perfectly simple mistake would ruin my whole day. *Why can't we have a fire?* Sam asks. *Quiet,* I say.

Imogen is already quiet. Her existence is perfect and complete with a Chelsea bun in her mouth, and she has no thoughts but paradise right now. Ed is quiet because he has taken the raisins out of the Chelsea bun and begun to insert them in his nose. I can't tell if he's hiding them from discovery, the way a lesser baby would give his peas to the dog, or saving them in case of starvation later. Sam and Thea still want to know why they can't have a fire tonight. I decide to tell them. I lean forward, fearful that my secret will get out. I could say we don't have enough money — it's an excuse they've heard before — but I try to be honest. *Because I don't know how to light a fire,* I say.

All my life this has haunted me, not that you need open fires very often as a grown-up, unless your union is on strike.

Lighting a one-match fire is like being able to tango, or spit, or whistle through your fingers, or make a rude noise under your armpit, or order a meal in Japanese. It makes you feel good about yourself. I still dream about the Cub Scout Pride day when I sat, nearly eight years old and even nearer tears, buried up to my neck in burned matches. You'd have thought I was learning to smoke a pipe. Our neighborhood is full of kids setting fires in garbage cans, there are posters from the fire department asking good citizens for cooperation in tracking down these petty arsonists, but if I ever see one I'm going to ask for lessons.

Thea doesn't care. *Oh,* she says, and then, *Why are cars called cars?* I shouldn't be surprised, I suppose. I remember answering a question about babies in embarrassing gynecological detail only to have her say, *And do baby cows say Moo like their mommies?*

The place is filling up. Most of the customers wear hats with phrases like FISH OR DIE on them. I wonder if there's a third option. Nice folks, they smile as they walk past our table. I suppose we do look cute in our short pants and sunburns. Today is the first rainy day of our holiday, the first day chilly enough to even think about lighting a fire. Sam is on his feet. He's finished his Chelsea bun and raring to go — anywhere. Imogen slowly licks icing off her fingers. Her eyes are closed. *Car,* I tell Thea, *is an old Blackfoot word meaning Horse with high insurance rates and mandatory seatbelts.* She searches my face. *Really?* she asks. You can't say Honest Injun any more so I say, *No.*

The rain lets up momentarily and Imogen opens her eyes. Time to go. On our way out of the restaurant, Ed sneezes. The woman at the next table cries out in pain. *Dad, why do you sneeze when you have a cold?* Thea asks. I strap Ed into his seat. *Sometimes,* I say, *you sneeze when you have a noseful of raisins.*

The air is dank and wet, and the scent of woodsmoke hangs heavily around the cottage. *Did you all have a good time in town?* My wife looks up from her work to find me staring at the fireplace. *It was cold in here, so I thought I'd light a fire — are you okay?* she asks.

The kids are hopping up and down in delight, shrieking *Let's cook lunch on the fire!* I hang firmly onto Ed. *Fine,* I tell them. Lunch is hot dogs. We all go outside to cut green branches to cook them on. *Just remember,* I tell them, *fire is hot. If you drop your wiener in the fire —* I try to smile but it's hard, this is another humiliating Cub Scout moment — *just leave it alone.*

Lunch goes well. We have a great time, but I notice Thea staring thoughtfully at the fire. Finally she asks, *Dad, why are there twelve wieners in the package, but only eight buns?* I shrug. Some questions are just unanswerable.

5. Share the Rod

AH, THE HEAVE AND SWELL of the open lake, the tang of the bait in a bucket under your feet, the anticipation as you let out your line and reel it in slowly, the heave and swell of the open lake, the excitement that spreads from your wrist through your body as you feel that first tentative twitch, the pull of a hungry large-mouthed fish, more heave and swell, and the whiff of diesel exhaust as you shut off the motor — the heartful contentment of a perfect summer afternoon on a perfect stretch of gently heaving blue water. The boat is drifting slowly, the line is trailing alongside, the blue horizon is lifting and lowering, lifting and lowering, lifting and ... I hear a tremendous shriek from the bow — *Immie's caught a fish!* — and the splash as something falls in. Startled out of my nauseous reverie, I take in the situation at a glance. We're all still in the boat, but Imogen, in her excitement, has lost our rod.

We have only one fishing rod. Strange, when you consider that we have four bowling balls, six badminton birds and a miniature working volcano. In fact the rod isn't even ours. My wife discovered it in the cottage broom closet beside the wasp blaster, and suggested a fishing excursion to the children, who immediately whooped and ran off to slam doors, the speed of their random movements increasing dramatically just the way the speed of water molecules increases as the water is heated, Yes, Mr. Lazure, I was so paying attention in Grade Six science. But then the long-distance phone calls started — not for me, the only long-distance calls I get are from friends who have gone into the insurance business. I was left face to faces with four would-be old salts. *No*, I begin, *I will not take you fishing. Fishing is evil and smelly and boring and then you fall in the lake and everyone bursts out laughing* — that may not be your experience or Ernest Hemingway's, but it certainly is mine, long time ago but I'll never forget it. *No*, I tell them again, but their faces fall at the same time, like Galileo's weights from the leaning tower, to land with a simultaneous thud on the cracked flagstones of my indulgence.

Oh, Dad. Please, Dad. We'll share nicely. We'll dig up worms. We'll be good, Dad. And that's how I end up in the middle of the lake in a rented two-horsepower contraption. You know how they bring old boats inside and turn them into wet bars — well, this is an old bar that someone has turned into a wet boat. Anyway, it's ours for the day, full of cheers and excitement, flotsam and jetsam, win some and lose some. And noisome.

ED SEES THE PLASTIC RED and white float bobbing in the water. He jumps up and down, up and down, the boat sways alarmingly and everyone ends up on the floorboards. *There it is!* he shouts at the top of his lungs, *THERE IT IS!* leaning right out of the boat. I keep my hand on the back of his lifejacket at all times. If I were a real sailor I'd lash him to the mast, if we had a mast. We're drifting away from the rod. We've been drifting all along of course, water lapping at the sides of the boat, wind whispering. By now we're a fair distance down the lake. Is that buzzing a mosquito?

Okay everyone, we're going to get the fishing rod now, I tell them and then, *Sit down!* It's not the first time I've told them to sit down, and no one seems to pay attention this time either. I carry Ed to the back of the boat, where sits one of those famous engines, the ones with the pull cord that only your neighbor can start. When I pull, nothing happens, so I pull harder and the entire cord comes out in my hand.

That's when the beach ball hits us. I look round, my heart racing, and I see that we're drifting inexorably toward — a party. Giggling teenagers and old-fashioned rock and roll, frisbees and dogs, beach blankets and secret kisses. Think of a beer commercial, doesn't matter which one. Good thing we fit right in — *Here you go!* I shout, sending the beach ball back into the splashing crowd. The buzzing gets louder and louder until it's right beside us. It's a jet-ski racer driven by someone named Brad — aren't they all. He waves, cuts his own engine and leaps right into our boat — Apollo Belvedere in a Day-Glo wetsuit — and before I can even suck in my stomach he has the top of our motor off and is rewrapping the cord. *That should do it,* he says. The kids are speechless and still, and when he pulls the cord and the motor starts, they cheer and he looks embarrassed.

His jet-ski is only a few feet off. He leaps aboard and starts it up, *Thank you,* we call, and he waves and speeds away. *Who was that man?* asks Ed. Thea stares after him. In ten years she'll be seventeen and he'll be working in an insurance office, but I can't tell her that.

We stop to pick up the fishing rod on our way home, and you'll never guess what's on the end of the line. *Can we eat it for dinner?* Immie asks, awestruck.

Of course, I say. *You should always eat what you kill, but in this case —* it's the smallest fish I've ever seen. How could it have swallowed the worm? *— I'll scramble some eggs too — just in case you're still hungry afterwards.*

Last Day

THE SUN CLIMBS UP the eastern sky while we shiver in the shade. Our beach doesn't get direct sunlight until noon, but this is our farewell to the cottage and we don't want to miss a moment. Imogen is upstairs helping her mom take that last look under beds, and Mom is upstairs because someone has to be there when the exterminators come. The rest of the children are dabbling their toes at the edge of the lake, and seeing which of their miniature plastic superheroes float. None of them, apparently. It doesn't seem to bother any of the children that their teeth are chattering and the water is cold. I can remember feeling the same way when I was their age.

Sunlight! The great golden disc slides across the brow of our cliff with all the silent majesty of a fried egg sliding off the plate and onto the floor. In less time than you would believe we are all of us blinded and squinting, and way, way too hot. Clothes fly off of little bodies like party snakes jumping out of a can. The mournful cry of the cicada announces that summer is dying. Isn't that an evocative sound? Maybe you're moved by geese honking their way north, or the wind soughing — if that's the word, I've never actually used it before, I feel as if I'm borrowing some poet's sports car for a joyride — through the pines. Or a kettle singing on the hob, or church bells or train whistles, or the sounds of "The

Pond," as heard in the background of *all* NFB films in my schooldays, even if the film was about ancient Egypt or atomic particles. Anyway, it's cicadas for me. And speaking of time's focus narrowing down to nothing, the inflatable canoe is here at the water's edge and the paddles are at the top of the bluff, up one hundred and fifty-eight stairs.

Frustrating. If I look straight up I can practically see the damn things, but I'm not Superman. I'm not even Tenzing of Everest. And the kids want to go for a ride in the canoe. But wait, what's this? Almost at the bottom of the stairs, hair flying behind her like a mane, so absolutely excited her face is all blue eyes and open mouth, is Imogen — with news. Last time she was this thrilled was when we were telling time and the second hand had gone *all the way around* the clock. Way up the stairs is my wife with a pitcher of grape Kool-Aid and, yes, the paddles. Also a concerned expression. Maybe something really has happened — something other than the passing of another minute.

He's ripping away the wall! Immie shrieks at the other kids. *Isn't it neat! And he's wearing a space suit!*

My first thought is that I called the wrong number in the Yellow Pages and got excavators instead of exterminators. I remember once calling a florist about a particular arrangement and getting a company that paved driveways. I was surprised at the price they quoted. They were surprised that I wanted it delivered.

Ed is so excited he starts off to tell Mom the news. *She already knows!* the other kids shout at him and he slumps to the sand.

Everyone always knows before I do, he cries. It's hard being the youngest, last with everything. *Knows what?* I ask, picking him up. His face brightens and he whispers wetly into my ear, *That Godzilla likes to eat seaweed.*

        *   *   *

MY WIFE EXPLAINS when she makes it to the bottom of the stairs. The bees in our bathroom are not your regular buzz-and-sip hive-dwellers, they're Mining Bees. I think of the dormouse's treacle well — wonder what a honey mine looks like? I picture the little helmets and pitchforks and bumble-while-you-work. *Their nests are underground,* my wife explains. *Oh,* I say and then, realization sinking in, *Oh.*

The exterminator has removed part of the siding so he can crawl underneath the cottage with his smoke to get at the bees. He promises to put back the siding when he's done. Mentally adding Exterminator to the long list of professions I could never be tempted to join, no matter what their benefit package looks like, I suggest a swim and then a ration of Kool-Aid. *Great!* say the kids, jumping into the canoe and abandoning their game of Beach Restaurant, where Nibbles the Pony serves seaweed to a variety of customers, including Snow White, The Human Torch, Cyborg Batman, and, yes, Godzilla. Of course a waterfront establishment like that is bound to have a mixed clientele.

I push the canoe out, Sam falls out, I get him back in, Thea jumps out, I put her back in, Ed jumps on Sam, I separate them, Thea and Sam lean the same way and fall out together, I right the canoe, tell them sternly to get back in, and catch Ed, who leaps at me without warning. By now we are three feet from shore. Everyone is giggling except my wife, who is laughing openly, and Imogen, who is sitting in the middle of the boat, singing quietly to herself. My ankles are getting cold. I give us a last push-off and jump in, just in time to hear Imogen say, *Daddy, I have to go to the bathroom.* I look back. My wife holds the paddles in her hands. We're drifting in circles, about twenty feet from the beach.

Only one thing to do in a crisis. I burst into a harsh crow of laughter. Then I grab Sam, he's nearest, hang him over the back end of the canoe with his legs in the water, and tell him to kick. *Dad,* he asks calmly, his face close to mine, *is this dangerous?*

I shake my head — *Only silly,* I say, and bring us to shore by a slow and circuitous route. Steering with a six-year-old outboard motor isn't as easy as it looks. High overhead, dense black smoke drifts over the edge of the cliff, dimming the sun momentarily. Good thing we've packed. Good thing the exterminator didn't come when we called, a week ago.

He's putting away his gear when we get up the stairs. He apologizes for the delay. The smell should disappear in a week or so, he says, cigarette in hand. *Oh, and I found this in the bathroom — figured it was yours.* I thank him. It's ours all right. Grimy, no longer blonde hair, sparkly blue eyes and positively reeking of smoke — Pastrami Barbie, I don't know how I'm going to break it to Thea. I climb into the van and start the engine. Sam bursts into tears. *I don't want to leave,* he sobs. *When are we going to be coming back?* And we haven't even left yet.

Envoi

I'M ON MY WAY OUT the door when the phone rings. *I'll bet you can't guess who this is,* says a deep voice on the other end of the line.

Mom? I say. Wouldn't it be interesting if it was — but it isn't. It's Bill from my college alumni fund who wants me to subscribe to the quarterly newsletter. *It's a great way to keep in touch with your old friends, and support the college at the same time,* he says. *And half of your subscription goes to famine relief.*

One of the best things about moving is that you get to leave behind all the worthy organizations you gave money to last year. Oh, they'll catch up to you — the mills of charity grind very fine indeed — but for a while you can lie low and draw your curtains whenever you see anyone approaching with that very specific smile. It's the moral certainty I resent and, right after the certainty, the money.

Mom, quit it, I say. *Quit your kidding. I'd love to come over for dinner on Sunday but I can't. The vet says Bowser will be back on his feet soon. I can't go very far without him, of course. Meanwhile I'm using the white cane. Maybe next week, all right? You call me then. And I'm so glad your cold is better, Mom — you sound great!*

I lock up on the way out. None of our stuff is valuable, but I don't want burglars stealing the boxes I've put everything in. I went to a lot of trouble to get those boxes.

LATE AUGUST, THE SUMMER IS DYING and the air is filled with memories and dandelion fluff. Everything moves slowly, quietly, to a set pace, like an old man getting ready for bed. I'm walking past the fruit store and a delicatessen and the lingerie store under a sky the color of a freshmint cough drop. I walk slowly, enjoying a rare and refreshing hour of solitude, also the charmingly thick ankles on the street-corner accordionist and the odor of dill-pickle soup coming from the Krakow Restaurant. Midafternoon sunshine glints off parked cars and store windows. It's my last day in the neighborhood and I need a haircut.

The moving truck comes tomorrow. Noon, they promised, but I know better — a moving truck on time is like a current issue of *Reader's Digest,* logically it has to exist, and yet I've never seen, or even heard tell of one. My doctor insists that her magazines are already five or six years old when she gets them from the distributor — kind of like pre-aged blue jeans, she says.

Some people drink under pressure, others get asthma or piles or migraines. My hair grows. Yesterday even my wife noticed, *You must be under a lot of stress,* she told me, staring at the top of my head. She's taken the children to the swings and slides down by the waterfront. They've always liked to play there, and this may be the last chance they get. Unless the moving truck is really late.

I walk past the phone booth at the corner and wave to the lady inside, I haven't seen her for weeks and weeks. She's short and dark-haired and angry. She'll sit on park benches frowning for hours on end, or else visit public telephones, pick up the receiver and yell into it — I don't know what she says, but it isn't Happy Birthday. Then she'll slam down the instrument and stomp away, her back bent under the weight of her world. She's been doing that as long as I've lived here. Hard to say how old she is under the dirt and anger.

I usually get my hair cut at *Tad's!* because I don't have to wait there — it's a dingy storefront with a painted barber pole and a flyspecked calendar and an old guy, Tad, I guess, though we're not on a naming basis, who does a pretty good job, considering his Parkinson's disease. *Tad's!* is closed today, so I go two doors down to *Pete's!* The only guy ahead of me is one of the local skinhead teenagers, he looks fine to me but I guess he's not happy with his lid. I don't know what he tells Pete, maybe which side the part would go on if he had enough hair to part. Pete nods and starts in with the razor. I don't see how he can take anything off, it's the Emperor's New Haircut, but the customer is satisfied and that's what counts. I make a little joke about it when I get into the chair, and Pete looks puzzled. *What for you?* he says. My wife goes to someone who understands her hair, I wonder if Pete understands me. I tell him short back and sides, illustrating with gestures to make sure he understands. I smile encouragingly, take off my glasses and settle back. I can't see anything. I hear a buzz and feel a gentle tickling, not at all uncomfortable, on my head and neck. Five minutes later I'm staring into the mirror at another skinhead. Me.

Well, I did tell him short. I'm so surprised I don't say anything. I move right up to the mirror, next to that tall cylinder full of blue sterilizing liquid with combs in it. Trying to get used to a newer, balder me, I am momentarily startled by the name on the side of the sterilizing container — Barbecide. Sounds like something a depressed doll would commit. *You like?* says

Pete, holding a hand mirror behind me so that I can see my shirt collar. I mean, there's nothing else back there. I smile mechanically. *It'll be easy to maintain,* I tell him, the haircut equivalent of the Miss Congeniality Award. But it takes some getting used to, the feeling of, well, nakedness where you're used to being completely dressed. Not well dressed, maybe, but covered. Walking down the street, peering furtively at my reflection in shop windows, I can't decide if I belong in a lobotomy clinic or death row. If I had an extra foot of height, a better tan and a magical on-court presence, I could be Michael Jordan — no, he doesn't wear glasses. My self-esteem gets a momentary shot in the arm when one of the neighborhood gang members shouts, *Nice cut!* as he cycles by. I've never had a compliment on my hair from a stranger before. But I can't help wondering what my wife is going to say about it.

Oh my God! Oh my God! That isn't my wife. That's Mrs. Klesko from down the street, who sees me waiting for the streetcar and comes over as fast as she can. *So that's why you're moving! When did they tell you? What are the children going to do? Are you in pain? I know the treatments are awful! You're so brave!* I've never had this kind of sympathy before — and it's all because of my hair. Mrs. Klesko's eyes glitter. *How long?* she asks. *Usually they give you six months, not that you can believe them. They gave my friend Myra six months and she ... but I don't want to depress you.* Mrs. Klesko crosses herself and looks heavenward. *Oh my God! How long did they give you?* I rub my hand over my head — feels like the skin of a ripe peach. *About an eighth of an inch,* I tell her as the streetcar pulls up.

THE RIDE DOWN TO THE BEACH is full of memories for me — Imogen's stroller rolling toward the back while I fumbled for change, like that scene in *A Streetcar Named* Potemkin. Sam choosing to sit next to a weeping woman so that he could tell her that everything was going to be okay. *You don't have to be scared,* he said, and she stopped sniffing and fumbled for a Kleenex. Thea commenting to the driver on her way out, *My dad doesn't use his hands either — and he's only got four passengers.* Ed, caught in mid-bounce by a sudden stop, rocketing forward to land in the empty lap of a nursing mother who was able, with a single placid smile, to establish an effective bond—of course she was pumping out bonding signals like an AM Radio station. Had it been Ed's stuffed animal in her lap, she would have bonded with it. Eddie cried when she got out at the next stop.

I ride past the laundromat and a couple of delicatessens, past the video store and the hardware store and the corner store and the St. Nicholas Donut shop, where the product is not nearly as tasty as the Christian Science one's up the street. I don't think of donuts as requiring a light touch, but somehow a Polish donut remains inedible by any of us except Ed — it's a lump of dough that has had every conceivable indignity heaped upon it, and then a currant on top. Not even Ed eats the currant. We make the big turn past the tenement hotel and hospital, down to the water. It's a cityscape, smokestacks and apartment towers and parking lots. It should be big and alienating, but the lake is so much bigger that it softens and shrinks everything, like our washing machine on the GENTLE cycle. The machine in our new house has six speeds and a turbocharger, I think she said, I can hardly wait to take it for a spin.

I see the kids before they see me. Thea and her friend Erin are swinging together, Imogen and Ed are digging like badgers, spraying the sand between their legs, and Sam and a boy I don't know are sitting on a typical playground Thing, kicking their heels and trading horror stories of bodily function — *And then the throw-up stuff comes out of your nose — Oh yes, I hate that too, or when you dirty your pants while you're sneezing, and there's snot all down your front and ...* I shudder and move on.

I stop when I find myself in shadow. A huge guy between me and the sun, he's got his hands on his hips and this really disgusted expression on his face. *Oh, no,* he says. I move to the side, shading my eyes against the glare.

Hi, Steve, I say. He must be here with Erin. *How's it going?*

He shakes his head. *I was sitting on the bench there, talking to your wife. I got up and came over here because I saw some weird punk kid staring at Sam.* I look around. *You,* he says.

I've forgotten about my haircut. *Does it really make me look young?* I say.

He sighs. *How could you do it?* he says. Then the children notice me and come running over with great whoops of joy and excitement, all of them insisting on running their hands over my head, even Erin and the stranger whose name I never do find out. Erin asks Steve if he could shave his head too, and he smiles at her and frowns at me and walks slowly away. *Can you play ball with us, Dad?* Sam asks me, and I tell him I'll be there in a minute. *Can you help us dig, Dad?* Immie asks and I tell her I'll be there in a minute. Thea and Erin ask if they can feel my head one more time. *All right, one more time,* I say, *and then I have to go and talk to Mommy for a bit.*

My wife doesn't get up. Maybe she can't. She's wearing sunglasses, so I can't tell what she's thinking. *Got my hair cut,* I tell her. She nods. *I didn't mean to —* I begin, rubbing my hand over my head. *It was a bit of an accident. Pretty extreme, eh?*

She nods again. Her hands are clasped tightly together. *Did Tad forget his medication again?* she asks with a tremble in her voice.

I sit beside her. She doesn't flinch or anything, but her shoulders are shaking. Steve is watching us from a distance — he's a sensitive guy, except when he has a power tool in his hands. *I went to another guy and we got our signals crossed. I'd have to say that the reviews so far have been — mixed,* I say. *Mrs. Klesko thinks I have cancer, but at least one of the gang members is impressed. And the kids seem to like it.*

My wife takes off her sunglasses to wipe her eyes. Now I can tell she's laughing. Hard. She bends over, the laughter coming out of her in great gusts. *Here.* She hands me her sunhat. She can't talk for a minute. *Better put that on or you'll get sunburned. I don't want ...* and she has to stop talking again.

Steve sidles up in a tactful way. *I'm going to take Erin home now,* he says. *I hope everything goes well tomorrow for you guys. You have our address, don't you? Be sure and write. Good luck.* He shakes my wife's hand. *I admire you,* he says to her. To me he says, *Don't take off that hat for the next two months.* Then he calls Erin over, puts her effortlessly onto his shoulders and heads toward the parking lot. She doesn't want to go, she pulls at his hair hard enough to bring tears to my eyes just watching. Ed used to do that to me, but he won't be able to do it any more.

So many good-byes since the SOLD sign went up on the front lawn. Friends, neighbors, babas, people I didn't recognize, stopping to say how much they'll miss us, patting the kids on the head, asking if we got a good price for the house, giving advice and best wishes and, in the case of Tim the body builder and Herodias, surprisingly painful handshakes. And now we're almost alone in the park, just the six of us and Sam's friend, spending a quiet moment or two before going home for our last night in the old house.

ED AND IMMIE ARE SITTING ON THE SAND, panting like a couple of tired dogs. *Digging is hard work,* they tell me. They've got a good-sized hole, maybe a couple of feet across and a couple more down. I ask where they are digging to, and Immie replies, *We're looking for a portal to another dimension.* Ed nods, he knows all about portals.

We used to try to dig to China, I tell them, hunkering down and scooping out a few handfuls of moist sand.

Did you ever get there? they ask. I shake my head. *We used to get bored and bury each other in the holes we were digging.* I immediately wish I hadn't said it, but there's no point shutting your mouth after your words have fled. *Don't you do it, though,* I tell them. *You won't like it.* They nod, unconvinced.

I divert their attention by suggesting a soccer game, and we pick teams, pick names for our teams, pick goal areas, pick positions, change team names, change teams because by now the stranger has to go home for dinner, and are ready to begin play. We have to stop almost immediately when Thea gets a stone in her shoe — she and Sam are playing against me and Imogen, with Ed sometimes on one team and sometimes on the other. My wife is the referee because she can whistle through her teeth.

Fifteen minutes later the incident happens. Play has just resumed after yet another blind-side tackle by Ed on someone not involved in the play — in this case, the referee. He has apologized and been forgiven, and now he throws the ball in to Sam, who for the first time gets all his weight behind his right foot. We are using a promotional ball with a picture of Ollie The Orange on it — very bright and bouncy and almost weightless—and Sam's kick travels way past the goal to the pebbly beach, where a gust of wind picks it up and skips it down to the water. I run after the ball, and everyone runs after me, and we get to the water's edge just as Ollie The Orange bobs out of reach.

It is a time for immediate action, and Ed responds, hurling himself at Imogen, who has bent over to pick up a pretty pebble. It is a time for decisiveness, and Thea responds, *I don't want to be the Maple Leafs any more. Let's be the San Jose Sharks.*

I make my decision. The ball is incredibly cheap and the lake is incredibly cold and dirty and the sun is setting and my pants are dry and the decision is the wrong one. The ball bobs farther and farther out of reach, and I do — nothing. After a minute it's clear that there's nothing to do. The ball isn't going to come back. *Sorry, Sam,* I say. His face convulses in a sudden flood of grief.

The ball is about fifty feet out now, moving swiftly. Sam is stripping off his clothes. *No no,* I tell him, trying to recover the discarded articles. He can't swim. I have to hold on to him to prevent him from dashing into the scummy ripples. He collapses to the ground, sobbing. *Is it dinnertime yet?* Thea asks. Sam sobs louder. My wife rounds up the other kids. I pick up Sam and we make our way, slowly, slowly, to the van.

Sam is curled up like a baby in my arms. I'd never have suspected this attachment, he hasn't played with the ball in weeks. His sense of loss is frightening in its intensity, unless — *Are you really worried about moving, Sam?* I ask him. Of course, that must be it. *It's natural to be a little upset. We've lived here a long time — most of your life. I remember bringing you here when you and Thea were —* I have to swallow *— just babies. We're all sad to be leaving a place we know —* Thea interrupts. *Not me.* I smile at her — *Leaving our friends and familiar surroundings,* I go on, strapping him into his seat while he sobs even more bitterly. Somehow I'm not making him feel better. I suppose it's important that he get all his feelings out.

The funny thing is that as I talk I'm starting to get a little bit teary myself. All that stuff about the familiar surroundings, I guess. I'm going to miss Steve and the Sagals and Mrs. Klesko's son Jerry. I'm going to miss the bearded prophet on the corner and the streetcars.

I've never lived in a small town before. What if they don't like me? What if there are bullies on the playground? What if the supermarket doesn't carry my favorite flavor of potato chips? What if they don't celebrate Kwanzaa? What if they don't like me? Our new house is on a septic bed. I don't know all that can go wrong with a septic bed, but I bet there's a lot and I bet it's bad. *Good-bye, lake,* I say, as we pull out of the parking lot. *It'll be a while before we see you again.* My wife is driving, she checks the mirror and then does a quick double-take over her shoulder. *What?* I ask. She shakes her head. Then Ed sees it — *Hey,* he says. *There's the ball!*

What a magnificent sunset, streams of fire hit the swiftly moving clouds, turning them first pink and then ruddy, as the shimmering red-gold circle sinks with infinite care into the sky-line. The lake darkens almost to purple — with a single small spot of bright orange in the middle of the deep-water channel. Sam gasps. It's the soccer ball all right, a few hundred yards out from shore, moving south southeast at a pretty good clip. My wife accelerates, and soon a big parking lot obscures our view. Sam's eyes are riveted on the back window. His lips move silently.

The next intersection has a lake view, very beautiful and ... yes, there's Ollie The Orange away in the watery distance. My wife apologizes to Sam for laughing so hard. She tries to speed up but traffic won't let her. For the next fifteen minutes we crawl along. Each time we come to a vacant lot or a space between two buildings I'm sure we won't be able to see the ball, and each time we can. Sam's voice is a steady drone. *Hail Mary, full of Grace,* he says, *the Lord is with Thee. Blessed are Thou among women, and Blessed is the fruit of Thy womb Jesus.*

I can't reach to pat him on the shoulder. I try to catch his eye, but he's concentrating. He prays all the way home. No parent can watch his child's distress unmoved, no matter how ludicrous the cause, but it occurs to me that if Sam's hopes and fears are bound up in Ollie The Orange, then — that's all right. There are lots of kids whose fears aren't ludicrous at all, and I'm not talking about Imogen, who discovers a spider in the bathroom when she's washing her hands before dinner.

My wife checks our phone messages while I slice cold meatloaf — I made this one by myself — and ripe field tomatoes, another good thing about August. And open a can of tuna fish for Ed before running upstairs to rescue Imogen.

When I get back, my wife is wearing a puzzled smile. *Why does the Braille Society want to put you on their mailing list?* she asks me. *They left a very friendly message. And they want to know how Bowser is doing.*

I nod distractedly and call *Dinner!* Heaven knows, I'm ready for it.

THE MOVING TRUCK ARRIVES to the minute. The three men inside are quiet, kind and courteous. They ask how I am doing and whether they will be discommoding the neighborhood too much by blocking off a portion of the street with their truck. I tell them not to worry. Their only problem will be fitting through our doorway, they all look like the biggest Billy Goat Gruff. Too bad Ed has gone on ahead with the rest of the family. He'd have enjoyed watching these guys toss our furniture around, it's what he's always wanted to do. The truck is loaded by two-thirty, well ahead of schedule, I feel like buying a lottery ticket or a subscription to *Reader's Digest*. The movers are not even sweating, a good thing because we'll be sitting on each other's laps for the next couple of hours. With a small lump in my throat and the song of the dying summer in my ears, I bid farewell to the first house I ever let the bank own for me. *Eastward Ho!* I say to the driver, and he puts the truck in gear and runs into a suddenly swerving bicycle. There's a screech of tortured metal and a volley of oaths, and one of our front tires goes *bang!* Even before I get out, I know what has happened.

*   *   *

Jeez, would you look at that! My bike's a write-off. And my equipment. I got forty or fifty dollars' worth of paint there, and brushes and rollers. You guys had better have some insurance. I'm not moving until the cops come. My neck isn't feeling so good, now that I think of it. Jeez, I got this shooting pain right here, and I see spots.

I peer through my window. I don't see spots. I see Roy lying in the middle of a pool of porch-gray exterior semi-gloss. He's got his arms behind his neck and he looks relaxed enough, and why not? We're all in the gutter, says the poet, but some of us are looking at an out-of-court settlement.